MEDITATIONS
OF A
MILITANT
MODERATE

MEDITATIONS OF A MILITANT MODERATE

Cool Views on Hot Topics

Peter H. Schuck

ROWMAN & LITTLEFIELD PUBLISHERS, INC.
Lanham • Boulder • New York • Toronto • Oxford

ROWMAN & LITTLEFIELD PUBLISHERS, INC.

Published in the United States of America
by Rowman & Littlefield Publishers, Inc.
A wholly owned subsidiary of The Rowman & Littlefield Publishing Group, Inc.
4501 Forbes Boulevard, Suite 200, Lanham, Maryland 20706
www.rowmanlittlefield.com

P.O. Box 317, Oxford OX2 9RU, UK

British Library Cataloguing in Publication Information Available

Library of Congress Cataloging-in-Publication Data
Schuck, Peter H.
    Meditations of a militant moderate : cool views on hot topics / Peter H. Schuck.
        p. cm.
    Essays previously published in various sources, some revised and updated.
    Includes bibliographical references and index.
    ISBN 0-7425-3960-1 (cloth : alk. paper) — ISBN 0-7425-3961-X (pbk. : alk. paper)
    1. United States—Politics and government. 2. Political culture—United States. I.
Title.   JK21.S253 2006
320.6'0973—dc22

                                                                    2005008318

Printed in the United States of America

∞ ™ The paper used in this publication meets the minimum requirements of
American National Standard for Information Sciences—Permanence of Paper for
Printed Library Materials, ANSI/NISO Z39.48-1992.

CONTENTS

PREFACE

What Is a Militant Moderate?

Barry Goldwater was wrong: Extremism in the pursuit of liberty—even *liberty*—is indeed a vice, and moderation in its pursuit is truly a virtue. I have written these essays for those readers who lack Goldwater's strident certitude—about what liberty is, how it can best be attained, and which other values must be sacrificed to attain it.

What does it mean to be a militant moderate, and why do I think that it is a good thing to be? These are important questions and thus the answers are not at all obvious. At first blush, one might even think that militant moderate is an oxymoron. When we think of militants, after all, we may conjure terrorists in Iraq, Crusader armies pillaging the Holy Land, or dead-enders holed up in Waco and Ruby Ridge. These are not pleasant images, much less icons of reasonableness. And Goldwater's motto remind us that moderation has no intrinsic merit; its value depends on what it is being moderate about. But I find no inherent contradiction in being a militant moderate. Moderation refers to an orientation to a substantive issue relative to other orientations to that issue, while militancy denotes a high level of conviction about that position and a willingness to act on it.

So much for definitions. Now let us set aside militancy for a moment and consider why one might want to be a moderate in the first place. Some reasons are not particularly admirable. We all know complaisant people who are prepared to pay almost any price in order to avoid offense or controversy. Some insipid politicians seek compromise, *any* compromise, for its own sake. Somewhat less contemptible are those who believe that (or act as if) the truth of any matter is *always* located in the middle of the space between contending positions. These people are blind to certain stubborn realities: that radical evil and heroic goodness exist, that some extreme positions are actually correct, and that even incorrect extremes can exert salutary pressures on status quos resting on little more than political inertia and embedded injustice.

But not all reasons for being a moderate are misguided. Approximately 2,500 years ago, the Greek philosopher Aristotle offered the (literally) classic defense of moderation, arguing that the nobility of individual character depends on achieving a middle point between the antipodal excesses of human conduct and feeling to which humans are inclined. For Aristotle, cowardice and rashness are vices but courage is a virtue. Surliness and flattery are vices, friendliness a virtue. Moderate temperament and disposition, in this view, are constitutive not only of private morality but of civic virtue and social health.

Aristotle's theory of the golden mean was intended to cultivate the character needed by a good society and polity. While sharing this goal, I embrace moderation for a somewhat different reason: the design of sound public policy requires it even (perhaps especially) when Aristotelian virtue is in short supply. Whether the issue is foreign relations, the war on terrorism, health care, tort reform, illegal immigration, tax simplification, Social Security, homelessness, AIDS, or deficit reduction, policymakers and ordinary citizens alike stumble in the dark, groping their way through what seems like crisis after crisis. In this daunting policy milieu, neither the simple ideology nor the simple morality of those on either end of the political spectrum provides much useful guidance for the hard work of social problem-solving. Ideology lacks the suppleness needed to apprehend and act on complicated, changing social facts, and morality in such matters almost always cuts in more than one direction. Ideology and morality may provide useful starting points for the pursuit of policy solutions, but the roads they mark quickly run out when they enter the morass of political and social complexity and conflict.

This morass, of course, is the best argument for *incrementalism*, one of moderation's vital techniques. If we are uncertain about where to go or how to get there but know that we are in quicksand, we are well advised to take small steps until reaching terra firma. But although incrementalism is very common, it is not exciting; it seldom makes the heart race or the spirit soar. And this timidity puts it at a severe political disadvantage. Americans are drawn, perhaps preternaturally, to novelty, boldness, self-confidence, and decisiveness. Politicians naturally try to exemplify these appealing traits. So do businesses seeking capital, scientists stalking research grants, and policy entrepreneurs looking for political openings. Indeed, all who yearn to make a big splash and be noticed tend to use a marketing style that features extreme but unsustainable claims of novelty and certainty. At this rhetorical dance, moderation is usually a wallflower.

Yet most really new policy ideas are, alas, bad ones. This statement is neither cynical, churlish, nor reflexively conservative. Consider that the same policy problems, more or less, have been around for a very long time—at least since the advent of the modern administrative state in the

New Deal and especially with its vast expansion during the 1960s. Unlike scientists and engineers who often discover new facts and techniques enabling them to solve problems with large social payoffs, public policy-makers must work with a limited set of familiar tools. Most plausible policy ideas are not really new; they have been proposed and debated before in some form or were already tried somewhere and found wanting. They are old wine in new bottles.

Indeed, if a policy idea is truly new, there is a good chance that it will be politically or administratively unworkable. Even policy ideas that are attractive in principle are often unsound, sometimes even disastrous, in practice. As numerous case studies demonstrate, implementation of a new idea in a complex, political, and decentralized policy environment inevitably produces many unforeseen consequences, some of which may perversely undermine the policy's goals. In this environment, even the most astute policymaker cannot predict most of what will actually happen once the policy is actually operating in the field. She comprehends few of the numerous implementation-relevant variables and exercises effective control over fewer still.

The hard realities of implementation mean that even creative policymakers are well advised to proceed with extreme caution. They do best not by instituting large, synoptic change in a single stroke but by muddling through. This fact, which only the most unregenerate ideologue will deny, is reason enough to turn even innovative and reformist policymakers into moderates—and it should do the same to the rest of us. We moderates should grow more militant as we recognize that every policy implementation failure today dims the prospects for genuine reform tomorrow.

The social value of militant moderates is also underscored by the 2004 elections. As both parties conspicuously played to their closed-minded, dug-in extremes, the broad mainstream of opinion—Schlesinger's "vital center"—received less attention and representation than it should have. As I explain in the final essay, the voters are more centrist on the issues than the politicians and the mass media pundits are, and this gap, which is worrisome for our democracy, can and must be remedied. Americans deserve better from their public intellectuals than axe-grinding, score-settling, and smug certitudes. The bitterness on all sides of the election testifies to our desperate need for calming, thoughtful, trustworthy interlocutors who understand complexity, respect diverse values, want to solve real problems, and (as Learned Hand put it) are not too sure that they are right.

The thirty-seven essays (and one poem) that follow are written in this pragmatic, reformist, nonideological, empirically minded spirit. In part I ("Civil Rights and Wrongs"), I focus on policies intended to improve conditions for blacks. Three essays on various aspects of affirmative action explain why this well-intended but profoundly misguided policy can be reshaped to better serve the interests of blacks and of the larger society in social justice and a robust diversity. This leads to my sharp critiques of two of the most eloquent and influential academic voices on affirmative action and race relations: those of Owen Fiss and Cornel West. Part I concludes by challenging the notion of reparations for slavery and supporting the use of housing vouchers rather than more coercive policies in order to integrate races and classes in suburban communities.

Part II ("The Culture Wars") takes up six incendiary issues: the Pledge of Allegiance's reference to God; school vouchers; elite universities' legal challenge to Pentagon recruitment on campus given its antigay policy; the constitutional status of political parties and private groups with discriminatory membership policies; tort litigation against gun manufacturers; and the cultural chasm between the legal academy and the legal profession. Part II ends with a sport: a poem that imagines what would happen if Tax Day came just before Election Day rather than six months later.

In part III ("The Rule of Law"), I discuss seven more hot-button issues that roil our legal and political systems: class actions; punitive damages; the law's approach to lying; the civil jury; institutional reform litigation; tort reform; and surrogate motherhood.

The five essays in part IV ("Dealing with Terrorism and Victims") take on some difficult problems arising out of the terrorist attacks on the World Trade Center on September 11, 2001. One argues that preemptive military strikes are essential under certain circumstances and that the United Nations Charter must either be reinterpreted or changed in order to legitimate them. Another justifies ethnic profiling in some situations while proposing ways to reduce its inevitable costs to minorities. A third essay considers why, when, and how the government should compensate some accident victims but not others. A fourth argues that the 9/11 Compensation Fund sets a worrisome precedent. Finally, I support a special kind of court to try suspected terrorists, one that can balance individual rights against effective law enforcement.

In part V ("A Nation of Immigrants"), I discuss five aspects of our immigration system: immigration politics; my proposal to protect more refugees by creating a regulated market for the trade of protection obligations; the need to reform the 1996 immigration law; the changes and continuities in the ideal of American citizenship wrought by the 9/11 attacks; and the doubtful case for noncitizen voting.

Part VI ("Developing Giants") draws on my working visits to the world's two most populous nations, China and India. The essays are intended to evoke their exotic cultures, depict their rapid economic and social development, and explore the very different paths they are taking toward institutionalizing a just rule of law.

The final part ("The Future of Liberalism") presents my heterodox views on five urgent issues in contemporary American life: liberalism's inconsistent approach to social engineering and environmental protection; the uses of ethnoracial diversity; the private punctilios that should guide Americans in a diverse, competitive society; the limits of civility; and this militant moderate's take on the 2004 national elections.

Although the essay "Rethinking Liberalism" was written back in 1981, almost all of the others appeared just in the last few years, the most recent in June 2005 (on civility). All of them, I believe, are as timely and true as ever. Sadly, I did not need to change either the one on rethinking liberalism or another written twenty years later for President Bush's *first* inauguration, urging reform of the unduly harsh 1996 immigration law. In the few instances where updating or explanation seemed useful, I have altered the text or added a short footnote. Although the original versions of some of the essays carried extensive footnotes, I have eliminated them whenever possible. Readers interested in the data sources, bibliographical references, and analytical refinements are urged to consult those versions.

Thanks are in order—to the first publishers of these pieces (*The American Lawyer, New York Times, Wall Street Journal, Jurist, Brookings Review, The New Republic, Reconstruction, Washington Monthly, National Center for Victims of Crime, Judicature,* and *Georgetown Law Journal*); and to Jennifer Knerr at Rowman & Littlefield, who shared my enthusiastic hope that collecting these essays in a single volume would enrich public discourse.

– PART I –

CIVIL RIGHTS AND WRONGS

The civil rights movement of the 1950s and 1960s constitutes the most important advance in liberal democracy, legal equality, and human rights in modern American history. Those of us who participated in it even peripherally felt this at the time; the passage of years has only fortified those feelings.

Looking back at this revolution (no lesser word will do) in policies, politics, and public attitudes with the advantage of hindsight, we can now see that the movement has actually gone through several phases. The first phase involved creating a regime of formal equality for blacks, other minorities, women, and to a small extent, immigrants. This phase understood equality as legal protection against discrimination by government or most private institutions on the basis of race, religion, gender, nationality, and certain other characteristics like age. Most striking about this regime was the contrast between its compelling universalistic moral premises and the immense struggle and sacrifice needed to establish it. A second phase, exemplified by preferential programs favoring particular minorities and all women, soon followed beginning in the late 1960s and 1970s. Here, the goal was not formal equality but equality of outcomes, although advocates often rationalized the preferences as a remedial policy that in time might succeed well enough that it would no longer be needed, enabling us to rely on antidiscrimination law to assure equal opportunity.

The third phase emerged in full in the 1990s and continues today. It is marked by a fundamental rethinking of preferences. The first three essays in this part contribute to this reappraisal. The initial essay, which distills a much longer analysis in my book *Diversity in America*, was published in 2003 just before the Supreme Court's decision in *Grutter v. Bollinger*. It proposed a distinction between legally mandated preferences, which I argued are constitutional (at least as to blacks) but unwise public policy, and those that private institutions choose to impose on themselves. The second essay criticizes the *Grutter* decision and predicts that it will simply usher in a new round of legal challenges to affirmative action. The third essay explains why even an opponent of public law preferences can support them in the context of Supreme Court nominations by the president.

The next two essays take on two noteworthy defenders of group preferences for blacks—my Yale Law School colleague and friend, Owen Fiss, and the prominent theologian and public figure Cornel West. I contend that Fiss's seminal 1976 article on groups and equal protection and West's manifesto, *Race Matters*, both fundamentally misconceive how the interests of ethnic groups, particularly blacks, can best be advanced in our increasingly diverse American society.

I then take up two specific remedies for racial injustice that many liberals favor. The idea of reparations for slavery, I argue, is seriously flawed in principle and unworkable in practice, and it would inflame race relations rather than ameliorate them. Finally, I show that the goal of integrating suburban neighborhoods racially and economically, which I strongly support, cannot be attained through litigation and judicial decrees. A far more effective remedy for racial and class isolation, I contend, is for the government to distribute more housing vouchers to low- and moderate-income families.

∿ **1** ∿

Affirmative Action I: Don't Mend It or End It—Bend It

Affirmative action policy—by which I mean ethno-racial preferences in the allocation of socially valuable resources—is even more divisive and unsettled today than at its inception more than thirty years ago. Affirmative action's policy context has changed dramatically since 1970.

One change is legal. Since the Supreme Court's 1978 *Bakke* decision, when Justice Lewis Powell's pivotal fifth vote endorsed certain "diversity"-based preferences in higher education, the Court has made it increasingly difficult for affirmative action plans to pass constitutional muster unless they are carefully designed to remedy specific past acts of discrimination.* Four other changes—the triumph of the nondiscrimination prin-

---

*After this essay was published, the Court in its 2003 *Grutter* decision did uphold a nonremedial plan but under arguably very narrow limits. See "Affirmative Action II" essay.

ciple; blacks' large social gains; evidence on the size, beneficiaries, and consequences of preferences; and new demographic realities—persuade me that affirmative action as we know it should be abandoned even if it is held to be constitutional. I discuss them below.

"As we know it" is the essential qualifier in that sentence. I propose neither a wholesale ban on affirmative action ("ending" it) nor tweaks in its administration ("mending" it). Rather, I would make two structural changes to curtail existing preferences while strengthening the remaining ones' claim to justice. First, affirmative action would be banned in the public sector but allowed in the private sector. Second, private-sector institutions that use preferences would be required to disclose how and why they do so. These reforms would allow the use of preferences by private institutions that believe in them enough to disclose and defend them, while doing away with the obfuscation, duplicity, and lack of accountability that too often accompany preferences. Affirmative action could thus be localized and customized to suit the varying requirements of particular contexts and sponsors.

TRIUMPH OF THE NONDISCRIMINATION PRINCIPLE

Why is change necessary? To explain, one must at the outset distinguish affirmative action entailing preferences from nondiscrimination, a principle that simply requires one to refrain from treating people differently because of their race, ethnicity, or other protected characteristics. Although this distinction can blur at the edges, it is clear and vital both in politics and in principle.

When affirmative action became federal policy in the late 1960s, the nondiscrimination principle, though fragile, was gaining strength. Preferences, by contrast, were flatly rejected by civil rights leaders like Hubert Humphrey, Ted Kennedy, and Martin Luther King, Jr. In the three decades that followed, more and more Americans came to embrace nondiscrimination and to oppose affirmative action, yet as John Skrentny shows in his *Ironies of Affirmative Action*, federal bureaucrats extended affirmative action with little public notice or debate. Today, nondiscrimination, or equal opportunity, is a principle questioned by only a few bigots and extreme libertarians, and civil rights law is far-reaching and remedially robust. In contrast, affirmative action is widely seen as a demand for favoritism or even equal outcomes.

SOCIAL GAINS BY BLACKS

Blacks, the intended beneficiaries of affirmative action, are no longer the insular minority they were in the 1960s. Harvard sociologist Orlando Patterson shows their "astonishing" progress on almost every front. "A mere 13 percent of the population," he notes, "Afro-Americans dominate the nation's popular culture . . . [A]t least 35 percent of Afro-American adult, male workers are solidly middle class." The income of young, intact black families approaches that of demographically similar whites. On almost every other social index (residential integration is a laggard), the black-white gap is narrowing significantly; indeed, the income gap for young black women has disappeared.

Even these comparisons understate black progress. Much of racism's cruel legacy is permanently impounded in the low education and income levels of older blacks who grew up under Jim Crow; their economic dis-advantages pull down the averages, obscuring the gains of their far better-educated children and grandchildren. These gains, moreover, have coincided with the arrival of record numbers of immigrants who are com-peting with blacks. To ignore this factor, economist Robert Lerner says, is like analyzing inequality trends in Germany since 1990 without noting that it had absorbed an entire impoverished country, East Germany. In addition, comparisons that fail to age-adjust social statistics obscure the fact that blacks, whose average age is much lower than that of whites, are less likely to have reached their peak earning years.

My point, emphatically, is not that blacks have achieved social equality—far from it—but that the situation facing them today is altogether different than it was when affirmative action was adopted. Advocates, of course, say that this progress just proves that affirmative action is effective; hence it should be continued or even increased. But this *post hoc ergo propter hoc* rea-soning is fallacious and ignores blacks' pre–affirmative action trajectory and the policy's growing incoherence and injustice.

SIZE, BENEFICIARIES, AND CONSEQUENCES OF PREFERENCES

When we weigh competing claims for scarce resources—jobs, admission to higher education, public and private contracts, broadcast or other spectrum licenses, credit, housing, and the like—how heavy is the thumb that affirmative action places on the scales? This is a crucial question. The larger the preference, the more it conflicts with competing interests and values, especially the ideal of merit—almost regardless of how one defines merit.

The best data concern higher education admissions where (for better or for worse) schools commonly use standardized test scores as a proxy for aptitude, preparation, and achievement. William Bowen and Derek Bok, the former presidents of Princeton and Harvard, published a study in 1999 based largely on the academic records of more than eighty thou-sand students who entered twenty-eight highly selective institutions in three different years. Affirmative action, they claimed, only applies to these institutions, although a more recent study suggests that the practice now extends to some second- and even third-tier schools.

Selective institutions, of course, take other factors into account besides race. Indeed, some whites who are admitted have worse academic credentials than the blacks admitted under preferences. Still, Bowen and Bok find a difference of almost two hundred points in the average SAT scores of the black and white applicants, and even this understates the group difference. First, the deficit for black applicants' high school grade point average (GPA), the other main admission criterion, is even larger. Thomas Kane finds that black applicants to selective schools "enjoy an advantage equivalent to an increase of two-thirds of a point in [GPA]—on a four-point scale—or [the equivalent of] four hundred points on the SAT."

Second, although the SAT is often criticized as culturally biased against blacks, SAT (and GPA) scores at every level actually overpredict their college performance. Third, the odds were approximately even that black applicants with scores between 1100 and 1199 would be admitted, whereas the odds for whites did not reach that level until they had scores in the 1450–1499 range. With a score of 1500 or above, more than a third of whites were rejected while every single black gained admission. And a recent study of forty-seven public institutions found that the odds of a black student being admitted compared to a white student with the same SAT and GPA were 173:1 at Michigan and 177:1 at North Carolina State.

These preferences, then, are not merely tie-breakers; they are huge—and they continue at the graduate and professional school levels. It is encouraging that an identical share (56 percent) of black and white graduates of the institutions in the Bowen and Bok sample earned graduate degrees; the share of blacks earning professional or doctoral degrees was actually slightly higher than for whites (40 percent versus 37 percent). But black students' college grades and postgraduate test scores are so much lower on average that their admission to these programs, disproportionately at top-tier institutions, also depends on affirmative action. In the early 1990s, for example, only a few dozen of the 420 blacks admitted to the eighteen most selective law schools would have been admitted absent affirmative action. A high percentage of these schools' black graduates eventually pass the bar examination, but some 22 percent of blacks' from these schools who take the exam never pass it (compared with 3 percent of whites), and only 61 percent of blacks pass it the first time compared with 92 percent of whites. Blacks who enter the professions do enjoy solid status, income, civic participation and leadership, and career satisfaction. But this hardly makes the case for affirmative action, for the higher-scoring applicants whom they displaced would presumably have done at least as well.

How much of blacks' impressive gains is due to reduced discrimination resulting from changing white attitudes and civil rights enforcement, as distinct from preferences? How would they have fared had they attended the somewhat less prestigious schools they could have attended without preferences? What would the demographics of higher education be without those preferences? We cannot answer these vital questions conclusively. We know that black gains were substantial even before preferences were adopted, that preference beneficiaries are overwhelmingly from middle- and upper-class families, and that most black leaders in all walks of life did not go to elite universities. We also know that many institutions are so committed to affirmative action that they will find ways to prefer favored groups—minorities, legacies, athletes, and others—no matter what the formal rules say. Although California voters banned affirmative action in state programs, their politicians press the university system to jigger the admission criteria until it finds a formula that can skirt the ban and produce the "correct" number of the favored minorities (excluding Asians, who are thought not to need the help).

NEW DEMOGRAPHIC REALITIES

The moral case for affirmative action rests on the bitter legacy of black slavery, Jim Crow, and the violent dispossession of Native Americans. Yet the descendants of slaves and Native Americans constitute a shrinking share of affirmative action's beneficiaries. Political logrolling has extended preferential treatment to the largest immigrant group, Hispanics, as well as to blacks from Africa, the Caribbean, and elsewhere, Asians and Pacific Islanders, and in some programs to women, a majority group.

Some affirmative action advocates acknowledge this problem and want to fix it. Orlando Patterson, for example, would exclude "first-generation persons of African ancestry" but not "their children and later generations . . . in light of the persistence of racist discrimination in America." He would also exclude all Hispanics except for Puerto Ricans and Mexican Americans of second or later generations and would exclude "all Asians except Chinese Americans descended from pre-1923 immigrants. . . ." With due respect for Patterson's pathbreaking work on race, his formula resembles a tax code provision governing depreciation expenses more than a workable formula for promoting social justice.

Centuries of immigration and intermarriage have rendered the conventional racial categories ever more meaningless. The number of Americans who consider themselves multiracial and who wish to be identified as such (if they must be racially identified at all) was seven million in the 2000 census, including nearly two million blacks (5 percent of the black population) and 37 percent of all Native Americans. This is why advocacy groups who are desperate to retain the demographic status quo lobbied furiously to preempt a multiracial category.

In perhaps the most grimly ironic aspect of the new demographic dispensation, the government adopted something like the one-drop rule that helped enslave mulattos and self-identifying whites before Emancipation. Under OMB's rules, any response combining one minority race and the white race must be allocated to the minority race. This, although 25 percent of those in the United States who describe themselves as both black and white consider themselves white, as do almost half of Asian-white people and more than 80 percent of Indian-white people. The lesson is clear: Making our social policy pivot on the standard racial categories is both illogical and politically unsustainable.

ALTERNATIVES

Even a remote possibility that eliminating affirmative action would resegregate our society deeply distresses almost all Americans. Nothing else can explain the persistence of a policy that, contrary to basic American values, distributes valuable social resources according to skin color and surname. But to say that we must choose between perpetuating affirmative action and eliminating it entirely is false. To be sure, most suggested reforms—using social class or economic disadvantage rather than race, choosing among minimally qualified students by lottery, and making preferences temporary—are impracticable or would make matters worse. Limiting affirmative action to the descendants of slaves and Native Americans would minimize some objections to the policy but, as Patterson's proposal suggests, would be tricky to implement and would still violate the nondiscrimination and merit principles.

Most Americans who favor affirmative action would probably concede that it fails to treat the underlying problem. Black applicants will continue to have worse academic credentials until they can attend better primary and secondary schools and receive the remediation they need. A root cause of their disadvantage is inferior schooling, and affirmative action is simply a poultice. We must often deal with symptoms rather than root causes because we do not know how to eliminate them, or consider it too costly to do so, or cannot muster the necessary political will. If we know which social or educational reforms can substantially improve low-income children's academic performance, then we should, by all means adopt them. But this does not mean that we should preserve affirmative action until we can somehow eliminate the root causes of inequality.

I propose instead that we treat governmental, legally mandated preferences differently than private, voluntary ones. While prohibiting the former (except in the narrow remedial context approved by the Supreme Court), I would permit the latter—but only under certain conditions discussed below. A liberal society committed to freedom and private autonomy has good reasons to maintain this difference; racial preferences imposed by law are pernicious in ways that private ones are not. To affirmative action advocates, it is a Catch-22 to bar the benign use of race now after having used it against minorities for centuries. But to most Americans (including many minorities), affirmative action is not benign. It is not Catch-22 to recognize what history teaches—that race is perhaps the worst imaginable category around which to organize political and social relations. The social changes I have described only reinforce this lesson. A public law that affirms our common values should renounce the distributive use of race, not perpetuate it.

There are other differences between public and private affirmative action. A private preference speaks for and binds only those who adopt it and only for as long as they retain it. It does not serve, as public law should, as a social ideal. As I explained in my book, *The Limits of Law*, legal rules tend to be cruder, more simplistic, slower to develop, and less contextualized than voluntary ones, which are tailored to more specific needs and situations. Legal rules reflect interest group politics or the vagaries of judicial decision; voluntary ones reflect the chooser's own assessment of private benefits and costs. Legal rules are more difficult to reform, abandon, or escape. Voluntary ones can assume more diverse forms than mandated ones, a diversity that facilitates social learning and problem solving.

Still, many who believe in nondiscrimination and merit and who conscientiously weigh the competing values still support affirmative action. If a private university chooses to sacrifice some level of academic performance to gain greater racial diversity and whatever educational or other values it thinks diversity will bring, I cannot say—nor should the law say—that its choice is impermissible. Because even private affirmative action violates the nondiscrimination principle, however, I would permit it only on two conditions: transparency and protection of minorities. First, the preference—its criteria, weights, and reasons—must be fully disclosed. If it cannot withstand public criticism, it should be scrapped. The goal is to discipline preferences by forcing institutions to reveal their value choices. This will trigger market, reputational, and other informal mechanisms that make them bear more of the policy's costs rather than just shifting them surreptitiously to nonpreferred applicants, as they do now. Second, private affirmative action must not disadvantage a group to which the Constitution affords heightened protection. A preference favoring whites, for example, would violate this condition.

THE COMMITMENT TO LEGAL EQUALITY

For better *and* for worse, American culture remains highly individualistic in its values and premises, even at some sacrifice (where sacrifice is necessary) to its goal of substantive equality. The illiberal strands in our tangled history that enslaved, excluded, and subordinated individuals as members of racial groups should chasten our efforts to use race as a distributive criterion. Affirmative action in its current form, however well intended, violates the distinctive, deeply embedded cultural and moral commitments to legal equality, private autonomy, and enhanced opportunity that have served Americans well—even though they have not yet served all of us equally well.

⌁ 2 ⌁

Affirmative Action II: The Supreme Court Botches the Job

The Supreme Court's long-awaited decisions in the *Gratz* and *Grutter* cases concerning the University of Michigan's affirmative action programs were greeted with deep sighs of relief by the numerous advocates of (euphemisms aside) ethnoracial preferences. Their relief at having dodged a judicial bullet is perfectly understandable. The Court's decision, however, should not give them too much comfort, for it will convince no one who is not already a true believer in preferences.

Let me count the reasons why. The majority's application of strict scrutiny amounts to a dilution of that indispensable standard. It relies on an unexamined, shallow conception of diversity and of what is required to produce its benefits. In the name of that diversity, it relies on the very stereotypes it opposes, stereotypes that it ironically believes preferences will discredit and dispel. Its constitutional test compels a conclusion that is precisely the opposite of the one it reaches. It hopes that preferences will be temporary, yet its own logic would perpetuate them. In another of the case's striking ironies, the decision will promote uniformity, not diversity, in the design of future affirmative action programs. Finally, its decision, far from bringing closure to the bitter, three-decade debate over preferences, will in fact inflame and enlarge it.

In what follows, I critique the *Grutter* majority's reasoning in upholding the preferences' *constitutionality*. I believe that there is a stronger argument for their constitutionality, at least as applied to preferences for blacks. This argument is based on statutory preferences for blacks that were enacted by the same Reconstruction congress that adopted the Fourteenth Amendment. The *Grutter* majority does not even mention this argument, perhaps because Michigan's plan favors Native Americans and Hispanics, not just blacks. In any event, my view is that the *moral* and *policy* objections to preferences are more compelling than the constitutional ones. Although I do not pursue these moral and policy objections here, I analyze them in detail in my recent book, *Diversity in America*.

STRICT SCRUTINY

Strict scrutiny is supposed to be, well, strict. Its raison d'être is to be rigorous, skeptical, and demanding enough to challenge the government's premises, flush out its true motives, and ensure a very tight congruence of evidence, legal categories, and policy justifications. Strict scrutiny is employed, of course, when there are especially good reasons to think that, as with racial classifications, the government may be playing with fire around highly combustible materials.

Many academic advocates of preferences, of course, argue that the strict scrutiny standard formulated by the Court in *Croson* and *Adarand* (per Justice O'Connor, no less) was *too* strict, even Procrustean, and that a "benign" preference adopted by self-abnegating majorities should be judged less rigorously. Whatever the merits of this argument—note that in fact no majority has, or is likely to, adopt preferences, so its benignity is decidedly in the eye of the beholder—the *Grutter* majority does not accept it. Nor does it even come close to applying the traditional standard. There may well be a middle ground of strictness, but the majority does not occupy it. *Grutter*'s remarkable latitudinarianism, as we shall see, pervades every aspect of its analysis. As the Chief Justice correctly notes, the majority's review of Michigan's preference system is "perfunctory" and "unprecedented in its deference." It remains a mystery why universities sponsoring preferences are more entitled to such deference than, say, the private employers or municipal procurement agencies whose plans have been struck down in the past under strict scrutiny. In adopting and structuring such plans, universities, no less than employers and agencies, respond to a variety of political, ideological, competitive, social, legal, and institutional pressures. They all presumably act in good faith, whatever that may mean in this context. But the sponsors' good faith, of course, is supposed to be irrelevant under any form of strict scrutiny.

Justice O'Connor's strict scrutiny has all the strictness of an indulgent mother who gives her affable son the keys to the family car without questioning him about his drinking. When the father warns that the youth has gotten drunk before and harmed some bystanders, she replies, "Oh, he's a good boy, and anyway he says he's only going to the library." In this spirit, O'Connor accepts the Michigan law school's assurances that she needn't worry, while shrugging off the hard questions posed by the dissenters—a kind of good-natured "Oh, don't mind dad; he's just being crabby" response.

Which are those hard questions finessed by the majority? One is about the nature of educational diversity and how the law school's preferences relate to diversity value. A second is how educational diversity relates to both the "critical mass" idea on which the school's theory pivots and the ethnoracial stereotypes that it claims to abhor. A third is about the majority's test for distinguishing between valid and invalid preferences, and about how well Michigan's program fares under that test. A fourth is about race-neutral alternatives. A fifth is about the future of preferences and of the politics surrounding them. I discuss each of these in turn.

DIVERSITY

The *Grutter* majority famously ratifies Justice Powell's embrace in *Bakke* of student diversity as a compelling state interest sufficient to justify university admissions preferences—even as it ignores the conditions, including rigorous individualized appraisal of an applicant's actual diversity-value, that Powell insisted were necessary to validate them. What the majority does not do is to provide a coherent account of diversity that goes beyond generalities and platitudes, or to explain why the Constitution allows the law school to define diversity in purely and narrowly ethnoracial terms, disfavoring minorities other than the three favored ones (blacks, Native Americans, and the Spanish surnamed) and treating other kinds of diversity either as much less weighty or irrelevant. Indeed, as Justice Thomas points out in a dissenting footnote, the school seems not to value the additional diversity that black men, who are greatly underrepresented relative to black women, would provide. (He might have added that the world views of these two groups, according to Harvard sociologist Orlando Patterson, are strikingly different.) The majority, I strongly suspect, takes the diversity rationale more seriously than the law school does. The dissenters also take it seriously but only out of formal necessity, because the majority does.

The only convincing explanation for the school's program has little to do with the goal of educational diversity and everything to do with a goal the Court has insisted is constitutionally insufficient to justify preferences: the laudable wish to remedy the historic injustices suffered in America by (at least two of) those groups. Every sophisticated observer who can see through the rhetorical fog thrown up by the now-obligatory diversity-talk (including all members of the Court, one supposes) understands that this remedy, not diversity, is the law school's true purpose. (Indeed, in a very recent article that discusses *Grutter*, Tobias and Robert Paul Wolff praise the opinion's interventionist approach to the social inequalities that they believe justify preferences. The fact that O'Connor departs radically from her earlier approach in *Croson* and *Adarand*, they think, is a cause for celebration, not censure).

If the law school's program were really about educational diversity rather than about remedying past injustices, why would its preferences extend only to a demographic characteristic (only a few favored races or ethnicities) that has the effect of confirming the very stereotypes that the program is supposed to break down, while ignoring those other demographic factors (religion or partisanship, say) that directly represent the different world views with which educational diversity is supposedly concerned? Would a fundamentalist Christian or a conservative Republican or an anarchist, for that matter, create less diversity-value for Michigan's students than an applicant whose only special claim to diversity-value is his surname or the color of his skin? The answer, obviously, is no—and it is no whether one defines diversity-value in terms of disparate world views, interacting with people of unfamiliar backgrounds, encouraging dorm room chit-chat, or even breaking down traditional stereotypes.

STEREOTYPES AND "CRITICAL MASS"

The majority insists that the breaking down of ethnoracial stereotypes is crucial to the constitutionally legitimated goal of educational diversity and that the "critical mass" of favored minorities intentionally produced by the school's preferences will also help achieve this goal. The connection between critical mass and stereotype destruction, in this view, is a close one: "when a critical mass of underrepresented minority students is present," the majority states (citing Dean Syverud's testimony), "racial stereotypes lose their force because nonminority students learn that there is no 'minority viewpoint' but rather a variety of viewpoints among minority students."

But how can this be? What alchemy enables the law school to prefer students on the basis of surname or skin color without at the same time strengthening the notion of ethnoracial essentialism and viewpoint determinism? What prestidigitation allows the school to admit minority students with academic records (whatever the school's metric) that are substantially weaker than those of their (other minority or majority) competitors without thereby reinforcing stereotypes of academic inferiority? How clueless does the majority think the nonpreferred students and faculty are that they will somehow not notice what is going on and draw the logical and stigmatizing inference about group differences in academic performance (which is what a stereotype is)? These are, after all, elite educational institutions. By definition, they attract the most competitive students and faculty, individuals who place a very high (often excessive) value on the particular coin of their peculiar realm, academic excellence, and do so partly because they themselves are so well endowed with it.

To recognize the importance that elite schools give to academic factors is emphatically *not* to say that test scores and GPA are or should be their only criteria of admission, and no critic of *Grutter* need say anything so absurd. A sensible institution will consider a variety of factors in selecting its student body, although an elite school that hopes to maintain its position will give the greatest weight to academic potential or performance. In any event, the assumption that a group favored by ethnoracial preferences is more likely than members of other groups to excel on these nonacademic factors is itself a stereotype, and a pernicious one at that. There is simply no a priori reason to believe, for example, that black applicants as a group are more likely to exhibit, say, leadership potential, community service, or other "soft variables" than applicants of other groups.

By the same token, a critic of *Grutter* need not deny the obvious fact that preferences of other kinds exist, and that some are objectionable. Preferences favoring legacies and athletes, for example, are also widespread even at elite schools. Recognizing the beneficiaries of these preferences as such also engenders stereotypes about their academic inferiority (e.g., "dumb jocks"). The important point, however, is that constitutional strict scrutiny does not demand special justification of such classifications as it does of ethnoracial ones (which, of course, is what the Equal Protection Clause was intended to invalidate), and the stereotypes arising from these other preferences are far less socially corrosive or individually stigmatizing.

CONSTITUTIONAL TEST

The majority defines a defensible test for the constitutionality of ethnoracial preferences: "each applicant must be evaluated as an individual and not in a way that makes an applicant's race or ethnicity the defining feature of his or her application"; members of different groups must be on the same "admissions track" and must compete "on the same footing." Having proclaimed this test, however, the majority, much like a high school principal determined to graduate the students regardless of their performance, proceeds to "dumb down" the test so that all can pass it, all the while insisting on the integrity of the original standard.

Race and ethnicity, O'Connor says, can be a "plus factor" in a system of "individualized assessments" so long as it does not constitute either a "rigid quota" (as in the undergraduate program) or "racial balancing." But as Rehnquist and Justice Kennedy show statistically in their dissenting opinions, the law school weighs the plus factor for race and ethnicity so heavily that it creates—in effect, although not in name—a two-track system tantamount to racial balancing in its offers of admissions with a view to achieving its numerically and racially defined critical mass. The majority, like the law school, wants to have it both ways: Ethnoracial factors are only a "modest" plus factor in admissions, yet few of the favored minorities would be admitted without them—unless one is prepared to assume, contrary to fact, that they are so far superior to other applicants on the nonacademic criteria that this superiority erases their academic deficits.

The truth, evident from the dissenters' analysis and indeed from common sense, is that the majority can approve the law school's affirmative action program under the majority's own constitutional test for one reason and one reason only: The program is sufficiently opaque by design and allows enough scope for subjectivity and discretion in the arbitrary and undisclosed weighting of the "soft variables" in individual cases that a skeptic cannot *prove* unmistakably that race-ethnicity is the predominant factor in the admission of preferred minorities. This fact, of course, renders the location of the burden of proof constitutionally decisive, which in turn makes the majority's unstrict scrutiny, discussed earlier, all the more pivotal in generating the outcome in *Grutter* and future cases.

RACE-NEUTRAL ALTERNATIVES

The majority's abject deference to the university is nowhere more apparent than in its treatment of race-neutral alternatives. All that is constitutionally required, it says, is for the law school to give "serious, good faith consideration of workable race-neutral alternatives." The school has satisfied that requirement, the majority continues, because none of these alternatives would give the school the number of preferred minorities that the institution wants. This is true enough, but it is an answer to the wrong question. The right question is: Given the constitutional presumption against ethnoracial preferences, a presumption so strong that strict scrutiny is required to enforce it, how imperfect must the race-neutral alternative be before the Court will allow the school to reject it in favor of a racialist, constitutionally disfavored one? Although there is no clear answer to this question, the majority does not even ask it. Nor, curiously, does it even mention what many regard as the most attractive race-neutral alternative, one based on economic disadvantage. This alternative is hardly ideal, as I explain in *Diversity in America*, but this imperfection in no way implies that ethnoracial preferences, whose defects go to policy as well as constitutionality, are therefore more acceptable.

THE FUTURE AND THE POLITICS OF PREFERENCES

Much has been made of the majority's expectation "that twenty-five years from now, the use of racial preferences will no longer be necessary." Justice Thomas's recitation, in dissent, of the grim statistics on comparative academic performance makes such a hope seem unrealistic, and I would add that the studies of ethnoracial preferences in other societies provide no support for it. To the contrary, they indicate that such preferences, once established, endure and indeed expand to new groups and new program benefits.

The only exceptions to this pattern of which I am aware are in California and Washington State, where voter referenda have banned

these preferences—and the exception, at least in California, is both revealing and disturbing. As I show in *Diversity in America*, relying in part on the
reporting of *Wall Street Journal* writer Daniel Golden, the University of
California has engaged in a series of stratagems expressly designed to circumvent Proposition 209. Some of the more egregious ones involve the
channeling of minority students to new "critical race studies" programs
that have lower admissions standards, the awarding of special admissions
credit for foreign language fluency by minority students who are native-
language speakers, "percentage" plans that rely on the efficacy of the continuation of segregated schooling patterns, greater use of unspecified (and
unspecifiable) "holistic" criteria, and of course the use of winks and nods
by admissions officials. We can expect that other bans on preferences will
be met by similar, if not more creative, evasions.

Indeed, legal commentator Jeffrey Rosen uses this very fact to contend
that preferences, which he seems to oppose in principle, should be maintained. All things considered, Rosen claims, it is probably better to have
a system that openly acknowledges and publicly justifies preferences
than one where they operate sub rosa and thus are even more susceptible
to abuse. In truth, Rosen's rationale may actually be the most persuasive
case for the status quo—but it is not one, of course, that is rhetorically
available to a putatively principled Court.

Nevertheless, one might view Justice O'Connor's opinion as an implicit effort to craft precisely the kind of compromised outcome that Rosen
reluctantly favors, to resolve this bitter debate once and for all and then
move on. If so, I doubt that it will succeed. First, we can expect much
future litigation over whether the use of race as a "plus factor" in a given
affirmative action plan is excessive, in effect amounting to the proscribed
"racial balancing." By modeling their plans on Michigan's, of course,
schools can make such challenges more difficult. *Grutter* seems to give
such schools a legal safe harbor. Ironically, the majority encourages uniformity, albeit in the name of diversity. For this reason, future litigation
will focus not on the form of these plans but on how they are actually
administered.

Second, our national experience suggests that difficult and divisive public issues in American life—affirmative action is certainly one of them—are
seldom resolved by the Court's decisions or indeed by any official fiat.
History (not to mention the professoriate) has not been kind to the Court
when it has attempted to settle such issues prematurely, peremptorily, or
amorally. *Dred Scott, Plessy, Lochner, Roe v. Wade*, and *Bowers v. Hardwick* are
among the decisions that illustrate the point. Will *Grutter* be another?
Probably not. After all, the Court merely *permits* ethnoracial preferences, it
does not *require* them—and it therefore allows democratic politics to have
the final say and get its way.

What will democratic politics dictate? The key political fact is that elite institutions and elite opinion aside, affirmative action has little public support. The vast majority of Americans, including more than a third of blacks and more than 70 percent of Hispanics, oppose preferences in hiring and promotion, with the level of this opposition rising somewhat over time. When the issue is college admissions preferences, opposition is substantial even among blacks and other minorities. Although the level of opposition varies with the precise phrasing of the question, no researcher in this field doubts that public opinion remains decidedly and intensely negative, pretty much regardless of how the questions are formulated, the state of the economy, or personal financial conditions. This opposition, moreover, appears to be principled; it is just as strong among whites on the egalitarian left as among those on the political right. Politicians, who have a feel for these things, have long assumed that the electorate staunchly opposes race-conscious programs.

My guess, moreover, is that if the public knew how large the weighting of ethnoracial preferences in selective college admissions actually is—a leading researcher finds that black applicants "enjoy an advantage equivalent to an increase of two-thirds of a point in [GPA]—on a four point scale—or [the equivalent of] four hundred points on the SAT"—its opposition to preferences would be that much greater.

We are about to find out. The prospect is for many state-level campaigns seeking to bar preferences, as California did in Proposition 209, and these campaigns will surely educate the public about how large the preferences actually are and how they operate. Indeed, the first such campaigns have already begun. For someone like me who believes that issues of this kind ought to decided primarily by politics, not by courts, this prospect is encouraging—although the conflicts may get ugly. But these campaigns do raise serious doubts about the notion, popular among pro-preference pundits like Laurence Tribe, that the *Grutter* majority somehow succeeded in crafting a pragmatic solution to this enduring controversy, capturing a social consensus favoring preferences. In reality, however, no such consensus exists, and the post-*Grutter* campaigns will destroy the illusion that it does.

ᣔ 3 ᣔ

Affirmative Action III: Racial Preferences in Supreme Court Nominations

In one of those delicious ironies that thrill supporters of affirmative action, the White House has leaked word that it plans to fill the next U.S. Supreme

Court vacancy with a member of a minority group, probably Hispanics, whose voters the Republican Party hopes to attract for future elections. The GOP has long made a point of opposing affirmative action—by which they (and I) mean giving special weight to ethnoracial minority status in choosing among candidates for valuable jobs, college admissions, or other social goods. The president's reported eagerness to use ethnoracial preferences in judicial nominations raises an obvious question: What principle, if any, can justify selecting Supreme Court nominees on ethnoracial grounds while condemning such preferences in other areas?

The question may seem more theoretical than legal or practical. Even after the Court's stunning and unprecedented use of the Equal Protection Clause, in *Bush v. Gore*, to determine the outcome of the 2000 presidential election, it is hard to imagine that any judge would actually entertain a constitutional challenge to a high-level government nominee in which ethnoracial factors affected the choice. The interesting question, however, is, why not? Answering it can help to sharpen the continuing debate over affirmative action by refining our understanding of why the practice raises intense moral and constitutional issues in some contexts but not in others.

At first blush, political expediency seems like a compelling explanation of the White House plan (if that's what it is). To paraphrase H. L. Mencken, one will seldom go wrong by underestimating officials' fidelity to high principles. After all, successful politicians have by definition mastered the art of compromising principles for tactical reasons and then covering their tracks with idealistic rhetoric. And those who manage to climb the greasy pole to the White House tend to be the most shamelessly masterful of all. How else to explain the first President Bush's insistence, with a straight face, that he was appointing Clarence Thomas not because of his race but because he was the most highly qualified candidate in the country?

More recently, the Trent Lott affair has intensified many Republicans' search for a pro-minorities fig leaf to cover the nakedness of the GOP's civil rights agenda. Lott's own groveling performance on TV, promising to reverse his career-long hostility to race-based preferences, followed by his resignation as Senate majority leader, prompted media speculation that the White House would soften its own opposition to preferences.

The Republican Party has always spoken loudly but carried a small stick where affirmative action is concerned. President Richard Nixon inaugurated the policy in 1969. Since then—and despite affirmative action's substantial and growing unpopularity among voters— subsequent Republican presidents have made few serious efforts to dismantle it. The Republicans' last appointee to the high court, David Souter, seems to support it. Nor is the Republican-controlled Congress likely to rock the affirmative action boat. Indeed, with minorities constituting swing voting blocs in many elections, and Hispanics now the largest such group, a White House determined to compete vigorously for their support will probably engage in more ethnic appeals—not fewer—all the while insisting that it favors color-blindness.

Political expediency, then, may suffice to explain why President Bush will make race or ethnicity a major, if not decisive, factor in his next nomination to the Supreme Court, even while denying that fact. But if we set politicians' motives to one side and consider the matter from a loftier, more detached perspective, the question becomes whether in principle the rest of us can simultaneously maintain that giving points to race or ethnicity in choosing Supreme Court nominees is permissible but that using such preferences in college admissions is wrong. My answer is that one can hold both of those positions and still be morally and (insofar as law follows morality) legally consistent.

To begin to make this case, we must examine more closely the most important concept or value that underlies the debate over affirmative action: merit. Opponents of affirmative action invariably invoke merit as the appropriate principle of distributive justice, especially when it is the government that is doing the distributing. They usually define merit to mean some notion of excellence or praiseworthiness.

This definition, of course, leaves unanswered the crucial question of precisely which characteristics signify that an opportunity or valuable resource is deserved by the recipient. Opponents sometimes try to sidestep this question by insisting that whatever merit may mean in this context, ethnicity and race almost never constitute a valid measure of it. (They may make an exception, for example, for religious groups that require religious affiliation as a condition for certain in-house jobs.) They will cite the terrible injustices that ethnoracial preferences perpetrated in the past, particularly when used to favor whites at the expense of minorities, and the unfairness of disadvantaging individuals with the wrong skin color or surname, especially those who are no better off economically than those who would receive a preference. Opponents may also emphasize the question of incentives—that, for sound policy reasons, such opportunities should reward individual effort and achievement, not ascriptive features, like race, over which one has no control. Worse, if jobs or admissions are set aside based on race, everyone who is hired or admitted who happens to be a minority group member will be stigmatized as unworthy even if they can compete fully on the prescribed standards. Distributing merit-based goods by ascription, they maintain, tends to stigmatize all recipients, including those who are in fact high achievers.

The question of what merit means, however, cannot be finessed so easily. Supporters of affirmative action seldom dispute the value of merit as an abstract ideal of distributive justice. Instead, they challenge how it is defined in practice and in context. First, they point to the many situations in which apparent deviations from merit are tolerated or even celebrated—for example, admission preferences for alumni children and athletes with inferior academic records, or job preferences for people with the right connections. These deviations, supporters argue, evidence hypocritical double standards, with society invoking the merit principle selectively in order to benefit the already advantaged and to exclude minorities. Such deviations, they say, imply that we do, and should, broaden our conception of merit to embrace a variety of other interests valued by particular institutions or society in general—for example, achieving a more demographically diverse student body or workforce, or removing the vestiges of caste. It follows, they contend, that merit is inevitably contextual; it depends for its meaning on the values that affect the specific job or opportunity in question, and the factual circumstances that shape those values.

I have argued elsewhere against government-sponsored, university-administered affirmative action plans that invoke a diversity rationale. Such plans typically define diversity narrowly in order to produce not a variety of viewpoints but the "right" number of favored minorities at the expense of more academically qualified minorities or whites, thereby violating even a flexible conception of merit and equal opportunity. Whether or not they would meet the Court's legal standards under *Grutter*, they constitute misguided public policy.

It is striking, then, that public opinion and legal elites hardly think twice before countenancing the use of ethnoracial preferences in nominating Supreme Court justices. Almost everyone seems to concede that, in principle, the president—a public official bound by the same constitutional norms that bind state university admissions plans—may legitimately base his decision on the nominee's race or ethnicity. Needless to say, people object to particular nominees for all sorts of reasons. They may claim, for example, that the president accorded too much (or too little) weight to the nominee's race or ethnicity, or that the nominee is not the best choice among members of the preferred group. But they seldom deny the president's right to use such factors despite the equal protection principle. Again, the question is: Why?

One reason is historical. During the nineteenth century, party organizations routinely used ethnicity, among other factors, to balance their electoral tickets, and by the mid-twentieth century, leaders of political machines in Chicago and elsewhere had added race to their balancing acts. These political practices, and their private-sector counterparts, are now so common as to have become normal and even normative. These ticket-balancing traditions almost never arouse principled criticisms. (Interestingly, the Supreme Court has rejected historical precedent in ruling that lower-level officials may not be appointed or dismissed for such reasons, including political party affiliation, and that even peremptory challenges to potential jurors may not be based on them.)

In addition, the conception of merit deemed relevant to Supreme Court nominations differs from that implicated by university admissions programs. Elite, competitive educational institutions—which is where affirmative action really matters, since most schools will accept almost anyone who applies—generally rationalize their admissions on the basis of each applicant's relative merit, defined largely, though not exclusively, as academic achievement or promise. In the admissions process, moreover, equal opportunity and individual consideration are central values. Supreme Court nominations, in contrast, implicate no agreed-upon criterion of merit, even at the first-order, default level (such as GPA or test scores in the admissions context). The criteria and the process are acknowledged to be exclusively political—by which I mean that the president is entitled and expected to take into account any and all considerations, while the Senate will have the final say, based on each senator's idiosyncratic criteria. Merit is not defined as legal craftsmanship, superior intellect, or prior judicial experience (although this last has become much more common in recent appointments to the Court). Nor are professional achievement and recognition necessarily required, at least as certified by the American Bar Association, although they are customary. Indeed, politicians have both criticized and marginalized the ABA's findings since the Bork case.

For Supreme Court nominations, merit is a purely political ideal, one that is truly in the eye of the beholder. From the beginning of the Republic, presidents and senators have viewed the Court as a representative institution— not in the sense of being accountable to an electorate or physically resembling it, but because it exemplifies the nation's commitment to the rule of law. Accordingly, politicians have always brought to the selection process whatever values they and their constituents want the Court to exemplify and advance through law—and, so far as one can tell, this was the Framers' intent. The values balanced by politicians are too numerous, diverse, fluid, and ineffable to be assigned particular weights or otherwise controlled by law. To integrate these values into a discrete choice is an inherently discretionary, subjective task—the kind of task that the Court in other contexts has characterized as "a political question" or one as to which "there is simply no law to apply."

But to say that Supreme Court nominations are, and should be, "lawless" in this sense is emphatically not to say that the president is entitled to have his way. Indeed, the very opposite is true. The stakes to the nation in a life-tenured appointment to the high court are far too high, and the precedents for rejecting presidential choices far too numerous, for the

Senate to adopt a posture of abject deference. Just as the president is entitled to take race or ethnicity into account, so senators are entitled to reject a choice that they think rests too heavily on those criteria or fails to weight the ethnoracial criteria that they prefer.

My personal hope—unrealistic, to be sure—is that the president and the Senate may instead conclude that using ethnoracial selection criteria debases the ideal of blind justice. Whatever was true before the civil rights revolution, electoral considerations, and other factors placed blacks and women on the high court, the use of ethnoracial criteria today provides only a spurious form of representation and adds little or nothing to the quality of the Court's justice. Indeed, it sends the wrong signal to a society struggling to move from a law too often shaped by racial and ethnic hierarchies to one based on group-blind conceptions of merit and more universal, inclusive social values.

~ **4** ~

Groups and Equal Protection: The Flawed Theory of Owen Fiss

In "Groups and the Equal Protection Clause," my dear colleague and friend, Owen Fiss, has written a characteristically elegant, subtly argued brief for providing an undefined array of social advantages to blacks at the expense of other minorities and whites.[1] That this brief is gussied up as a theory of equal protection should not deceive us. Fiss forthrightly acknowledges that his theory is "a redistributive strategy" on behalf of blacks—one that he says might be not only a policy option for government but one that is *constitutionally required*.[2] Although he notes the possibility of using equal protection law to redistribute to other groups should they exhibit the requisite social disadvantage, he does not dwell on this possibility—a point that I discuss immediately below. Blacks, he writes, are "the prototype" of the beneficiary group, "the wards of the Equal Protection Clause." Fair enough—though Native Americans, Hispanics, Asians, other ethnoracial minorities, and still other groups prepared to make similar claims (e.g., gays and lesbians) are lined up to demand, well, equal protection.

Fiss's explication of his group disadvantage theory (as I shall call it) exhibits several attractive features. He exhumes the deeper structures of equal protection doctrine and analytical methodology, and then throws them—and their underlying assumptions—into sharp relief where we can scrutinize them closely. He reminds us that the courts' application of the familiar equal protection doctrine is neither objective nor straightforward but entails difficult value judgments at every turn. He usefully compares this doctrine and his group disadvantage theory with respect to their normative underpinnings and other elements, including the former's greater congeniality to judges. Perhaps most important for supporting his theory, he shows that even existing equal protection doctrine, despite the textual reference to "persons," inevitably rests on certain notions about the identity, cohesiveness, social status, and other traits of *groups*. All of this contributes significantly to our understanding of the concept, theory, and practice of equal protection.

A group-disadvantage theory, however, can be no more persuasive than the notions of groups and group competition that frame and infuse it. In this brief essay, I shall contend that Fiss is unconvincing on these very points— and not simply because of the quarter century that has passed since his article. While readily acknowledging that the concept of a group is both "problematic" and "messy," he goes on to make it the foundation of his theory. Unfortunately, his understanding of how groups work in American culture is too superficial to support the theory's normative weight. The title of my essay suggests why. The diversity, dynamism, and competition of group life and the individualistic culture in which groups are embedded constitute the generative social context in which groups form their identities, achieve and compete for status, and form relationships with other groups in civil society, including the state. Fiss's failure to take adequate account of this context renders his theory mistaken in fundamental respects, and his failure to provide a coherent account of status and status harm leaves it radically incomplete. These deficiencies should have been evident even in 1976 when he wrote his article, but they are greatly magnified by blacks' subsequent gains in almost every area of American life.

EMPIRICS: BLACK PROGRESS
AND POLITICAL INFLUENCE

I noted earlier that Fiss says little about how nonblack minority groups would fare under his theory. He suggests only that they might receive levels of protection somewhere between that afforded to blacks (maximum) and whites (minimum). In a society that generates an enormous number and range of groups, however, this suggestion has far too little resolving power. Fiss does distinguish between "natural" and "artificial" groups, noting that only the former are serious candidates for special protection under his group disadvantage theory. But as he himself seems to recognize, his criteria for identifying such groups ("perpetual subordination and circumscribed political power") have no clear referent other than blacks—a point to which I shall return in the next section.

The question-begging character of these fundamental Fissian criteria, especially as applied to other groups, is obvious. To illustrate the point, let us consider how these criteria apply to blacks, who are the easiest (in Fiss's word, prototypical) group for his theory and the hardest for a defender (as I am) of the antidiscrimination principle that he condemns as inadequate, if not incoherent. For centuries in America, blacks were cruelly subordinated, by any definition of that term. This proposition needs no elaboration. But is their subordination *perpetual*? What does this mean, and how would we know if it were true? If blacks' income, educational attainment, intermarriage, and many other indicia of social status have improved markedly over time in relative as well as absolute terms, and if their status improvement is continuing, what basis is there for contending that their past subordination will be *perpetuated*? In fact, young black women achieve roughly equal levels of income and education as their white counterparts, and young blacks of both sexes are now about as likely to have graduated from high school as young whites.[3] Indeed, blacks do better than Hispanics in these respects. The evidence on the white-black wage gap strongly suggests that as early as 1980, almost all of the gap could be explained by differences in basic skills acquired before youths enter either the labor market or postsecondary education. The gap, then, largely reflects family and early schooling factors, not labor market discrimination.

Should we not say instead, then, that the rising generations of blacks—those whose life chances have been and will be shaped by current social ideals and conditions rather than being frozen by the educational deprivation and caste subordination that permanently crippled earlier generations—are competing more effectively from more equal starting points? Note that I say "more equal," not "equal." This dramatic progress by blacks, of course, is very far from having produced full equality. Although blacks made significant residential integration gains during the 1990s, for example, their neighborhoods remain more isolated than those of other minority groups, even among the middle class. Wealth is more unequally distributed than income. The enduring problems of the black underclass—the tragically high rates of crime, substance abuse, violence, ill health, incarceration, unemployment, illegitimacy, single-parent households, school drop-outs, social isolation, discrimination, and many others—constitute American society's most daunting challenge.[4] But even conceding these problems, the notion of perpetual black subordination gravely misrepresents the conditions and ignores the steep trajectory of black achievement, which began even well before *Brown v. Board of Education*.[5] Their upward trajectory was discernible, albeit less clearly, even in 1976 when Fiss published his article. This criticism, then, cannot simply be dismissed as a case of 20-20 hindsight.

Similar questions are raised by Fiss's other criterion—circumscribed political power—again, even when we apply it to blacks, the prototypical disadvantaged group. In what sense politically circumscribed? The Voting Rights Act was enacted almost forty years ago and during that time, the courts and the Justice Department have implemented the Act in ways calculated not simply to protect blacks' right to vote like everyone else but also to maximize the number of legislative seats held by blacks—and simultaneously by other protected groups, no mean feat—as well as to protect their incumbency. These advantages (if that is what they are; political scientists differ about this) are enjoyed neither by whites nor by any other minority (so far). Blacks constitute a swing voting bloc in many federal, state, and local elections. They are perhaps the most reliable constituency in the Democratic Party coalition. Indeed, blacks' electoral support for Democratic candidates is so strong and unswerving that the Party leadership often takes their votes for granted. This creates a potentially large political opening for the Republican Party that some of its moderate members hope to exploit, along with appeals to socially conservative and entrepreneurial immigrants.

Blacks, who were well represented at the highest levels of the Clinton administration, occupy high-profile positions in a conservative Republican administration, including secretary of state, national security advisor, and deputy attorney general. Blacks, who constituted only 4 percent of the lawyers in the United States in 1998, hold 8.7 percent of the federal judgeships and almost 6 percent of the state judgeships—more than twice the Hispanic share of judges. Blacks have won mayoral elections in hundreds of municipalities, including most of the major cities, as well as in a growing number of statewide elections. The number of black elected officials increased almost sixfold from 1970 to 1999—almost 70 percent more than the number of Hispanic officials. (Only one black, Douglas Wilder, has been elected governor in the modern era, though another, Carl McCall, was the unsuccessful Democratic nominee in New York in 2002). It is entirely possible that a black, Colin Powell, Condoleeza Rice, or Barack Obama will be elected president in the future. For a group that comprises under 13 percent of the population, is losing ground demographically to other groups, and whose policy preferences tend to be much more liberal than those of the average voter (a point discussed below), these political achievements are stunning.

Perhaps Fiss means something else by "politically circumscribed." Perhaps he means that blacks as a group, despite their strong descriptive representation (i.e., black members) and growing access to legislative and executive power at all levels of government, fail to enact their substantive policy agendas and that this failure is systemic—that is, due to the nature of their group—rather than simply reflecting the vicissitudes of political struggle. If this is what he means—that blacks qua blacks are unable to form effective political coalitions to achieve their objectives—he would need to develop a convincing argument to that effect. No such argument, however, can be mounted.

The fact is that blacks have won many political battles at the federal level—and even more in states and localities where they are more demographically concentrated. The most remarkable victory, in some respects, is the survival for more than thirty years of affirmative action programs that are under broad constitutional challenge in the courts and the states, and that arouse broad public opposition. Another example of black political effectiveness is the vast expansion of the welfare state since the 1960s, an expansion that has continued in virtually every federal program targeted at low-income people. These means-tested or low-income-targeted redistribution programs include health care, food stamps, assisted housing, the Earned Income Tax Credit, energy assistance, disability, Title I, Head Start, and others. The only possible exception is the old AFDC program, which Congress fundamentally reformed and capped (at a higher level) in the 1996 welfare reform law and which has been replaced (and in some cases, augmented) by many states with large low-income populations.

I mention government redistribution programs and affirmative action programs for two reasons. First, they have long been at the top of most blacks' political agenda—along with equal opportunity laws, which of course are already on the books. If we ask which programs most blacks say they most want, the answer is redistribution programs and affirmative action. The second reason I mention these particular programs is that most Americans oppose them. Affirmative action, I just noted, has always been opposed by a large majority of voters, and public attitudes toward welfare programs, which the media and public associate with blacks, are also decidedly negative. Indeed, blacks are far more liberal—in terms of support for large-scale governmental wealth redistribution programs and other policies—than Americans generally, so one would expect a centrist polity to reject many of their candidates and their policy positions. One would expect these rejections even if Americans were, as I think the vast majority are, sympathetic to black social aspirations.

For these two reasons, then, affirmative action and redistributive programs pose the hardest test for blacks' political efficacy. Significantly, however, blacks have passed this test, winning and sustaining political support for these unpopular programs for decades. Blacks as a group are in relative demographic terms both small and declining, yet they have succeeded in amassing and exercising considerably more political influence than their numbers would predict.

It is worth emphasizing that my concern here is with blacks' political influence, as my purpose is to refute Fiss's characterization of them as a perpetually subordinated, politically circumscribed group. I do not propose to consider the quite different, more complex, and highly contestable question of how wisely and effectively blacks have deployed the political resources they have so painstakingly mobilized—except where Fiss takes a position on this question with which I disagree. The main example of this is his strong support for the decision by black leaders to invest so many of their hard-won political assets in the pursuit and defense of legally mandated ethnoracial preferences. In my recent book, *Diversity in America*, I have explained why, contrary to Fiss, I view their decision to do so as poignantly misguided.

PRINCIPLE: ANTIDISCRIMINATION

After explaining some reasons why courts find the modern antidiscrimination principle attractive, Fiss comes to the heart of his dissatisfaction with it: its individualistic and, in that sense, universalizing premises, the fact that "it is not in any way dependent on a recognition of social classes or groups." He hastens to point out, correctly, that various elements of the doctrine—means-end rationality, the "fitness" of classifications, and the categorization of suspect classes, for example—cannot be applied without reference to particular groups. With this fact in mind, he goes on to speak, incorrectly, of "[t]his illusion of individualism."

This is an illusion only if we conflate two things that are actually quite different. First, there are the individualistic and universalistic aspirations of the equal protection norm; as Fiss puts it, "no person seems to be given more protection than another." Second, there is the just-mentioned operational fact that the norm, in its doctrinal form, cannot be applied by a court without some explicit or implicit reference to groups.

But how one perceives the relationship between the norm's aspiration and its operation determines how one will assess the group disadvantage proposal. As I have already noted, Fiss disparages the individualistic aspiration—either in its own terms or because he thinks it can only be achieved by treating individuals differently depending on their group's relative social status. These two possibilities amount to much the same thing, and they drive him to embrace a different norm, his theory of group disadvantage. In contrast, I view the individualistic-universalistic aspiration as socially sound and normatively just, and believe that the antidiscrimination principle should constantly strive to reach it by demanding appropriate levels of classificatory fitness. (For present purposes, I accept the conventional doctrine defining this fitness inquiry, and I do not address the question of whether courts might design or apply the doctrine better, except to say that they should use the best current information about the group's social and political status). In this view, the fact that courts applying the antidiscrimination norm must assign people to groups for this limited and temporary purpose is but a necessary means to the ultimate end of treating individuals as equally as the law can.

I say that the antidiscrimination doctrine's ascription of individuals to groups is *limited* because it is the legislature's ascription that is used as the basis for conducting the means-end and fitness inquiries. The court does not place its own imprimatur, much less the Constitution's, on this ascription unless it upholds the classification. In that case, its judgment is only that the group ascription in question was a permissible one for the legislature to have made. I say that the purpose is *temporary* because the inquiry, and hence the ascription, lasts no longer than the litigation for which it is conducted. I say that the ascription is *necessary* because I can think of no other satisfactory way to determine whether individuals have received equal protection of the laws.

Fiss's alternative—his group disadvantage theory—is plainly unsatisfactory. Indeed, he unwittingly condemns his own theory when he criticizes the antidiscrimination principle (here, as applied to preferences) for not supplying any nonsubstantive basis or standards for making the judgments required by the principle. This observation about the antidiscrimination principle, and his corollary observation that a court applying it must therefore exercise some independent judgment in doing so, are true enough. But this aspect of the antidiscrimination principle, which Fiss sees as a vice, is actually a virtue—at least when compared to Fiss's group disadvantage theory. He favors his theory precisely because it "talks about substantive ends, and not fit, and . . . recognizes the existence and importance of groups, not just individuals."

I contend, in contrast, that the antidiscrimination principle is desirable precisely because the ascription of individuals to groups that it requires is limited, temporary, and minimizes judicial prescription of substantive ends that are, and in a liberal democracy should be, contested and adopted by citizens and politically accountable officials, not judges. To put my point another way, Fiss's group disadvantage theory depends on and indeed invites judges to embed in the law their own normative views about particular groups as the reified bearers of equality rights, while the antidiscrimination principle encourages judges to view groups more descriptively, ascribing individuals to them only to the extent necessary to resolve the individuals' own equality claims through a methodology that seeks to minimize such judicial normativity.

My account, then, raises a crucial question that Fiss does not ask. Which is more socially and constitutionally problematic—a familiar antidiscrimination principle intended to constrain the substantive choices that judges make and to focus their analysis on the fitness of the group ascriptions the legislature has made? Or a group disadvantage principle that requires judges to determine the relative social status, mobility, and political efficacy of competing groups, guided only by the ill-defined criteria that Fiss's theory provides?

My answer to this question is clear. The antidiscrimination principle is less problematic. Although it exhibits a number of notorious problems, including some of the methodological difficulties noted by Fiss, these problems are not peculiar to equal protection law but are of a

familiar sort in legal doctrine. Their familiarity makes them manage-
able. They constitute the devil that we know—and the one, Fiss all but
concedes, that Americans strongly prefer.

In contrast, as I showed above, the criteria necessary to apply Fiss's
principle are not only breathtakingly vague; they also beg precisely the
kinds of questions—about group identity and achievement, political efficacy, intergroup competition, the distinction between unfair practices
and group-disadvantaging practices, and distributive justice—that
judges have no business answering, questions that should be allocated to
other more politically accountable institutions. Even the most courageous
social scientist would hesitate to answer such questions without having
first conducted rigorous, methodologically demanding empirical studies
and searchingly debated with a broad range of interests about the most
controversial normative issues. Indeed, even Fiss's uncannily wise, fair,
and prescient judges, if not Ronald Dworkin's Hercules, might forswear
such a task, which goes well beyond the already challenging analysis
required of judges applying the antidiscrimination principle.

Fiss's theory, however, expressly eschews any pretense of analytical
rigor. "Imprecision," under his theory, "is not itself a constitutional vice"
so long as the government action "seeks to improve the position of a disadvantaged group and is in fact related to that end." Fiss offers no other
limiting principle or decisional guidance. He would subject governmental
actions that prefer one racial group over another to only the rational-basis
standard of judicial review. Under this most permissive of standards, he
says, government can prefer one disadvantaged group over another disadvantaged group so long as the preference does not impair the latter's
"status." Fiss quickly adds that this necessitates "a theory of status-harm"
showing how the government action improves or aggravates the status of
a disadvantaged group.

What, then, is this theory of status and status-harm on which Fiss's entire
group disadvantage principle squarely rests? Alas, he does not provide such
a theory, conceding that it "may be highly problematic" and noting that the
requisite status-harm would not be satisfied by showing differential impact
or even unfairness to the disadvantaged group. But apart from this, we are
told only that the pivotal status-harm test is clearly met by blacks, and that
other disadvantaged groups could also meet it, at least in principle.

Which other disadvantaged groups might qualify for preference under
Fiss's theory? And what happens when the social resource at issue is zero-
sum so that preferring blacks would disadvantage Native Americans or
other already-disadvantaged groups?[6] Obviously, this is an important question. After all, such zero-sum conflicts are ubiquitous, as Fiss readily
acknowledges: "What is given to one group cannot be given to another."
His answer, evidently, is that blacks win all such conflicts unless the prefer-

ence is patently irrational. This is because "[p]referring blacks may limit the number of places open to other disadvantaged groups, but it is not clear that it impairs their status." Fiss's "not clear" is an egregious understatement, of course, especially in the absence of any theory of status-harm.[7]

In truth, Fiss lacks more than a theory of status-harm. He also lacks any theory of group identity (beyond acknowledging that any individual has a multiplicity of group identifications) and any theory of group competition (beyond acknowledging that it is often zero-sum). This is no small deficiency given that his group disadvantage principle calls for active, perhaps constitutionally compelled redistribution from one ethnoracial group to another. It is like advancing a theory of taxation without discussing who will pay what and why.[8]

Any serious theory of group identity and group competition would be obliged to confront certain facts of group life in America today and certain dilemmas arising out of those facts. These facts were perfectly obvious in 1976 when Fiss wrote his article but they have become much more salient since then. First, as *Diversity in America* shows, racial discrimination against blacks—Fiss's "prototype" disadvantaged group—has by any measure declined dramatically, and the same is true of black disadvantage more generally, though important inequalities remain. As noted above, this record of black progress, which Orlando Patterson calls "nothing short of astonishing," belies Fiss's image of a perpetually subordinated caste. How much of this progress is due to the racial preferences Fiss advocates is hard to say. *Diversity in America* explains that the combined effects of the antidiscrimination principle and more secular economic dynamics were far more significant. In any event, the factual assumptions underlying Fiss's theory are far more doubtful today than they were then.

Second, blacks constitute a far more differentiated group than Fiss supposed, and their heterogeneity is steadily increasing. To take only the most obvious example, many American blacks are immigrants or the children or grandchildren of immigrants. As Harvard sociologist Mary Waters explains, they did not experience the depredations of American slavery and share with the descendants of those slaves little more than skin color and the risk of discrimination by racists who lump them together. In addition, the enormous growth of the college-educated black population has widened the already broad chasm separating them from the small, increasingly isolated black underclass. Many blacks, like other groups, militantly oppose the government's effort to ascribe to them a single ethnoracial identity and claim multiple ones. Treating blacks as a monolithic group for preference purposes, as Fiss expressly favors, is a Procrustean deformation of their social reality that misrepresents, disserves, and disrespects them. This deformation, moreover, also fuels or inflames much of the public opposition to affirmative action.

Third, the emergence of other ethnoracial groups has vastly complicated the competition for public resources and recognition that Fiss depicted. The ancient struggle of black aspiration against white oppression has been transformed into a far more confusing political battleground in which many more internally heterogeneous and externally diverse groups form shifting alliances to advance discrete agendas on a wide variety of issues. To take just one example, legislative districting under the Voting Rights Act, the claims of blacks for special protection in electoral arrangements now run headlong into the claims by Hispanics and to a lesser extent, Asians, who advance similar political demands based on similar moral and other arguments. Many other such examples could be discussed—disputes over the location and educational policies of public schools, competition for immigration quotas, the design and implementation of affirmative action programs, claims for judgeships and other official positions, ethnically related religious conflicts, policing strategies, and on and on *ad nauseam*. Like the vanished bipolar world of the Cold War, Fiss's biracial world of equal protection is a dangerous anachronism.

Race, the pivot of Fiss's group disadvantage theory, is perhaps the worst imaginable category around which to organize group competition and social relations more generally. At the risk of belaboring the obvious, racial categories in law have played an utterly pernicious and destructive role throughout human history. This incontrovertible fact should arouse wonder at the logic of those who view racial preferences as no more troubling than athletic scholarships, and at the hubris of those, like Fiss, who imagine that we can distinguish clearly enough between invidious and benign race discrimination to engrave this distinction into our constitutional order.

Vast human experience mocks this comforting illusion, as does the fact that most Americans, including many blacks and other minorities, think of racial preferences as invidious, not benign. Whether benignly intended or not, using race to distribute advantage and disadvantage, as Fiss urges, tends to ossify the fluid, forward-looking political identities that a robust democratic spirit both inspires and requires. The earnest hope of Fiss, Justice Blackmun, and many other well-meaning reformers that we could get beyond race by emphasizing it has not been borne out.

Quite the contrary. Ironically, the proponents of ethnoracial preferences now have the greatest stake in infusing our private and public discourses with a relentlessly racialist rhetoric and sensibility that in tragic fact tends to deform these discourses and impede further progress.

NOTES

1. 5 *Philosophy & Public Affairs* 107 (1976).

2. The constitutional text in question, of course, refers to "equal" protection, not special protection, but this obstacle presents no greater difficulty for Fiss than it does for current doctrine, which also affords groups varying levels of protection.

3. See Orlando Patterson, *The Ordeal of Integration: Progress and Resentment in America's "Racial" Crisis* 27 (1997). In fact, Patterson's failure to break out the different age cohorts actually conceals the greater gains of young black women.

4. They also exert a strong downward bias on group averages for blacks. But even in the underclass, some gains occurred during the 1990s.

5. Another recent example of this progress is stock ownership by middle-class blacks. Of blacks with annual income of $50,000 or more, 74 percent own stocks, up 30 percent in five years. The comparable figure for whites is 84 percent, up only 3.7 percent.

6. Here I do not consider preferences that disfavor whites; under Fiss's theory, whites—even poor whites in Appalachia—are ipso facto high-status and thus their claims will always lose out to those of a disadvantaged group.

7. Speaking of preferential law school admissions for blacks, Fiss "doubt[s] whether anyone believes" that such preferences impair the status of that group. But as I show in *Diversity in America*, many whites do believe it, as do many blacks, including some who oppose preferences and some who at least qualifiedly support them.

8. Fiss does not say how thoroughgoing this redistribution must be, but his logic implies that it must continue until the status of disadvantaged groups is equal to . . . what? the status of the most privileged group? of the average group? of the lowest-status group that is not "specially" disadvantaged?—and that since blacks are "perpetually subordinated," new redistribution must be undertaken over and over again in order to maintain their legally mandated gains. Fissian redistribution, then, must be a kind of perpetual-motion machine.

⌒ 5 ⌒

Race Matters: The Incoherence of Cornel West

Cornel West's "basic aim in life," he tells us in his slender collection of essays, *Race Matters*, is "to speak truth to power with love so that the quality of everyday life for ordinary people is enhanced and white supremacy is stripped of its authority and legitimacy."

This is a tall order, of course, and it would be gratifying to report that West fills it. Alas he does not, although perhaps no one could. Truth, after all, is notoriously elusive, even for one as talented and broadly educated as Cornel West, who is professor of religion and director of Afro-American studies at Princeton. The powerful have already heard most of what he has to say, although he says it in a distinctive, attractive voice at once passionate and rational. While he speaks the language of love, he cannot resist disparaging the motivations and aspirations of many of those with whom he disagrees. His sympathy for ordinary people is evident, but his conception of them seems too thin for one to have confidence that his sketchy prescriptions would help them much. And since West uses white supremacy as an all-purpose label to excoriate whatever he dislikes about American society (especially "cultural conservatism" and capitalism), his effort to de-legitimate it is scattershot at best, counterproductive at worst.

Before elaborating and defending these criticisms, I should note some of the book's considerable virtues—beginning, appropriately enough, with its title. West's double entendre cleverly captures both the sweep of the topics that the essays (some of which were written for other, disparate audiences) embrace and West's core assumption that attitudes about race continue to shape the structure and spirit of American culture at every turn. A more important strength is West's attentiveness to the importance of values and even spirituality to any proper understanding of, and remedial approach to, the dilemmas surrounding contemporary race relations. West identifies distinctively "liberal" and "conservative" views on race issues. Liberals, he says, favor government programs premised on structural explanations of white discrimination and black poverty and crime; they fear that discussing values will produce "blame the victim" politics inimical to black interests. In contrast, conservatives eschew such programs, stressing instead blacks' need to change their values and behavior; conservatives fear that discussing structural reforms rather than culture would threaten the sanctity of the status quo. Seeking to debunk this conventional division, West correctly notes that culture, being rooted in a variety of mediating institutions such as families, churches, and the mass media, "is as much a structure as the economy or politics." The polity and economy, moreover, both shape and are shaped by cultural values. This concern for values is underscored by West's strong critique of what he calls "racial reasoning" by blacks—a heightened, defensive racial consciousness emphasizing "black authenticity, closed-ranks mentality, and black cultural conservatism." Appraising blacks' responses to the Anita Hill–Clarence Thomas affair, he argues that this mode of reasoning helps to explain and sustain the pervasive sexist and homophobic attitudes and abusive treatment of women that he finds among black males. Here, as elsewhere, West exhibits an admirable humanistic sensibility, one attuned to injustice and degrading treatment wherever they may be found. In addressing highly sensitive issues that few commentators are prepared to tackle head-on—racial reasoning, leadership failures and anti-Semitism among blacks, the connection between attitudes about black sexuality and about race, Afrocentrism, the merits of affirmative action, and the psychology of the black middle class—he displays audacity and a kind of courage.

West, however, would probably take this celebration of courage as faint praise. After all, he is at some pains to depict black conservatives who also raise these issues (though often resolving them in different ways) as confused and careerist, not courageous. Moreover, the enthusiastic blurbs on the book jacket from Marian Wright Edelman, Henry Louis Gates, Jr., and Johnetta Cole will surely immunize him against most attacks from the left, which is clearly where his heart is. Finally, fine scholars like West are paid— and at Princeton (and Yale), paid well—to take on controversial issues like these, and they receive tenure precisely in order to insulate them from some of the career risks that might otherwise attend heterodox thinking. We do not ordinarily praise as courageous people who are simply doing their job. I suspect that West would agree that the fact that his essays seem courageous says less about him than it says about the impoverished state of public debate on race issues today. West aims at an analysis that acknowledges the merits of both liberal and conservative views of "race matters" and then goes beyond them to construct new, more encompassing formulations and solutions. His openness to opposing points of view and his call for greater humility on the part of black leaders and intellectuals certainly compare favorably to much of today's commentaries on race, which exhibit a predictable, one-sided rigidity and self-righteousness. But here again, praise for West must be qualified, for his balance and transcendence turn out to be more apparent than real. While he presents what he terms conservative views, his assessment of them is almost uniformly hostile. At the same time, his own positions fall comfortably within the traditional liberal consensus; one should not be beguiled by his rhetorical bells and whistles about a "prophetic framework of moral reasoning" and his proud but misleading description of his analysis as "radical." My point is not that West's essays should be more balanced. Although he is a distinguished scholar, these essays do not pretend to be scholarship but are instead a mode of tendentious discourse conducted at a high level of generality and proceeding by way of moral *ipse dixit* and conceptual development rather than through the marshaling of empirical evidence. Even in scholarship, of course, balance is a mixed blessing. While we want scholars to adduce and assess evidence and claims with scrupulous fairness, we usually have no reason to want or expect that they will find the merits of those claims to be in perfect equipoise. And on that score, at least, West does not disappoint us.

He introduces the book with a reference to the conflagration arising out of the first Rodney King verdict in 1992. (The book was published before the second verdict.) He observes that it was "neither a race riot nor a class rebellion" but was instead a "justified social rage" transcending race and class. Although West makes his own abhorrence of violence and pillage perfectly clear throughout, he fails to explain why he thinks this particular outbreak of mayhem and arson was "justified," a rather disturbing omission under the circumstances. He immediately goes on to denounce the regnant liberal and conservative views of race in America which, he says, constitute a "paralyzing framework" for dealing with such a tragic event.

In place of this framework, which begins with "the problems of black people," he insists that we focus on "the flaws of American society," which subordinate blacks but which victimize whites as well. His list is long. It includes "unemployment, hunger, homelessness, and sickness for millions," the "collapse of the spiritual communities" that sustained earlier generations of Americans, a politics obsessed with media images and public opinion polls, a "powerless citizenry that includes not just the poor but all of us," the "cultural decay in a declining empire," and the "profound hatred of African people [that] sits at the center of American civilization." These corrosive conditions have engendered in blacks a pervasive "nihilism," which he defines as "the lived experience of coping with a life of horrifying meaninglessness, hopelessness, and (most important) lovelessness."

How did this corrupting, disabling nihilism, this "disease of the soul," come to afflict blacks? In the past, West says, blacks were equipped with a "cultural armor"—religious and civic institutions and informal support networks—that enabled them to "beat back" these demons. This armor, however, has now disintegrated under the pressure of two developments: the degeneration of black leadership and the market's increasing intrusion into every aspect of black life. West deplores both of these factors, and views them as deeply connected. No black leadership group escapes his fierce (but loving?) invective. The black middle class today, he insists, is not simply much larger than in the past; it is also "more deficient, and to put it strongly, more decadent." Obsessed with status and addicted to stimulation as a way of life (West's words), middle class parents no longer enroll their children in black educational institutions but instead send them "to Harvard, Yale, and Princeton to get a high-paying job (for direct selfish reasons)." This is a fascinating allusion. It is impossible to believe that West does not intend it to underscore the irony of such a condemnation coming from one who has chosen to teach these Ivy League children rather than teaching their counterparts at, say, Morehouse or Lincoln. Is this, then, an instance of self-mockery? Or is it a veiled claim that no one in the black middle class, even a prophetic moral philosopher, can escape from this "decadence"? If the latter, can he really mean this?

Black politicians come in for even worse criticism. Some of it is plain silly. For example, West contrasts the black dress suits worn by Malcolm X and Martin Luther King, which "signified the seriousness of their deep commitment to black freedom," with contemporary politicians' expensive tailored suits, which "symbolize their personal success and individual achievement." Like Houston Baker, who discerns in the wearing of X-caps "a national blackness oppositionally testifying against American legal obscenities," West is evidently taken with sartorial metaphors. In West's view, the Victorian three-piece suit with watch chain worn by W. E. B. Du Bois "dignified his sense of intellectual vocation, a sense of rendering service by means of critical intelligence and moral action," while "the shabby clothing worn by most black intellectuals these days may be seen as symbolizing their utter marginality behind the walls of academe and their sense of impotence in the wider world of American culture and politics." (In light of this iconographic theory, what are we to make of West, who presents himself on the cover of his own book nattily dressed in a three-piece suit complete with stick pin, cufflinks, and possibly [his hands are in the way] watch chain? To this shabbily dressed [white] intellectual, West's suit looks expensive and tailored, like those worn by the politicians, but perhaps he purchased it on sale. Who can say?)

The quality of black intellectuals' work, he insists, "has suffered more so than that of others" both because they have permitted themselves and their "radical critiques" to be co-opted and disarmed by the elite "Academy" and its "dominant paradigms," and because black intellectuals lack supporting infrastructure. These reasons are no more convincing than the assertion—that black intellectuals' work is degraded—which they purport to explain. The charge that black intellectuals have been co-opted is pure ad hominem argument unless West is willing to engage the substantive positions of those he derides and demonstrate that they are in fact wrong. After all, the fact that these (unspecified) paradigms are "dominant" does not mean that they are wrong; if anything, the working presumption should be the opposite, at least until someone comes up with a better paradigm (i.e., one that explains the existing data better). Even if these paradigms do turn out to be wrong, blacks may have embraced them for the same intellectually plausible (even if false) reasons that drew the white "elite" to adopt them. His claim about infrastructure is also curious. It makes one wonder how James Baldwin, Zora Neale Hurston, Langston Hughes, Du Bois, and numerous other writers of distinction whom West admires managed to create an extraordinarily rich black literary tradition in a world with far less infrastructure for black artists. Among black intellectuals, conservatives like Thomas Sowell and Glen Loury receive West's heaviest fire. He seeks to depict them (lovingly?) as rather pathetic, hypocritical careerists. One particularly clear example of this merits extended quotation:

> Mobility by means of affirmative action breeds tenuous self-respect and questionable peer acceptance for middle-class blacks. The new black conservatives

voiced these feelings in the forms of attacks on affirmative action programs (despite the fact that they had achieved their positions by means of such programs). The importance of this quest for middle-class respectability based on merit rather than politics cannot be overestimated in the new black conservatism. The need of black conservatives to gain the respect of their white peers deeply shapes their conservatism.

This passage is triply ad hominem. It states that black conservatives (since no qualification appears, he presumably means all of them) owe their positions to affirmative action—a cruel, irresponsible charge absent evidence, which West does not bother to supply. Then it seeks to belittle their policy views by imagining, and then disparaging, their ulterior motives for holding those views, as if one could not justly criticize a state of affairs from which one has personally benefited—a precept that is absurd on its face and would also discredit most reform movements, which tend to be led by the relatively privileged. Finally, it accuses them of what amounts to psychological weakness and intellectual dishonesty. (A few pages later, West observes that far from being courageous critics of the liberal establishment, "their salaries, honorariums, and travel expenses are payed [*sic*] by well-endowed conservative foundations and corporations.")

West also distorts their views on one of the most sensitive subjects of all: white racism. Black conservatives, he writes, have not won support in the black community because "most blacks conclude that while racial discrimination is not the sole cause of their plight, it certainly is one cause." This clearly implies that conservatives like Sowell and Loury do not believe that discrimination is one cause of poverty, yet this implication is false. In fact, they maintain that discrimination is indeed one cause but they emphasize that it cannot fully explain the extent of poverty among blacks. This is a point that West makes himself only two paragraphs earlier! "Obviously," he remarks, "the idea that racial discrimination is the sole cause of the predicament of the black working poor and very poor is specious." The conservatives and West would probably disagree about the proportion of poverty for which racism is responsible, but that is a different issue and one that West does not discuss.

Another distortion occurs several pages later. In a very confusing passage about the role of intermediate associations such as churches, mosques, and schools, West states that black conservatives believe that these institutions support the "prevailing class subordination of American capitalist social relations"—as if that were the reason why conservatives approve of such institutions. Whatever West's phrase means here, it seriously misrepresents the conservatives' ardent praise for intermediate associations on the grounds that they buffer the individual against governmental power, enhance social diversity, and provide the best opportunities for people to achieve satisfying relationships and civic fulfillment.

West's across-the-board attack on today's black leadership, political and intellectual, is only one prong of his explanation of black nihilism. The other, more fundamental cause, in his view, is the intrusion of market capitalism into the black community. I say more fundamental because he holds market values responsible for at least much of the moral corruption of the leadership. (Remember the symbol of the politicians' tailored suits?) West, moreover, reserves his most vituperative, vivid rhetoric for the market; indeed, he can hardly mention it without appending a violent or sexual metaphor or epithet.

The market culture, he says, is "dominated by gangster mentalities and self-destructive wantonness"; this "growing gangsterization . . . results in part from a market-driven racial reasoning that links the White House to the ghetto projects." He writes of the "market-driven shattering of black civil society," the "jungle ruled by a cutthroat market morality devoid of any faith in deliverance or hope for freedom," and "[t]he reduction of individuals to objects of pleasure . . . in which gestures of sexual foreplay and orgiastic pleasure flood the marketplace." He denounces the "unregulated corporative and financial expansion and intense entrepreneurial activity" that lead to a "culture of consumption." Referring to Thomas Sowell (representing other black conservatives), West asks a "descendant of slaves sold at the auction block" a "provocative and slightly unfair question": "Can the market do any wrong?" While West surely would not suggest that the conservatives are apologists for slavery (that would be more than "slightly unfair"), he must be suggesting that it was a quintessentially capitalist practice. In fact, of course, slavery was an ancient, precapitalist practice that capitalist development in fact helped bring to an end.

Since the market is the root of most evil in West's cosmos, one would expect him to offer some analysis to support his claim that it has in fact caused the pathologies that he sees in the black ghetto. Yet one searches his text in vain for such an analysis or even a coherent argument, Marxist or otherwise, to that effect. Indeed, his notion of the "market" is wholly undefined. It appears to be a portmanteau synonym for unbridled greed, conspicuous consumption, and amorality; if it has any virtues in promoting efficiency or protecting individual freedom, he does not acknowledge them. Thus while mocking the promarket views of black conservatives, he does not bother to engage their argument that on the whole the market has been a much better friend to blacks than government has.

Reading between the lines (which is all his sketchy discussion permits us to do), West's critique of capitalism appears to be moral and spiritual, not economic. Not only is this moral and spiritual critique undeveloped; it is also hollow and unpersuasive without an economic counterpart. Where sympathetic observers of the black struggle applaud growing entrepreneurial activity, he laments it because it produces a "culture of consumption." He seems to believe not that the market makes us less prosperous or even less equal or happy than we might be under some other system of production and distribution, but that it somehow makes us less noble. We must infer from this that if black economic progress were far greater and more widely distributed than it is, black nihilism would be that much deeper; the black middle class for which he expresses such contempt would in that event presumably be even larger and more "decadent."

Since West scorns blacks' hard-won economic gains in the market, readers are entitled to ask about his alternative vision of black progress. That vision, it turns out, is neither novel nor "radical" (his own touchstone for reform), but it is remarkably vague. First, "we must admit that the most valuable sources for help, hope, and power consist of ourselves and our common history." Fair enough. Second, "we must focus our attention on the public square. . . . The neglect of our public infrastructure, for example—our water and sewage systems, bridges, tunnels, highways, subways, and streets—reflects not only our myopic economic policies, which impede productivity, but also the low priority we place on our common life." West's statement about society's growing neglect of infrastructure is one of the few empirical claims that is specific enough to be tested, and it appears to be false—or at least debatable. Heywood Sanders of Trinity University has recently pointed to a pattern of steady long-term increases in investment in the infrastructure categories West mentions; the exception is mass transit, which fluctuates more but has risen steadily under 1990s legislation. According to Sanders, total public infrastructure investment growth in these categories has exceeded the rate of population growth, except in the highways category. Unfortunately, as Brookings Institution studies show, this spending is grossly misallocated.

An essential step, West says, is "some form of large-scale public intervention to ensure access to basic social goods," a "mixture of government, business, and labor that does not follow any existing blueprint." He does not elaborate what he has in mind; indeed, he devotes but one short paragraph to the subject. This omission, given the circumstances of this book, strikes me as highly objectionable. No one expects Cornel West to be a policy entrepreneur with a fully developed, workable, politically viable plan for black community development, especially since even the policy wonks have not managed to devise such a plan. Nevertheless, if one's project is to excoriate black politicians in the most uncompromising terms for their incompetence, moral obtuseness, and indifference to constituents, one is obliged to take seriously the severe political and policy constraints under which those politicians have to work. One must also raise more probing questions than West does about the character of the voters who put and keep these politicians in office in the first place.

The compromises that even the most morally scrupulous politician must make in order to win election and pursue some conception of constituent and public interests with effectiveness make it difficult for black leaders to get away with the kind of vaporous formulation that West uses both to seize the moral high ground and to discredit them. As Max Weber pointed out three-quarters of a century ago, the morality of politicians, which he called the "ethic of responsibility," differs radically from the morality of prophets, which he called the "ethic of ultimate ends." The latter appears to be West's chosen province, yet he seems innocent of the distinction.

If "speaking truth to power with love" means anything, it must mean respectfully acknowledging that those who undertake to exercise authority and stewardship on behalf of others are constrained by larger, more demanding responsibilities. This in no way immunizes the politicians from criticism, of course, and there is in any event precious little danger of that in our polity—even for black legislators guaranteed safe seats under the current interpretation of the Voting Rights Act. But it does mean that one like West who aspires to reshape black politics in the real world should hold politicians to standards that they can meet in the real world.

To what standard does West hold them? The answer is far from clear. He groups contemporary black politicians into two categories—"race-effacing managerial leaders" (he cites former Los Angeles Mayor Tom Bradley) and "race identifying protest leaders" (he mentions Marion Barry and Louis Farrakhan)—and dismisses all of them as misguided, co-opted, or ineffective. A third category, "race-transcending prophetic leaders," is what West admires but he claims that it is today an empty set. A "prophetic" politician, he writes wistfully, would possess "personal integrity and political savvy, moral vision and prudential judgment, courageous defiance and organizational patience." Such a politician is one who "critiques the powers that be (including the black component of the establishment) and who puts forward a vision of moral regeneration and political insurgency for the purpose of fundamental social change for all who suffer from socially induced misery." As his prophetic heroes among elected officials, he names only Harold Washington, Adam Clayton Powell, Jr., and Ronald Dellums, while omitting distinguished leaders like William Gray, the highly respected former chairman of the House Budget Committee and (like West) a minister and fiery orator. (West makes clear that Jesse Jackson, whom he views as demagogic, does not yet qualify as a prophetic politician.)

This is odd, especially for a commentator who claims that his project is to transcend stale, unnecessarily divisive race-baiting. His favored politicians include rhetorically flamboyant legislative mavericks like Dellums (who are notably ineffective) and Powell (who in his later years did little but cavort in Bimini while his constituents struggled in Harlem). At the same time, he excludes those like Gray who consistently managed to get important legislation enacted. This puzzle only deepens when West goes on to denounce a black "obsession with white racism [that] often comes at the expense of more broadly based alliances to affect social change and borders on a tribal mentality." It was this obsession, after all, that marked the political careers of Powell and to an extent Dellums, in contrast to the political styles of Gray, Maynard Jackson, Andrew Young, and other leaders who managed with great effort to construct such alliances but whom West dismisses with silence.

Answers to the puzzle may be found in West's discussions of black anti-Semitism and affirmative action. After all, both of these practices jeopardize the broad-based alliances that West seeks. His treatment of black anti-Semitism is insightful and his firm denunciation of it is welcome. (He makes special mention of the many black ministers who condemned from their pulpits the murder of Yankel Rosenbaum in Crown Heights but were ignored by the media.) Unfortunately, however, the moral authority of this denunciation is tarnished by his judgment that the anti-Semitism of Farrakhan and Leonard Jeffries is "the same mean-spirited game" as the past support for Likud policies by mainstream American Jewish groups. This moral equivalency is crude and false. Both positions may have been wrong, but they are certainly not, morally speaking, the "same . . . game." The merits of Likud policies toward the Palestinians were at least arguable in the face of a genuine, continuing, violent Arab threat to Israel's survival. The Farrakhan-Jeffries venom, however, is not. Given the importance of affirmative action in today's race relations discourse, his discussion of it is remarkably brief, covering only a few paragraphs. It is almost as if he viewed affirmative action as a distraction from more significant issues, without quite saying so. If he could write on a clean slate, West would favor affirmative action policies based on class, not race. But while continuing to favor this transracial principle, he believes that the historic opposition to broad-based economic redistribution made it prudent for blacks during the 1960s to take advantage of the momentary public support for narrower civil rights measures, while opening the door to future expansion to other low-income groups. Without race-based affirmative action, he maintains, white racism would persist and the plight of blacks would be even worse. In this sense, he finds it to be an imperfect, incomplete policy—"part of a redistributive chain that must be strengthened."

This is certainly a plausible justification for race-based affirmative action, but it is also a highly contestable one. My point here is simply that the issue deserves far more discussion than West gives it. For example, he might have considered the appropriateness of contextual distinctions between affirmative action in the allocation of, say, factory jobs, graduate school admissions, legislative districts, and subsidized housing. He might also have considered the danger that affirmative action can stigmatize black successes not simply in the minds of whites (a risk that he might attribute to white racism) but also—most poignantly and corrosively—in the minds of blacks (a risk that is grimly confirmed by his categorical assertion that black conservatives "achieved their positions by means of such programs"). Finally, he might have considered the extent to which non-European immigration is weakening the moral and political underpinnings of affirmative action. Since competition with the newer groups is certain to intensify in the future and poses the most difficult challenges for blacks, his failure to mention immigration and interethnic tensions is especially regrettable. His insights would be valuable.

This is in the end a disappointing book, all the more so because of Cornel West's towering reputation as "the preeminent African American intellectual of our generation" (according to Gates's self-denying blurb on the book jacket). His emphasis on the demands of the spirit and the importance of cultural values and institutions in thinking about "race matters" is praiseworthy, but his categorical devaluation of those blacks who by dint of hard work in the face of great odds have succeeded in conventional economic, political, and intellectual terms is not. His alternative vision of "prophetic moral reasoning" is gentle but vapid; it amounts to little more than a norm of respectful tolerance for "the variety of perspectives held by black people" in contrast to "putting any group of people or culture on a pedestal or in the gutter." Given how minimal the demands of this moral norm are, it is truly remarkable that so much of West's writing in this book flagrantly violates it.

Americans, regardless of race, are entitled to more wisdom and better counsel from our preeminent intellectuals. Because race does indeed matter, we need all the help we can get.

∿ 6 ∿

Slavery Reparations: A Misguided Movement

Let us stipulate—because it is manifestly true—that American slavery was a horrendous crime and a moral abomination. Let us further stipulate that this crime had countless victims and that their descendants still experience adverse effects today, seven generations later. Finally, stipulate that our society subscribes to an ideal of corrective justice that recognizes a legal duty compelling wrongdoers to remedy wrongfully caused losses and to surrender wrongfully obtained gains. Does this require the payment of reparations by the federal government to . . . somebody? Does it justify such reparations?

My answer to both questions is no—and not just because of uncertainty about who the "somebody" would be, although as we shall see this poses a serious practical problem. My objections to reparations fall into three general categories: instrumentalist, consequentialist, and horizontal equity.

By instrumentalist objections, I mean problems of a practical or administrative nature that would be created by any serious effort to move from the status quo to an effective and just reparations regime. By "serious effort," I mean one that takes full account of the practical requirements of implementation. I take up the meaning of "effective and just reparations regime" in the discussion of the consequentialist and horizontal equity objections.

It may seem churlish to begin with the practical or technical obstacles to engineering a solution. These problems will surely strike some reparations advocates as too small-bore and nit-picking to mention in the same breath with the moral project of reparations. But mention them we must, especially because of the project's moral purpose. As the saying goes, if one wills an end, then one also wills the necessary means to that end. Ought implies can. Means, moreover, are not merely instrumental to desired ends; often, they also have normative dimensions of their own that must be considered. Finally, when policies that are attractive in principle fail at the level of actual implementation, the policies themselves are discredited.

Here are just a few of the numerous implementation problems that a reparations law would need to solve:

First, how would it define the beneficiary class? Would it include all blacks in the United States or only those descended from slaves? If the former, what about immigrant blacks and how would "black" be defined in an increasingly multiracial society? If the latter, what about descendants of free blacks?

Second, how would the beneficiaries prove their entitlement? Absent a clear definition of black (who would judge?) or reliable documentary evidence of descent (surely lacking in most cases), what presumptions would be accepted and how could they be rebutted?

Third, would beneficiaries have to show that American slavery caused their current condition? What if they would otherwise have been killed or enslaved by their African captors, or sold to non-American masters?

Fourth, should all taxpayers bear the cost of reparations, or only those descended from slave owners or from those who lived in the slave states? The list of such technocratic questions—none of them fanciful—could be extended endlessly.

The actual effects of a reparations program, of course, will depend partly on the answers to these and other instrumental questions and partly on developments about which we can only speculate. To inform this speculation, however, we can draw on some historical experience with reparations or quasi-reparations programs to suggest what we might expect of this one, even conceding as I readily do that each program is different in any number of ways. Consider four such programs: postwar reparations; the September 11 compensation fund; affirmative action; and the payments to Japanese internees. (Again, space permits only the briefest characterizations). The treaties ending World War I required the Central Powers, especially Germany, to pay war reparations to the victorious Allies. In fact, the payments were grudging, delayed, incomplete, and raised new conflicts. For this reason, the payments brought little satisfaction to the recipients and the bitterness it engendered among Germans was skillfully exploited by Hitler and, according to many historians, contributed to his political support. The post–World War II reparations that Germany paid to Israel, although criticized by many as insulting and inadequate "blood money," were far more successful and helped to launch the new state.

The September 11 compensation fund has now completed its work and certain patterns are already evident. Although Congress assumed that this catastrophe was as sui generis as any event could be, the precedent it set produced pressure—so far unsuccessful—to include the victims of other terrorist-related disasters such as Oklahoma City and the Khobar Towers in Saudi Arabia. And while the grieving, deeply sundered families who received their substantial awards so far surely value them, many recipients complain that the compensation's failure to remedy their loss adequately has inflicted an additional dignitary harm and reopened painful wounds. Far from assuaging their suffering, it seems, monetization sometimes aggravates it—no matter what compensation scheme is chosen.

Even though affirmative action does not entail direct payments for past discrimination, most supporters view it as a compensatory program; the greater economic opportunities it affords its beneficiaries do constitute a kind of reparations and are intended as such. After more than thirty years of affirmative action, several effects seem clear. (Many other effects, both good and bad, are more debatable.)

First, the number of individuals who are now eligible for preferences dwarfs the group that they originally and most compellingly targeted—the descendants of slaves and the victims of Jim Crow. Today, the eligible groups include other categories (women, Hispanics, Asians, and sometimes the disabled) as well as millions of immigrants of color whose ancestors did not experience slavery here.

Second, law's inherently technocratic modalities have tended to (literally) demoralize affirmative action programs. By implementing preferences through a system of contestable definitions, measurements, sanctions, regulations, and litigation, the law has politicized, bureaucratized, and trivialized what was once a moral project. As I discuss below, this moral imperative can be served better in other ways.

Third, affirmative action's unpopularity, even among many members of the beneficiary groups, has created new barriers to interracial reconciliation and heightened the salience and divisiveness of race—precisely the opposite of the advocates' original goals.

The most attractive model for black reparations is the program for the Japanese interned during World War II. The program is very recent, of course, and I know of no analysis of its effects but let us assume that they have been altogether positive—that the recipients are satisfied by the federal government's contrition and compensation, while the program is causing other Americans to reflect on the lessons of that dark chapter of our history. Perhaps this putative success augurs well for a black reparations program, but I doubt it for reasons already discussed. The surviving Japanese internees are a relatively small, easily identifiable group of victims who had been harmed in specific ways by a discrete event limited in time and space. None of the instrumentalist objections mentioned above applies to this group; for example, the beneficiaries are the surviving victims themselves, not innumerable, far-flung, anonymous descendants up to seven generations removed from us.

The German compensation schemes for Holocaust victims and slave laborers are not a close model for black reparations either, for many of the same reasons that distinguish the Japanese internment program. These German schemes, moreover, resulted from the settlement of strong legal claims based on unjust enrichment of specific banks, insurers, employers, and other companies that inflicted calculable losses on specific individuals and families.

Justice and fairness demand that similar cases be treated alike. We all know that every case is different in some respect from every other case, that the criteria of factual relevance and similarity are neither self-evident nor self-defining, and that classifying cases into categories for purposes of comparison is often a matter of judgment. We also know that the victims of grave injustice—slavery, the Holocaust, other genocides, enforced subordination—often regard their suffering as distinctive, if not unique; they tend to resist the notion that the victims of other grave injustices suffered more or in ways more deserving of remedy. To cite an extreme and maudlin but perhaps revealing example, Daniel Jonah Goldhagen, in his book *Hitler's Willing Executioners,* argues that even slaves were treated as less "socially dead" (in Orlando Patterson's phrase) than Jews were in Germany during the Nazi period.

The competition for greatest victimhood is almost inevitable both for political reasons and for a legal one; standard equal protection doctrine invites such comparisons in order to determine the appropriate standard of review. This competition is not an edifying sight—and not just because we lack a common metric for measuring and comparing injustices of this kind. It often descends into an ugly struggle for public resources, recognition, recrimination, and moral status among people who have already suffered enough and who should be the last to view injustice as a zero-sum game. Is slavery the greatest injustice in American history? Probably so, but I would not expect Native Americans whose ancestors were systematically exterminated by the U.S. Army to readily cede the point. Were the indentured servants of the colonial period or the Chinese coolies of the nineteenth century more harshly treated or less deserving of reparations than the Japanese internees? What about the internees' Japanese ancestors who were not permitted to own farmland, marry whites, or enter professions? What about the Irish immigrants who were forced by hateful discrimination to live in conditions arguably as degraded as slave cabins? Should we view their whiteness as an emblem of privilege sufficient to redeem their long suffering without further recompense?

I do not know the answers to these questions—or even how to think about answering them. There is much to be said (as equal protection doctrine allows) for taking one step at a time toward a more just society. My point, then, is not that giving reparations to the descendants of black slaves would require, legally or otherwise, that they be given to the descendants of liquidated Native Americans or near-enslaved coolies, much less that the former should not be first in line. Rather, it is that the politics and psychology of the competition for victimhood will make it difficult to stop there, and that the very effort to justify this stopping point will arouse new bitterness and magnify existing feelings of injustice.

The movement for black reparations, however well intended, is misguided. Indeed, it is perverse in its propensity to discredit the very ideal of corrective justice that it invokes, to aggravate bitterness rather than assuage it, and to make reconciliation more difficult. Our obligation now is to engage with and learn from the past, and then to move forward by turning the page. As we turn it, we must not forget that we are leaving behind an endless catalog of crimes, tears, and scars of the lash, of prejudice, and of poverty. We must leave this human misery and injustice behind, but not out of mind or conscience. We already have a long agenda to challenge our moral faculties and remedial imaginations as we assess our responsibilities to one another both now and in the future.

ᔕ 7 ᔕ

Housing Integration: Use Vouchers, Not Courts

Advocates for the poor proclaimed a rare victory in 2002 in their long campaign for more affordable housing in the suburbs. They hailed the latest court decision upholding New Jersey's so-called Mount Laurel doctrine, a set of rules designed to open suburbia to low-income families. But if past is prologue, the ruling by the New Jersey Supreme Court will mainly benefit builders of midpriced and luxury homes.

For more than three decades, the court has tried to prevent New Jersey suburbs from using zoning laws to exclude the poor. The goal is admirable, and the court's legal solution has attracted national attention. But as other states and municipalities have learned, a judicial remedy is not the best tool for reforming housing markets. Instead, the lesson to be learned from New Jersey's experience is that the most effective way to enable low-income families to live in better communities is for government to directly subsidize the poor who rent housing.

The Mount Laurel doctrine began more than thirty years ago. In 1971, a group of low- and moderate-income families sued Mount Laurel, a growing suburban township in New Jersey, claiming that its zoning practices excluded them from the community in violation of the state constitution's provision requiring the state to "promote the general welfare."

In 1975, the State Supreme Court sided with the families. In an unprecedented decision that stunned the housing industry and government officials around the country, the Court condemned land-use policies that discourage multifamily housing and ordered every developing community in the state to bear its "fair share" of housing for low- and moderate-income families. But it left the definition of "fair share" and other key issues unresolved, prompting an avalanche of lawsuits seeking to overturn local zoning, planning and environmental laws.

In 1983, the State Supreme Court prescribed a detailed set of rules for assigning specific "fair shares" to each community. Under the rules, communities must not only eliminate restrictive zoning but also offer developers inducements to build affordable housing. Most controversial was something called the "builder's remedy," which allows developers to sue to override local laws and construct more units of market-rate housing if they also build low-income housing.

By 1985, builders had challenged laws in about 140 communities. The legislature then reluctantly entered the fray, creating an agency to calculate the mandated fair shares. Communities that implemented their own plan for developing low-income housing would be immunized from further Mount Laurel litigation.

Twenty years and many lawsuits later, this judicial campaign for affordable housing has done little for low-income families. Statewide, developers have built almost fifteen times more market-rate units than affordable units—and most of the latter would probably have been built anyway. The affordable units, moreover, are disproportionately occupied by people of relatively high socioeconomic status, like graduate students, who happen to be at a low point in their earnings cycle. The market-rate units will eventually filter down to lower-income families in the normal housing cycle, but this takes time and does not target those who need the housing most.

This result is not surprising. Other states have attacked exclusionary zoning in a variety of other ways, also with little effect. The obstacles to affordable housing, especially in more prosperous suburbs, include factors like high land and construction costs. The Mount Laurel approach, with its focus on zoning litigation, addresses only one part of the problem. An alternative strategy would be to reform outdated building codes and other regulatory barriers that raise housing construction and renovation costs (and encourage bribery) while producing few safety benefits. But the most direct and effective strategy to aid poor families is to give them housing vouchers that they can use to rent units in more desirable neighborhoods.

The federal Section 8 voucher program has been supported by both Democratic and Republican administrations. While no panacea—especially in markets with low vacancy rates—Section 8 and other renter subsidies served 1.8 million low-income families in 2003, enabling them to move from inner-city neighborhoods to better urban and suburban ones—and at a much lower cost than legal mandates.

The Mount Laurel approach is a throwback to a time when judges ordered top-down social change. Housing markets, however, are too complex and dynamic for courthouse engineering. A better approach to improving options for low-income families is to give them vouchers and help them find housing in places where they want to live.

– PART II –

THE CULTURE WARS

I s American society waging a twenty-first-century equivalent of Bismarck's *kulturkampf*? Judging from the media's promiscuous use of the phrase, many commentators think so. They seem to perceive politically polarized blocs of citizens angrily confronting one another across a yawning, perhaps unbridgeable, ideological chasm. Sometimes the two sides (why are there always only two—is it because so many pundits see things only in black and white?) are described as liberals versus conservatives, sometimes as blue versus red states, sometimes as progressives versus traditionalists. In any event, the notion of a culture war divides people into mutually uncomprehending, bitterly opposed, and uncompromising camps driven by fundamentally inconsistent ways of seeing the world.

I view our politics quite differently—as do some of our finest political scientists. By and large, Americans resist being pigeonholed. They are uncomfortable being defined by abstract principles (other than "democracy" and "freedom") or by broad political theories whose rigidity leaves them little wiggle room to maneuver, compromise, or adapt to particular circumstances. For centuries, perceptive visitors to America—from Crevecoeur to Tocqueville to Bryce to Churchill—have found Americans to be distinctively pragmatic, privatistic, and diverse. Compared with other nations, and especially since the civil rights era of the 1960s, we are also remarkably tolerant of differences, exhibiting a dominant "live-and-let-live" ethos. (In the 2004 elections, 62 percent of the voters indicated support for gay marriage or civil unions, social practices that few straights had even considered a decade earlier.) Americans are drawn to political leaders who make them feel comfortable personally and programmatically, and to policy proposals that seem workable rather than to those that pie-in-the-sky idealists and purists have deduced from fixed principles.

The essays in this part are written in this pragmatic spirit. I begin with a meditation on the constitutional challenge to the "under God" phrase in the Pledge of Allegiance recited in the public schools, arguing that the Establishment Clause should be understood in this context to prohibit coerced religious expression, not to protect young people who do not utter those words from peer pressure. An essay on school choice contends that the tragic failure of many public school systems to perform the vital task of effectively educating low-income children demands that we experiment with promising choice-based alternatives, including vouchers. Next, I criticize the challenge by my beloved Yale Law School to a federal statute that gives Pentagon recruiters equal access to our students. Although I share Yale's strong opposition to the military's "don't ask, don't tell" policy, I find that the school's principled exclusion of on-campus military recruitment is morally, pedagogically, and practically perverse. My essay on whether a political party or private group like the Boy Scouts should be able to exclude those whose conduct or values it rejects explores the tension between antidiscrimination laws and a liberal commitment to diversity.

Another cultural conflict, one conducted for the most part with good humor and mutual respect, is that between two pillars of the law: the profession and the professors. In this essay, I explore the tensions between practicing lawyers and judges, on the one hand, and legal academics (especially at the elite law schools), on the other. In part, this is a conflict about what new lawyers need to know and how they should be taught to think, but it also reflects deeper differences about the role of theoretical ideas in shaping the future of the law. Part II concludes not with an essay but with a poem designed both to amuse and to instruct. In it, I imagine what would happen if we moved the day for paying taxes from April 15 to a date just before we go to the polls as voters. The poem, then, observes the eternal war between two familiar but opposed cultures: favor-currying politicians and tax-weary citizens.

8

The Pledge of Allegiance: A Noncoercive Endorsement of Religion

When a federal appeals court struck down the Pledge of Allegiance as an establishment of religion in 2003, public indignation was immediate, intense, and unprecedented. Whereas even the infamous *Dred Scott* opinion, which helped precipitate the Civil War, had plenty of defenders in Congress, not a single politician was willing to support the court's decision in the Pledge case. All rushed to vilify it, predicting that it would be swiftly overruled.

The constitutional issue is much harder than this almost universal condemnation suggests. In its 2004 decision (*Newdow*), the Supreme Court vacated the lower court decision because the plaintiff, a noncustodial parent, lacked standing. He has now obtained custodial parents and their children as plaintiffs and filed another suit. If and when the Court reaches the constitutional issue in this new case, it should uphold the Pledge—but only for the right reasons.

Some support the Pledge's constitutionality based on original intent—the claim that the First Amendment's establishment clause was not intended to invalidate a public ceremony simply because it mentions God. After all, the Declaration of Independence expressly invokes God, the Creator, divine Providence, and the Supreme Judge. Our currency contains the motto "In God We Trust" (though Teddy Roosevelt opposed this). Congressional chaplains invoke God in every session, and presidents routinely do so. "God Bless America" is sung on many public occasions.

These practices do bear on the Framers' original intent, but an equally relevant original intent was evident when Congress added the words "under God" to the Pledge in 1954. That effort to proclaim an American orthodoxy of religiosity and deism and to condemn Communism's godlessness does not constitute an "establishment" in the Framers' sense. But it was a clear governmental endorsement of religion, which the Court says is equally invalid.

Pledge supporters respond that the clause prohibits only an establishment of a particular religion and that the Pledge is nondenominational in using the word "God." But this argument misunderstands Establishment Clause jurisprudence, which makes it clear (as the appeals court majority emphasized) that the clause requires governmental neutrality—not only among religious denominations, but also between religion and nonreligion. The clause protects atheists, agnostics, and nontheistic believers, as well as religious sectarians.

This is why the fact that America is a religious nation, a reality often cited by Pledge supporters, is constitutionally beside the point. They frequently quote Justice William Douglas's statement in *Zorach v. Clauson* that "We are a religious people whose institutions presuppose a Supreme Being," but they ignore his insistence later in the very same opinion that the government "may not make a religious observance compulsory." Is the Pledge a religious observance? If the words "under God" mean anything, the answer must be yes.

Indeed, two recent Court decisions invalidate privately led prayers at public school events (*Lee v. Weisman* and *Santa Fe Independent School District v. Doe*). I oppose these decisions for reasons explained below, but if they are good law, they would seem to bar the Pledge a fortiori. If private speakers at school graduations or football games cannot invoke God communally, it is even harder to see how the Constitution permits teachers to lead the Pledge in the classroom. Is the Pledge compulsory? Not as a formal matter, but as we shall see in a moment, the Court in these two cases discussed the voluntariness interest in nonformal terms.

Some Pledge supporters try to buttress their argument by supposing that schoolchildren recite it by rote. (An old TV segment confirms this, showing some saying—to audience laughter—"and to the Republic for Richard Sands" and similar uncomprehending errors.) Even adults, supporters contend, treat the Pledge as a routinized, general affirmation of allegiance, without attending much to the words. This may be true, yet the logical implication of their ceremonial theism argument is that the more the Pledge is misunderstood or ignored, the stronger its claim to constitutionality. This cannot be taken seriously.

Perhaps the weakest arguments for the Pledge's constitutionality are its offensiveness to the polity and the well-grounded fear of the backlash it has already unleashed against the judges who struck it down. But the First Amendment was meant to be a safeguard against popular majorities using their legislative power to impose political and religious orthodoxies on minorities. Like other Bill of Rights guarantees, it gives courts the grave responsibility of vindicating constitutional principles when majorities violate them, even—or especially—when those principles are threatened by public criticism. In a system of judicial review, this criticism goes with the territory. If the court is right, and if Congress is unwilling to amend the Pledge, Congress's constitutional remedy is clear: Try to amend the Constitution.

I certainly am not suggesting that public support for a practice should be constitutionally irrelevant or that judges should not take seriously the likely political responses to their decisions. The real issue is how judges should use this political information. Americans' overwhelming support for the Pledge should give pause to a court being asked to invalidate it—not because a mobilized majority is always entitled to have its way or because the majority's demand is *de minimis* but because long-standing, widely venerated practices (religious invocations in legislative assemblies, for example) usually have a substantial constitutional basis. When the Court applies to the Pledge the existing establishment clause doctrine under the three-prong *Lemon v. Kurtzman* test (which is widely criticized), it should count the public's political veneration of the Pledge as evidence that it has a secular purpose and does not have the primary effect of advancing religion. (*Lemon's* third prong, the risk of church-state entanglement, should not bar the Pledge.)

If the standard reasons in favor of the Pledge are constitutionally insufficient, is there a better, more decisive reason for upholding it? I think so.

The most important reason is that the Pledge and the words "under God" are voluntary and thus do not impose an orthodoxy on those who are asked to recite them. Those who do not wish to affirm God's existence need not utter the words that offend them. No one is likely to notice what they say, but this is beside the point. (As a Jewish child participating in the communally sung Christmas carols that I loved, I often did not sing certain words whose truth I doubted or felt did not apply to me; presumably many atheists did the same.) Silence is a choice that the First Amendment firmly protects.

Where I see choice, however, others will see coercion. Indeed, the Supreme Court did so in *Lee* and *Santa Fe*, wrongly in my view. In barring privately led prayers at school-sponsored events, the Court ruled in these cases that although students are free to remain seated or silent rather than participate, they are still psychologically coerced in a constitutionally decisive sense. But this ipse dixit trivializes the idea of coercion. It presumes that young adults are more fragile than they are. It seeks to protect them from having the courage of their convictions even to the minimal extent of possibly courting some unpopularity by not uttering two words that others utter. It transforms individual choice into a legal harm— indeed, into an unconstitutional one.

It is true that the Pledge is also recited by elementary school pupils, unlike the prayers in *Lee* and *Santa Fe*. But this fact does not make the recital any less voluntary in a constitutional sense. In reality, most children will decide whether to say "under God" under their parents' suasion. The parents may discuss their reasons with the child, though some may simply dictate the choice. Even so, this is not what society (or the Constitution) understands as compulsion. To the contrary, parental guidance in religious matters is normative. Peer pressure may also affect children who do not utter the two words, creating conflicts between their convictions (or those of their parents) and their desire to be popular. But we should not see this conflict as problematic, much less as constitutionally impermissible. In fact, it is an essential part of the difficult process by which young people develop their moral views and identities and then learn to defend them. The essential lesson here as elsewhere is: no pain, no gain. The law should not dilute this lesson.

The Court should not apply to the Pledge the overly expansive definition of harm it used in *Lee* and *Santa Fe*. This definition is particularly ill-suited to a society as diverse as ours. In today's America, almost every cultural practice is bound to contradict some group's values or offend its sensibilities. Moral disagreements and unpleasant interactions are legion. In a society like ours, the law does better, as the dissenters in *Lee* urged, to limit the idea of coercive harm to a threat of official sanctions; it should not expand this idea to include mere competition among different informal norms.

Absent official compulsion or private violence, feelings of discomfort produced by social pressure or value conflicts over cultural practices like the Pledge are not constitutionally actionable.

Indeed, creating such a right might well multiply those feelings rather than reduce them. Consider the new right to be free of secondhand smoke—a great boon to nonsmokers like me, but one that increasingly relegates smokers to a despised group that must practice its habit in alleyways. Whether or not the law struck a better balance between the competing interests, my point is about how rights transform the nature of relationships. By remedying a sense of injury, they also foster it. Rights are also entitlements to be rigidly intolerant, to stand firmly and self-indulgently on the law if one chooses, rather than engaging in the kind of informal, give-and-take compromise that takes some account of the other's interests.

The Constitution already protects Americans' freedom to follow their own consciences and choose what they wish to affirm without legal sanction. Giving a legal remedy to those who are offended by "under God" would go beyond this protection. It would empower them to prevent the overwhelming majority of their fellow citizens from saying those words communally in a governmental setting. At a time when growing cultural diversity demands new forms of mutual accommodation (see "Punctilios for a Diverse Society" essay), freedom of choice for minorities is often a better way to mute social conflicts than a categorical solution through legal prohibition, which may only inflame those conflicts. The Pledge honors liberty and justice for "all," not just for those who share our beliefs.

✍ 9 ✍

School Vouchers: A Compelling Case for Choice

A *New York Times* advertisement asks whether we would favor giving people a choice of only one car, one physician, one place to live, and then asked why we should feel differently about having a choice of only one school system for our children and perhaps a bad school at that. It is an excellent question, and a good point of departure for discussing the controversial proposals to give parents publicly subsidized vouchers redeemable for tuition at private schools, including religious ones. (Some proposals use tax credits for the same purpose.) The Supreme Court's 2002 decision upholding Cleveland's voucher scheme properly leaves the adoption of such programs up to state and local legislators.

The *Times* ad suggests that the burden of proof rests on those favoring the current public school monopoly, not on voucher advocates. Politically, however, reformers must overcome the immense inertia favoring a status quo defended by the powerful teachers' unions under the banner of public education. Despite this burden, the case for allowing parents to test vouchers by using them for their own children is compelling.

Let us begin where the ad begins—with bad schools in a monopoly public system. A shocking number of public schools in our large cities do not effectively teach the most rudimentary skills needed to support even a modest existence in twenty-first-century America. Consider the New York City school system after a long succession of highly touted chancellors, blue ribbon recommendations, bureaucratic shake-ups, and higher teacher salaries and school expenditures. In 2004, the state reported—and this was an *improvement* over prior years—that 64.4 percent of the city's eighth graders who took state tests failed to meet standards in English and language arts, and 57.6 percent failed to meet them in math. Among black eighth graders, 72.3 percent failed to meet standards in English, 63.7 percent in math. The results for fourth graders were also appalling.

Experts, of course, offer diverse explanations for this abject failure: chaotic family lives, parental neglect, poor teaching, low expectations, overcrowded classrooms, outmoded curricula, disciplinary problems, lack of English fluency, the effects of television, and many others. No one knows the answer for sure; all of those factors probably play some part. But parents naturally don't want to wait and find out. They simply want their children in a better school environment.

All parents have options, at least in principle. After all, a local public school is not the same kind of monopoly as an electric utility. Dissatisfied parents can move to the suburbs to find public schools they admire, as countless families have done. They can remain in the city but send their children to private secular or religious schools while still paying taxes to support the public schools. The public system may even offer some choice. Perhaps that would mean busing outside the neighborhood. It could also mean providing a publicly funded charter school whose operational autonomy depends on how much independence the chartering law gives it from the school board, which tends to be strongly influenced by powerful teachers' unions. Most upper- and middle-income families choose one or another of these options to rescue their children from bad city schools.

Low-income families, however, have no such options. Just as a predator traps people by cutting off their escape, the public school monopoly keeps poor children in failing, often fearful schools. Some determined inner-city families have taken refuge in higher-performing parochial schools, charter schools, and privately supported academies. But the vast majority must stumble down educational dead ends in their low-performing local public school. Would any of the teachers whose unions oppose vouchers accept this future for their children? In fact, few teachers who have any choice send their children to inner-city public schools. Would any readers of this essay accept such schools for theirs? To ask this question is to answer it.

How, then, can we justify maintaining a monopoly that in effect forces lower-income parents to stand by helplessly as their kids' hopes are dashed in failing schools? We can't, which is why Milwaukee, Cleveland, and the state of Florida have established publicly funded voucher programs for many of their schoolchildren and why private philanthropists are funding more than forty thousand vouchers nationwide. In a typical program, parents receive a voucher worth some fraction (usually 50 percent) of the state's per pupil expenditure (PPE) for the public schools. They can use the voucher for any private school that meets certain standards, such as nondiscrimination on racial grounds. The public schools keep the rest of that pupil's PPE.

Will choice through vouchers improve children's education? The answer depends on how we measure improvement. The standardized test score data is still preliminary, but there are some encouraging signs. The best, most recent evidence was published in 2003 by Paul Peterson, a Harvard social scientist. Peterson compared the scores of students randomly selected for vouchers with those of students who sought but did not receive them. (The available vouchers were awarded through a lottery among poverty-eligible students.) In New York City in particular, the average performance of the black students who used the vouchers was significantly higher on math and reading tests than the scores of those who stayed in the public schools. Peterson's data were mixed in the two other cities he studied, but black students showed some progress.

Other measures of improvement were more unequivocal. Dramatically fewer of the parents receiving vouchers reported serious problems with fighting, cheating, truancy, or property destruction, and far more parents reported that they were very satisfied with the quality of academics and teachers. Parents, of course, measure improvement along other dimensions as well, such as religious and moral values, racial or social composition, bilingualism, athletics, neighborhood, and many others. Peterson's study found that only a tiny percentage of the families declined the voucher because of the school's quality, and almost none did so because they preferred a public school. Vouchers leave these trade-offs up to the parents, who assess their kids' progress in many different ways, rather than to the government, which can't or won't. Parental choices (if they have choices) will reflect their child-specific conceptions of educational value, especially if they can obtain information about different schools, information that a well-designed system would elicit.

The lobbying against vouchers comes mainly from the teachers' unions, who have a powerful economic stake in the status quo, and from some groups concerned about the use of public funds in religious schools. These arguments are even weaker than arguments against other government-protected monopolies, partly because the stakes in education reform are so much higher:

1. Vouchers will "cream" students by moving middle-class ones into the private schools, concentrating the neediest ones in the public systems, and tarnishing the public school ideal in which Americans cross racial and class lines and learn a common citizenship. Peterson's data indicate that vouchers milk the public schools, not cream them. Test scores between those who leave the public schools and those who stay are about the same. In any event, the sorry state of public education in the large cities has already creamed most of the families with any choice in the matter, and there is no sign of a reversal. We do not force all poor people to suffer a common fate by making them all use substandard hospitals so that others will not be able to use better ones. Medicaid and Medicare do just the opposite. Education should be no different.

2. Vouchers will marginalize the public schools. But they would only do so if those schools deserve to be marginalized. Evidence that choice in fact works to improve public schools should not surprise us, given what we know about how competition serves consumer interests in other areas. And since vouchers only represent 50 percent of current PPE, voucher use should actually increase the net resources remaining in the public schools.

3. Vouchers favor the wealthy, not the poor. The huge waiting lists of poor people seeking vouchers in every community that has tried them constitute powerful evidence to the contrary. If we trust even unsophisticated people to make wise choices about every other aspect of their lives, why not about their children's education? And if vouchers are properly targeted on children in failing schools, as is the case in Florida (but, alas, not in the California plan), vouchers will go to those who need them most. Even a universal program could be made progressive, as Robert Reich, nobody's idea of an apologist for the rich, proposed back in 2001.

4. Voucher amounts are too low and private schools too few to give parents meaningful choice. It is true that a $4,000 voucher (roughly the amount proposed in Michigan) will not pay the tuition at Andover or elite New York City schools, but it will cover full tuition in the vast majority of private schools. If increases proved necessary, moreover, voucher amounts could be raised considerably without reaching the PPE in the public schools. For example, Milwaukee's vouchers are now up to about $5,000, yet its public schools still have more money to spend per pupil than ever before. And we can expect that once private schools can compete for voucher dollars, many more of them with diverse educational approaches will arise. Some will be better than others, and some will be

downright bad. This, however, is true in every large group, and certainly in urban school systems.

5. Vouchers are unpopular with voters, as evidenced by the defeat of pro-voucher ballot measures in California and Michigan. These measures, however, were poorly designed and poorly promoted. The sponsors failed to target them on the most needy children, allowed the hostile teachers' unions to outspend and outfox them, and let vouchers become a code word for an attack on the public schools rather than emphasizing choice—a more appealing banner to march under, as abortion rights groups have found. These defeats show that many voters still need to be persuaded of vouchers' merits. Only experience with local programs can do that.

6. Vouchers used in parochial schools violate the First Amendment. The Supreme Court validated voucher programs channeling funds to parents rather than schools and assure parents an independent choice. Just as many government contracts with faith-based organizations to provide social services now forbid proselytizing of clients, voucher programs would probably also do so. Whether such prohibitions are constitutionally required or permissible or are even sound policy—assuming that parents make a knowing choice of the schools' religious policies—are important questions, but they do not bear on the more basic case for vouchers.

Vouchers are certainly no panacea. They cannot assure excellence in the schools where they will be used. Even existing programs do not yet reach all children in bad schools. Not all parents will make the wisest choices, nor can vouchers free families from crime, substandard housing, and limited economic opportunities in declining neighborhoods. What vouchers can do is enable such families to make choices that may enrich their children's lives. This would be no small thing.

∽ 10 ∽

Military Recruitment on Campus: The Solomon Amendment

The Pentagon's mighty war machine is fighting on more fronts than you might imagine. As if its hands were not full enough with campaigns in Iraq and Afghanistan, it has just been thrown into a defensive engagement with another formidable foe—the American legal academy. Moreover, the law schools may enjoy a kind of home-field advantage in court, even though their firepower is merely rhetorical, not lethal.

The conflict actually began in 1978, when New York University Law School adopted a policy denying its placement program to employers who discriminated in hiring on the basis of a student's sexual orientation. This policy, which simply added sexual orientation to the list of protected attributes (race, religion, national origin, veteran status, disability, and others), was quickly adopted by Yale Law School and many other law schools. The American Association of Law Schools (AALS) adopted this nondiscrimination policy in 1990, and its members applied it to military recruiters.

The Pentagon now had its casus belli. Congress supplied it with strong weapons in the mid-1990s, when it enacted the so-called Solomon Amendment, which in its current form denies federal funds to any institution that prevents the military from gaining "entry to campuses" or access to information enabling it to recruit students. If one "subelement" of a university (a law school, for example) violates Solomon, it jeopardizes almost all of the university's federal grant funds, not just those from the U.S. Department of Defense (DOD).

This provision remained essentially a dead letter until the September 11 terrorist attacks. In December 2001, with the Afghanistan war under way, DOD complained that many schools were discriminating against military recruiters in violation of Solomon. DOD's correspondence about Yale Law School's campus interviewing program reveals the agency's militant stance. Yale argued that it was in compliance with Solomon, in that military recruiters can visit the campus, access student information, and use law school classrooms for informational meetings on student request. Students can reserve rooms for interviews, and Yale staff, if asked, will even help military interviewers meet with law students in non-law school university venues. DOD replied that even this arrangement discriminates against the military, because Yale denies DOD some placement services that Yale makes available to nondiscriminating recruiters. DOD therefore threatened to withhold Yale's $300 million in grants. Succumbing to this pressure, Yale and other law schools suspended their nondiscrimination policies as applied to military recruiters, while urgently asking DOD to clarify its interpretation of Solomon and explain why the schools' policies violate it.

In 2003, the Forum for Academic and Institutional Rights (FAIR), an umbrella group of law schools, sued in federal court in New Jersey, seeking declaratory and injunctive relief against DOD's interpretation of Solomon, citing constitutional and statutory grounds. The suit, which did not challenge (indeed hardly mentioned) the military's "don't ask, don't tell" policy, contended that law schools teach students to judge people solely on merit rather than on the basis of race, sexual orientation, and other traits that "bear no relation to merit." DOD's reading of Solomon, FAIR claimed, forces schools to use their personnel, facilities, and funds to propagate an abhorrent, homophobic message in violation of the schools' First Amendment rights of academic freedom, expressive association, and free speech. With affidavits from faculty and students, it insisted that coerced surrender to Solomon's demand is eroding the credibility of the schools' commitment to the nondiscrimination ideal. Asserting that the schools' interview rules do not interfere with military recruiting, FAIR argued that DOD's real purpose is to punish those who oppose "don't ask, don't tell." (Given the universities' notorious, long-standing opposition to this policy, however, the more likely motive is DOD's prideful resentment of the schools' unequal treatment of its recruiters).

There is much to applaud in the schools' legal challenge. "Don't ask, don't tell" is not a principled policy of tolerance or equality. Instead, it is an uneasy political compromise between the earlier flat ban on gays in the military and the full acceptance of them that equality demands. It places both gay and straight soldiers in a painfully ambiguous situation, encourages dissembling and exploitation (if not outright blackmail) of gays, and reinforces their existing stigmas. In practice, the policy has caused the cruel outing and arbitrary discharge of many gay soldiers who boast proud records of devoted military service. Solomon, like all categorical fund cutoffs, is a crude enforcement tool designed to exert pressure on institutions that do the government's business. Some of its supporters in Congress and many in DOD were eager to pick a fight with the elite schools where antiwar and anti-Bush sentiment are very widespread among students and faculty. (Perhaps we should view Solomon as a case of the Powell Doctrine, which permits the military to wage war only when it enjoys overwhelming supremacy!) DOD's refusal to clarify its own policies under Solomon, moreover, created needless uncertainty, contention, and, now, litigation. At the same time, its opaque regulatory process, which seems to permit the government to cut off funds without affording the schools administrative review, raises serious due process questions. For all these reasons, a legal test of the Pentagon's policy is welcome.

Still, one is struck by ironies in the law schools' litigation positions— as to both Solomon and their own interviewing policies. Consider how the schools define merit. Only a few months before suing DOD on the ground that Solomon prescribes an alien, illiberal conception of merit, the schools advanced a different view. In *Grutter v. Bollinger*, they persuaded the Supreme Court that the very same attributes that the schools now say bear no relation to merit can be used to discriminate against white and Asian applicants. (See "Affirmative Action II" essay.) It seems odd for the schools to insist that they may define merit in a way that disadvantages white, Asian, and indeed straight applicants (if schools deem other minorities or gays "diversity enhancing") but that the military may not define merit in a way that disadvantages gays. Just as the schools cite pedagogical diversity, DOD cites combat effectiveness. Although neither of these claims is convincing, the relevant point here is that the schools, in the name of high principle, are defining merit as they choose and asking the courts to defer to their institutional autonomy and expert judgment in the matter. At the same time, they deny the same deference to the institutional claims of the military.

A second irony concerns the schools' position on the government's threats to cut off federal funding as a means to enforce its own nondiscrimination policy. When the Reagan administration opposed ending Bob Jones University's tax-exempt status and its access to federal educational loan funds, the law schools did not exactly fly to BJU's defense. Indeed, many of them were indignant about government policies that in effect subsidized an institution that discriminated against blacks as a matter of (in BJU's view) religious principle. Nor do the law schools now oppose fund cutoffs under Title VI of the Civil Rights Act of 1964 to prevent discrimination by private grantees. (Politicians of all ideological stripes use cutoffs to threaten practices they don't like; Ted Kennedy, for example, has proposed to bar funds to colleges with "early decision" policies.) Given this background, the law schools' claim that Solomon constitutes an illegitimate, indeed unconstitutional, effort to enforce an official orthodoxy seems a bit inconsistent.

But whatever one thinks of "don't ask, don't tell" (again, I oppose it), Congress duly enacted it after focused debate. Both the Clinton and Bush administrations ratified it. And the federal courts upheld it. None of this legal legitimation is true of race, sex, or other forms of discrimination that can cause fund cutoffs. The schools' position on the use of grant funds to enforce public policy, then, seems to depend not on whether the policy is legal (as "don't ask, don't tell" is), but on whether the schools happen to favor it. Varying positions on fund cutoffs depending on whose ideological ox is gored may be a common political tactic, but it is hardly setting the moral example that schools say in their pleadings is one of their chief raisons d'être.

Another moral irony of the lawsuit is that the pleadings do not identify the schools opposing DOD's policy, but instead use FAIR's anonymity to conceal them. According to press accounts, FAIR has done so in order to protect the schools' federal funding. (Some scholars and students, including many at Yale, have come forward and sued in their own name.) Whether or not this anonymity weakens their legal position (the government has challenged FAIR's standing), it does seem to mock a moral imperative—to stand up for one's rights and risk the consequences—that law schools should be teaching their students. Since it would be clearly unconstitutional for DOD to pick and choose among schools in cutting off funds according to which schools had opposed their policy or sued, the actual risks of self-identification in the lawsuit seem minimal.

In 2004, a federal appeals court reversed the district court, ruling that DOD's reading of Solomon violates the schools' First Amendment rights by coercing speech and interfering with their expressive integrity. The Supreme Court will decide, but let us assume that the schools are right on the law—that their interviewing rules as applied to the military do not violate Solomon (now amended to require "equal access" by recruiters) or that the First Amendment prevents Defense from sanctioning them. A key question remains: Should law schools have such policies in the first place?

Virtually all the schools (and the AALS) long ago answered affirmatively, but I have my doubts. I strongly favor barring discrimination against gays and protecting academic autonomy in the face of political pressures. But law schools should be dedicated to a third norm, too, one that would discredit their position on this question. As a matter of principle, law schools should treat their students as mature individuals who have absorbed enough education, legal and otherwise, to assess the evidence and make their own choices among employers without needing to be "protected" by the schools.

Why should the schools screen employers' practices for some of the most critical and well-informed young adults in the country? Can't students make up their own minds on this? What vision of intellectuality, character, and maturity do the schools convey when they relieve students of their duty as autonomous adults and citizens to make their own moral choices? Given the schools' vaunted quest for diversity, is it not inconsistent for them to discourage students from hearing a world view—opposition to gays in the military—that was resoundingly endorsed by a democratic (and Democratic) Congress, affirmed by administrations of diverse ideological stripes, upheld by the courts, and preached by some of the great religions to which many of the students subscribe? How much liberality and subtlety of mind do law schools exhibit when their interviewing rules treat all versions of that world view as a single species of invidious homophobia to be indiscriminately condemned—regardless of whether it proceeds from the kind of blind hatred that murdered Matthew Shepard or from ethical traditions or prudential concerns shared by many thoughtful, morally scrupulous people?

In truth, the law school interviewing policy is not meant to be even-handed. Rather, the policy is designed to make a political and moral statement by placing extra (small, as a practical matter) obstacles in the path of those students who wish to interview with certain employers whose practices offend the schools. To see why this differential treatment is inconsistent, consider an analogy. Suppose the Acme Corporation made it a bit more difficult for black applicants, but not for others, to arrange job interviews—say, by making blacks call an additional number or travel farther. Acme could not legitimately defend this practice on the ground that it did not discriminate against black applicants but instead merely denied them the benefit of the faster-track option available to other students. This analogy, I think, indicts the schools' interviewing rule *a fortiori*. After all, it discriminates against an employment practice that is perfectly legal and reflects a hard-won political and moral consensus, although one that I do not share.

The schools should allow their placement resources to be used on an equal basis by all employers whose policies with regard to sexual orientation are legal in the jurisdictions where their lawyers work, so long as they disclose those policies and certify their legality. The issue is not what the schools think about the military's position on gays—the schools and AALS have made that very clear—but how their students view it. A school's moral and pedagogical duty to its students is to cultivate their capacity for independent thinking, explain its own view (if it has one) on "don't ask, don't tell"—and then get out of the way. The students' duty is to listen carefully—and then make their own decisions.

ᨑ 11 ᨑ

Expressive Groups: Political Parties and Gays in the Boy Scouts

As Americans grapple with the challenge of diversity, the Supreme Court has given us a lot to think about. In two fascinating decisions rendered in 2000, the justices confronted some questions that increasingly preoccupy us as individuals, as group members, and as democratic citizens: Why and when is diversity among groups a good thing? When is the law justified in punishing deviant groups? Who should decide which groups are deviant, and on what basis?

At first blush, the two decisions *California Democratic Party v. Jones*, and *Boy Scouts of America v. Dale* seem to have little in common. *Jones* involved California's blanket primary electoral system while *Dale* involved the Boy Scouts' exclusion of an avowed homosexual from a leadership position. *Jones* seems to be about party competition in the public sphere, *Dale* about a private group's membership policies. What the cases share, however, is a struggle, waged under the banner of the First Amendment, over groups' freedom to define themselves in a society strongly committed both to diversity and to equality. *Jones* and *Dale* are pointed reminders of the conflict between these values, sometimes forcing us to choose one over the other.

In *Jones*, several political parties challenged a California statute, adopted by voters in a 1996 statewide referendum, that substituted a "blanket" primary for the traditional closed one for choosing party candidates for the general election. Whereas a voter used to receive a ballot limited to candidates of her own party, she now receives one listing every candidate regardless of party; voters may choose freely among them. The state defended the blanket primary, arguing that it traditionally regulated public elections and, following the referendum, had opted for a system that promised to increase turnout, produce more mainstream candidates, and give voters more meaningful choices in one-party districts where primaries are the crucial elections. The political parties contended that a blanket primary, by allowing nonmembers to help select their nominees, violated the parties' First Amendment right to associate only with those who shared their views and interests, which implied a further right not to associate with those with different views and interests.

Seven members of the Court, led by Justice Antonin Scalia, agreed with the parties, but first had to overcome practical and doctrinal difficulties. Earlier decisions had recognized that states may sometimes regulate primaries; indeed, the "white primary" cases held that parties must open their processes to blacks. California cited these cases to justify opening party primaries to nonmembers. The trial and appellate courts in *Jones*, moreover, had found that the California law protected valid state interests without significantly infringing on the parties' associational rights. Another problem for Scalia was that a broad right not to associate might invalidate open primaries, adopted by more than half the states, that allow nonmembers to vote in a primary, as well as the common system allowing voters to register with a party on Election Day and vote in its primary. A Court ostentatiously committed to federalism and states' rights would not want to invalidate diverse choices of different states concerning their governmental arrangements.

Nevertheless, the Court ruled that the states' interests must yield to a party's right not to allow nonmembers to vote in its primary. At the same time, it reaffirmed its earlier decision in *Tashjian v. Republican Party of Connecticut* allowing a party to open its primary to nonmembers despite a state closed primary law. *Jones*, then, protects group autonomy and self-definition by affirming a right of organizational privacy. If a party, as a private group, wishes to reach out to nonmembers, the state cannot prevent it. If it prefers to limit its processes to members, the state may not interfere with that choice either. But is a party really a private group? All the justices assumed that it is, which is in tension with the fact that U.S. states regulate parties more than European states do, even though the latter subsidize their parties. In any event, the justices agreed that the primaries are clearly public proceedings and divided only over the issue of how much state intrusion on organizational privacy was permissible in such proceedings.

Dale, the Boy Scouts case, raised a similar issue of organizational privacy but in an altogether different setting. James Dale, who was by all accounts a distinguished Boy Scout and admirable human being when he was appointed an assistant scoutmaster, was dismissed when the organization learned that he had publicly acknowledged his homosexuality and had become a gay rights activist. The Scouts stated that the organization barred homosexuals from membership, and Dale sued under a New Jersey law barring discrimination on the basis of sexual orientation in places of public accommodation. When the state supreme court construed the law to cover the Scouts and upheld Dale's claim, the group appealed to the U.S. Supreme Court, claiming that the state violated its First Amendment right not to associate with homosexuals like Dale.

The Court's 5-to-4 decision in the Scouts' favor is actually less interesting and important than the competing methodologies the justices offered for resolving such conflicts. All of them agreed that the First Amendment right of private groups not to associate with those whom they view as different also includes a right of "expressive association" allowing the group to avoid associating itself with messages that might lead outsiders to ascribe to it values or characteristics that it opposes. The justices disagreed, however, over how this right to exclude unwanted messages applied to the Scouts' exclusion of Dale. Specifically, they split over (1) how to interpret the group's internal and public communications concerning homosexual membership, (2) what its "morally straight" and "clean" tenets meant as applied to homosexuality, and (3) whether those tenets would be applied only to Dale's conduct (homosexual acts) or also to his condition or orientation (homosexuality); and, if only to conduct, whether only to conduct undertaken in his Scouts work.

They also disagreed sharply over the question of proof. Chief Justice William Rehnquist, writing for a narrow majority, deferred almost completely to the Scouts' self-depiction. It was enough that the group had expressed itself by taking an official and sincere position on homosexuality; the majority would not second-guess it by asking whether its position was a "purpose" of the group or whether the group had chosen an effective method of expressing itself. The group should enjoy complete control over how it defined and presented itself; an unwanted message that others might impute to the group could violate its right of expressive association even if its preferred message was controversial within the group, illogical, or even internally inconsistent. Only the group could say how salient its own message was and which other messages might so impair its own that the state's interest in eliminating discrimination, which the majority acknowledged was compelling, should be overridden.

The flip side of the *Dale* majority's wholesale deference to the group was its refusal to give any credence to the state courts' findings of fact on these questions. This was the same back-of-the-hand that the *Jones* majority gave to the lower federal courts in that case. Justice John Paul Stevens, writing for the dissenters, tested the Scouts' claims quite differently. Relying on the Court's earlier *Jaycees* and *Rotary Club* decisions, which rejected the groups' exclusion of women because admitting them would not significantly burden the groups' self-definitions, he also distinguished the Court's more recent *Hurley v. Irish-American Gay, Lesbian and*

Bisexual Group of Boston decision upholding the right of a private St. Patrick's Day parade organizing group to exclude a group wishing to march under a gay rights banner strongly opposed by the organizer group. Shifting the burden of justification, in effect, from the state to the Scouts and then raising the standard of proof, Stevens proceeded to parse the Scouts' memorandums, and even its silence, with the kind of literal, logic-chopping precision more appropriate to the construction of bond indentures or tax codes than to discerning the fluid, often ineffable nature of group identity. To avert sham claims (a possibility unmentioned by Rehnquist), a group "must at least show it has adopted and advocated an unequivocal position inconsistent with a position advocated or epitomized by the person whom the organization seeks to exclude." The Scouts, he concluded, did not come close to passing this test.

However one interprets the facts about the salience and consistency of the Scouts' position on homosexuality (I think reasonable people might differ), and however one feels about gay rights (I strongly favor them), Stevens's approach to the conflict between diversity and equality is too intrusive. It ignores the fact that private groups, like the individuals who constitute them, need breathing room in order to survive and flourish. The meanings and satisfactions derived from many group memberships have everything to do with who and what the group excludes, and only the members can decide what those meanings and satisfactions are. Although most obviously true of religious groups and political parties, this is also true for most other social groups from families to bridge clubs to labor unions to witches' covens.

If we want a civil society and polity in which private groups can sustain their meaning-giving value and function effectively, the state must keep its distance. (Ironically, the ability of a national polity to provide meaning and satisfaction to its members is very much under challenge not by litigants but by porous borders, limits on its traditional sovereignty, globalism, and other factors. The state, as principal regulator of private groups, is finding it harder to maintain the loyalty, cohesiveness, and distinctive political identity of its own members. (I have addressed this subject elsewhere.) It is not simply that those who exercise state power may use it cynically to serve their narrow or partisan ends—a serious risk of state laws regulating parties and primaries, though one not mentioned by the justices in *Jones*. It is also that even a benign regulatory state may stifle a group's vitality, spontaneity, and authenticity. Stevens's formalistic approach to discerning the Scouts' organizational values ignores the possibility that the Scouts had never really had to focus on homosexuality until sued by Dale, which would not necessarily be inconsistent with authentic homophobic values.

Were this approach to prevail, groups like the Scouts would be well advised to have lawyers scrutinize every communication that could possibly be used to challenge their value-defining choices. The fact that this legalization of private, not just public, life is already far advanced is no reason to extend its reach even further. Does rejecting Stevens's approach nullify the viability of antidiscrimination protections? A full answer must be found in real-world consequences as well as in legal rules. In practice, the Scouts and other such groups will and should pay a heavy price for their homophobia; many families will defect to scouting groups that welcome gays (others, unfortunately, may be more drawn to the Scouts because of its position), and public officials will withhold patronage and recognition, at least where they can legally do so.

This is as it should be. A group's principles are best tested when they bear a cost, and the cost of homophobia should be high indeed. In doctrinal terms, a group seeking exemption from generally applicable laws should have to show that its self-definition is not concocted for tactical purposes, but its standard of proof must be low if those laws are to protect the group's autonomy and the richness and diversity of a vibrant civil society.

ᔕᕪ **12** ᔕᕪ

Professors and Profession: An Odd Couple

The relationship between the bar and the academy is as old as law schools themselves. It has never been an easy one. Some tension, of course, is perfectly predictable, even desirable. Practitioners and professors have different goals, respond to different pressures and rhythms, and even speak different languages. In terms of size, income, social influence, and some other objective standards, both enterprises have never been healthier. Observing their mutual prosperity, one is tempted to say vive la différence! and be done with it.

The natives, however, are definitely restless—on both sides of the divide. Practicing lawyers often complain that legal scholarship is now so esoteric and theoretical that they cannot read or comprehend it, much less use it in their work. Some also doubt the value of the instruction that students receive in law school. Young lawyers who come to firms well grounded in the nuances of feminist theory seem utterly clueless about how to take a deposition or draft a contract. The professors, for their part, are no more enamored of law practice than the lawyers are of today's legal education. The best evidence of academics' attitudes, after all, is their career choice: They turned their backs on practice, deciding that they would rather spend their time in the library or classroom than with clients or in the courtroom.

Has this split widened in recent years? Some shrewd, sophisticated observers of the profession think so. In well-regarded books, Mary Ann Glendon, Anthony Kronman, and Sol Linowitz (respectively, a Harvard Law professor, Yale Law's dean, and a distinguished lawyer-statesman) decry the supposed decline of the bar. We are a "lost profession" (in Kronman's title) and a "betrayed" one (in Linowitz's). Gone is the lofty vision of law and professionalism that the schools have traditionally cultivated in their students. Judges and lawyers like Antonin Scalia, Alex Kozinski, Robert Bork, Philip Howard, and Peter Huber join this chorus of lamentation while adding a few grace notes of their own. In today's academy, they say, theory-driven professors concoct novel and perverse legal doctrines that eager lawyers foist on gullible, activist judges. In turn, the bench, egged on by its leftist, elite-schooled clerks, swallows these pernicious ideas hook, line, and sinker.

But this issue is more than a conservative hot button. Even certified liberals express anxiety about it. In a 1992 speech (later an article) entitled "The Growing Disjunction Between Legal Education and the Legal Profession," Judge Harry Edwards of the U.S. Court of Appeals for the D.C. Circuit voiced alarm about the different directions the two groups were taking. The schools, he charged, are moving toward "pure theory," the firms toward "pure commerce," and "the middle ground—ethical practice—(is being) deserted by both." His speech struck a raw nerve. In a thick symposium issue of the Michigan Law Review, leading deans, professors, and judges debated Edwards's claims. The fact that only one practitioner wrote for this symposium, compared to sixteen academics and judges, raises a pertinent question: Might this debate simply be another example of academic and judicial navel-gazing, of little real concern to real world lawyers?

Unlikely. The American Bar Association devotes much time and money to studying the content of legal education and certifying its quality. Most lawyers who have never heard of Edwards's speech surely retain an interest in it, particularly at their alma maters: Lawyers are not surprised that law schools and law firms have different preoccupation. They always have and always will. What troubles lawyers, just as it troubled Judge Edwards, is that the gap between these worlds seems to have widened.

Imagine a practitioner in, say, his midfifties thumbing through today's law school catalogs and law reviews. He would probably feel as if he were gazing across a Yellowstone of change and in comprehension. He would spot some familiar landmarks: Tax, property, trusts and estates, commercial law, and other traditional subjects still dominate both the curricula and the law reviews. But much of the landscape would seem quite alien. The abundance of highly theoretical courses and multidisciplinary topics described in the catalogs, with their often unintelligible jargon, abstract concepts, and abstruse references, would probably amaze, if not repel, him.

When he (and I) attended law school in the early and mid-1960s, many of these now-familiar offerings were not viewed as subjects at all, much less subjects for serious legal study. Many are "law and" courses—law and economics, law and society, law and sexuality, law and race, law and popular culture, law and literature, law and the risk society, law and theology, law and . . . almost anything that instructors want students to ponder for a semester. This change is apparent in many other course titles that reduce the substantive subject matter (such as torts) to the status of an adjectival modifier of the noun "theory"—tort theory, feminist theory, critical race theory, communications theory, and . . . well, you get the idea.

This curricular shift toward cross-disciplinary and theoretical courses reflects the instructors' academic attainments and ambitions, as well as the students intellectual interests. For many reasons—disenchantment with law practice's rewards and demands; schools' affirmative action in hiring; higher academic salaries; more emphasis on publication; and a large increase in female teachers—today's market for law teachers is far more competitive. Knowing this, candidates often come to that market with advanced degrees from nonlaw graduate schools (the "law and" fields). In fact, many law schools are now more eager to hire those who hold nonlaw master's and doctorate degrees than those with LLMs and JSDs (the more traditional routes for aspiring law teachers pursuing postgraduate training, and still the preferred route for foreign law teachers studying in the United States). My own institution (Yale), which is admittedly an atypical case, now has about fifteen full-time, permanent professors with doctorates in nonlaw subjects; many of the others have earned nonlaw master's degrees. The same is more or less true of many other law faculties, including those at some state institutions.

Cross-disciplinary and theoretical analysis, of course, is precisely what PhDs are trained—and like—to do. The social scientists on law faculties are also trained to do quantitative and statistical analysis, as are many of their law students. Their research usually reflects this training, which makes their law review articles even more impenetrable to most practitioners. However, the fact that reviews—now about six hundred strong, many cross-disciplinary or specialized—are more unintelligible and uninteresting to lay lawyers does not simply reflect the law schools' greater numeracy and the technical, abstruse argot of even nonquantitative specialists trained in the humanities or just plain law. It is also that the reviews contain some highly speculative or politically radical articles that they would not have published in the old days. Even though these articles are really political advocacy dressed up as scholarship, today's law review editors, who as college and law students are immersed in critical theories that debunk claims of objectivity, run them. The genre is illustrated by a *Yale Law Journal* article advocating that black jurors engage in race-based nullification in criminal prosecutions of black defendants.

This divide between the profession and the professors is more an impasse than a war, more a case of mutual incomprehension, disappointment, and disdain than of active hostility. It is not enough, then, simply to describe this divide; it must also be assessed. This necessitates answers to some questions: Has this divide always existed? Is it getting wider, as Judge Edwards and some other notables claim? How problematic is it? And what, if anything, can be done about it?

In brief, my answers are these: The divide has always been with us and is indeed increasing, although not as much as many critics claim. It poses no serious problems, however, and it can be reduced but never bridged completely, which in my view is fortunate for both sides.

Historians usually date the modern era of legal education from the 1870s, when Dean Langdell at Harvard developed the case method and casebooks. Nevertheless, today's modes of legal education and legal theory really began in the 1920s, when the Legal Realists, led by William O. Douglas, Robert Hutchins, Thurman Arnold, and Karl Llewellyn, became established at Yale and Columbia. Prefigured by Holmes (himself a practitioner-professor), the Realists debunked traditional ideas about the sources and logical consistency of law. They were imaginative empiricists eager to show that the law that officials and citizens actually used was not the law inscribed in the treatises. They were also theorists seeking to rationalize and reform law by drawing on economics, sociology, psychology, political science, and other social science disciplines just then emerging. Their practitioner colleagues had less time and inclination for this more painstaking academic work, and preferred legal treatises that met their practical need for practical legal doctrine.

The trajectory of separation set in motion by the Realists has grown steadily steeper in some ways. Law teaching, like law practice, has become a full-time profession with its own distinctive language, incentives, norms, and preoccupations. Many of the commonalities that the profession and academy once shared no longer exist. This separation, of course, is by no means peculiar to the law. Similar divisions have occurred in medicine, business, journalism, theology, and all other professional fields.

Still, the divide in law is not nearly as wide as its most severe critics claim. Judge Richard Posner, surely one of the most astute analysts of both sectors of the law, points out that scholars are still writing compendious, doctrinal, practitioner-oriented treatises at a healthy clip. Although today's treatises are usually more specialized than the traditional ones, this change reflects, as it should, the dramatically increased specialization of legal practice itself. Doctrinal scholarship—the kind that presumably is most useful to the bench and bar—has not declined in quantity, according to Posner. Instead, he writes, "its production has shifted toward scholars at law schools of the second and third tier."

An empirical study comparing law review articles in 1960 and 1985 seems to bear out Posner's contention. The study confirms that the 1985 articles were longer and more likely to be written by professors than by judges and practitioners, but viewed as a whole the 1985 articles were equally useful to practitioners as those in 1960, and more useful to judges, legislators, and scholars than the earlier ones. But in the nonelite (middle quintile) law reviews, the 1985 articles were judged "significantly more useful" to practitioners than those in 1960. The 1985 articles were relatively more theoretical and more critical of existing doctrine than the 1960 ones, but much of this was not "high theory" but rather an effort to synthesize and rationalize larger areas of doctrine in light of more general principles. In addition, the proliferation of publications meant that the total number of practical articles had grown substantially. Indeed, doctrinal analysis was the focus of about 60 percent of the articles in both years.

As for the law school curriculum, the divide is actually narrowing in some respects. For example, consider two of the most striking developments in legal education during the last thirty years: the creation of clinical courses as a core element in the curriculum, and the rapid growth in the number and prominence of courses on the legal profession and on professional ethics. Today, as never before, the academy has transformed the profession itself into an object of serious, sustained, and specialized study, complete with its own casebooks, conferences, law reviews, clinical programs, and even jargon.

Perhaps the best evidence that the profession-academy divide has not reached crisis proportions comes from the market. In financial terms, the profession is now supporting the law schools more generously than ever, while the schools in turn are training more practicing lawyers than ever. The bar's substantial increase in donations strongly suggests that it generally approves of what the law schools are doing. Similarly, the schools are dearly attentive to the bar's demand for well-trained law graduates: The schools are producing a lot of them. What's more, the position a school holds in the fiercely competitive marketplace depends almost entirely on the ability of its graduates to find employment—a performance index that is well publicized. Were there a serious mismatch between the supply of qualified graduates and the profession's requirements, lawyers could readily express their dissatisfaction by using their considerable influence as alumni and donors to press the schools to fundamentally reform legal education. This does not appear to be occurring. Instead, the common interests of the bar and academy are growing even as the differences between their worlds grow.

These differences—within broad limits that we have not yet approached—should be cause for satisfaction and pride, not lamentation. Despite the many regrettable rigidities of our legal system, American lawyers are still better positioned than lawyers elsewhere to facilitate the social and economic transformations that are convulsing the legal world. (Everything, after all, is relative.) Although this flexibility surely has many causes, much of it reflects the teaching and learning capacities of our law schools and lawyers. Law and legal institutions are changing more rapidly than can any curriculum that simply teaches current doctrine.

It is essential, then, that our law schools teach specific legal rules only within the larger frameworks of abstract theory, multidisciplinary analysis, and complex fact-finding. Only these forms of knowledge can equip young lawyers to exploit the remorseless change and competition they will confront when they leave the classroom. Older lawyers can in one way or another use the academy to stay abreast of new ways of thinking about and practicing law. At the very least, they can inform themselves about what is going on at their alma maters and tell the schools what they think of it. You can bet that the deans, who are always planning the next fund drive, will listen attentively.

⤳ 13 ⤳

Tax Day: Deficit Reduction Made Easy

As I pondered o'er my forms
Seeking haven from tax storms
I reached judgments quite severe
'Bout the pols who put me here
Taxes are beyond the ken
Of any of us mortal men
Schedules we can't comprehend
Calculations without end
Cross-reference leads to cul-de-sac
Definitions double back
Instructions that do not instruct
All to take my usufruct
How can ordinary Joes
Deconstruct IRS prose?
Who (save those with MBAs)
Can navigate this maddening maze?
1040 is the hardest part
But that, alas, is just the start
States, of course, must have their say
Each taxing in a different way

Heaven help the folks like me
Who live in A and work in B
Then New York City, for my pains,
Takes a piece of what remains
As soothsayer, I must estimate
Or be fined next year for paying late
If, God forbid, dependents work
I file more forms—a parent's perk
I guess I have myself to blame
For playing in this ghastly game
I could have hired a CPA
To get me through this dismal day
But since I trod those many miles
Compiling records, forms, and files
It seemed that I should be the one
To frolic in this springtime fun
Justice Holmes said long ago
(When governments small kept taxes low)
Tax was civilization's price
Purchasing what Holmes found nice
'Tis true enough, but Holmes omits
To mention that those benefits
May cost us more than they repay
When politicians join the fray
They love to spend our hard-earned wealth
It buys them votes—but *not* by stealth
For we, like fish, respond to lures
The more one gleams, more it obscures
Those lures add up to deficit
And though 'twas dropping bit by bit
Fiscal balance—o halcyon day
Is always several years away
We warm to politicians' smile
Their promises do us beguile
We forget that bills come due
(I pray mine will be sent to you)
The problem's ancient, I suppose
Yet simple answer I propose
The goal? Forge links 'twixt choice and cost
Tightening discipline we have lost
How, you ask, can this be done?
Can deficit wars be truly won?
Can voters learn that what they buy

Is what on Tax Day makes them cry?
Reform our calendar—this I urge
It separates what we should merge
Election Day is too remote
We should pay tax just 'ere we vote
Like hanging, as Sam Johnson said,
We'd focus on both hope and dread
As we elected in November
Just-paid taxes we'd remember
No six months' lapse would dissipate
The pain we felt on payment date
No April songbirds, budding trees
Would salve that wound or suffering ease
A Tax Day on November first
Would regulate the voters' thirst
By entering the polling booth
With tax in mind, we'd vote the truth
Memory on Election Day
Would limit wants for which we'll pay
By sharpening our civic nerve
We'd get the government we deserve

– PART III –

THE RULE OF LAW

No single idea is more precious to a free society than the rule of law. This is so for the simple reason that we cannot achieve any of our other public and private values, including justice, without it. (So widespread has the recognition of this fact become that the idea has earned its own acronym, ROL, for easy use by democratic reformers throughout the world.) In this part, I seek to make my own small contribution to the debate over what particular institutions, principles, and social practices are required to sustain the rule of law in a liberal society like ours.

I begin with an essay about class actions. This subject is particularly topical in light of the enactment of class action reform legislation in February 2005, legislation that was pending in Congress when I published the essay, five years earlier. The new law will move many class actions from state to federal courts and may bar altogether some class actions that, before the new law, could have been maintained in some state courts, but it does not address many of the issues raised in my essay. Another essay considers an equally controversial aspect of our legal system: punitive damages. Despite the relative rarity of such awards, they cast a large shadow over the civil litigation system, raising some substantial due process concerns that courts and legislatures should take more seriously. Next, I discuss lying—the most ancient human activity (initiated, after all, in the Garden of Eden) and among the most common. Taking off from a newspaper account of a small town mayor in Iowa who wants to criminalize falsehoods in the interest of "Midwestern honesty," I explore the many different, if not necessarily inconsistent, ways in which the law deals with lying in various contexts.

One of the most distinctive features of the rule of law, American style, is the civil jury. Every other nation has either abolished or severely limited the use of lay juries in civil cases, yet the United States has actually expanded their influence in a number of ways. My essay on the civil jury explains why this is so and suggests some ways in which its functioning and legitimacy could be enhanced. I then turn to courts, the other great institution shaping our rule of law. Few if any other legal systems permit courts to play the extensive constitution-shaping, policymaking, and bureaucratic management roles that they do in the United States. Focusing on what is known as institutional reform litigation—the supervision of large public bureaucracies that have violated constitutional or other legal norms—I analyze two aspects of the courts' performance in such cases: judicial competence and democratic legitimacy.

Another essay illuminating the rule of law in America takes on a perennially hot topic: gun control. Specifically, I examine the strategy of pursuing gun control through tort litigation seeking damages from gun manufacturers based on theories of defective products, nuisance, and negligent distribution. Here, a widely admired and famously creative federal trial judge has attempted—too zealously, in my view—to fashion innovative doctrines to support the claims of victims of gun violence in the face of traditional legal rules that would bar their suits. His well-intended legal innovations, I suggest, are not only doomed to failure as a legal matter but have had perverse effects, compounding the terrible losses already suffered by the victims he seeks to help. My next essay moves to the subject of tort reform more generally, analyzing the most important aspects of legislation that the insurance industry, product manufacturers, and others have been pressing in Congress for more than two decades, legislation that President Bush hopes to enact in his second term as a complement to the class action reform of 2005.

The final essay in this part concerns one of the most poignant dilemmas with which the law must deal: the use of paid surrogate mothers by infertile couples, a practice often denounced as baby-selling and, given the human values at stake, a difficult challenge for the rule of law. Focusing on the first and most widely discussed case of this kind, *Baby M*, I review the social and legal contexts in which surrogate motherhood occurs and argue that state governments should regulate but not choke off contracts of this kind, and that courts should generally enforce them.

⤷ 14 ⤶

Class Actions: Analyzing the Issues

Class actions are front-page news. Toshiba pays more than a billion dollars due to a potential glitch. Governments file massive suits against gun makers. Lawyers suing tobacco companies want to issue bonds on their multibillion-dollar recoveries. Consumer class actions piggyback on the government's case against Microsoft. Once an arcane subspecialty of a few trial lawyers, class actions have entered the mainstream of American popular culture.

Lawyers have used class actions, in one form or another, for centuries, but the practice is under attack today as never before. Its growing public prominence has intensified the backlash. During the last decade, Congress restricted federal securities class actions, barred Y2K cases, and has come close to enacting across-the-board limits on state class actions. Even before the Supreme Court stifled federal mass tort class actions in the late 1990s, the lower federal courts were refusing to certify them in many such cases. With class actions seemingly on the ropes, business groups are multiplying their attacks on them in the courts, legislatures, and media, while plaintiff lawyers are mounting new defenses.

Understanding the public's stakes in the class action battle is difficult because each of the major participants is conflicted. The plaintiffs' lawyers, who specialize in amassing claims and pressuring defendants into lucrative settlements, thrive on them. Other plaintiffs' lawyers, however, fear that class actions will bundle strong claimants with weaker ones and that they will lose litigation control, and the lion's share of the fees, to the class action specialists. Defendants are also ambivalent. Even an unmeritorious class action can persuade a defendant to settle at a premium rather than gamble its future on one roll of the dice. Yet the same company may see the class action as the only way to buy peace by binding present and future claimants. And judges who view class actions as unmanageable also use them to reduce backlogs, caseload management being an increasingly important criterion for judicial promotion.

Class actions engage competing ideologies as well as interests. By suppressing the uniqueness of class members' claims and stressing their commonalities, class actions magnify tensions between individual interests and group welfare. By allowing settlement specialists to control the litigation, they transform a claimant's right to her "day in court" into acquiescence to an opaque bargaining process conducted by strangers. In the struggle to shape the goals and performance of the tort system, the plaintiffs' bar, industry groups, and insurers all vie to shape the class action's image. Ideological and political conflicts, like legal ones, thrive where essential facts are in dispute. Class actions are no exception. RAND's Institute for Civil Justice conducted the first thorough empirical study of class actions, and its most striking finding was uncertainty: "No one can reliably estimate how much class action litigation exists or how the number of lawsuits has changed over time. Incomplete reporting of cases also means that it is impossible to select a random sample of all class action lawsuits for quantitative analysis."

As a result, combatants can confuse the issues surrounding class actions, exaggerate their claims, and cite misleading analogies, atypical cases, and unrepresentative anecdotes. All the more reason, then, to clarify the debate. Here are seven issues.

1. *Class action types.* All class actions are not created equal. They pursue diverse kinds of relief based on disparate theories, which can affect their legitimacy. Those that seek injunctions to restructure public prisons or school systems are controversial not because of the class form but because they empower courts to make political and operational decisions. Those seeking money damages for a large, diverse group (e.g., smokers or workers) are objectionable when they homogenize claims that merit more individuated treatment. The most essential class actions are those aggregating many small but similar claims (e.g., for an illegal commercial practice) that cannot practicably be litigated except on a group basis.

2. *Individual and collective claims.* The dichotomy between individual and collective interests can be misleading. Harvard Law professor David Rosenberg argues that defining in individual terms the legal duties owed by mass producers to consumers and others affected by their products may destroy the very uniformity that creates the mass production efficiencies on which we all depend. His point is not only that "mass production torts require mass production justice to assure mass production goods"; it is also that, ex ante (before we know whether we will be injured), most of us would prefer more mass, collectivized justice than the individualized tort system can provide, especially where our real choice is between class action and nothing. Still, Rosenberg may underestimate how ardently Americans embrace the ideology and symbols of individualism even when, as with the vaunted right to a day in court, reality often mocks the ideal.

3. *Class representation.* Courts may not certify a class that counsel or named plaintiffs would not adequately represent. But that depends on future conduct that is hard to predict. Class actions inevitably raise ethical dilemmas and conflicts of interest among lawyers, among class members, and between lawyers and clients. These problems are especially acute in asbestos and other mass exposure cases involving latent diseases that for decades will generate claims whose number, timing, and gravity are largely unknowable. When the product in question will continue to be marketed, like tobacco, future claims are even harder to predict. No structural changes can fix these conflicts. Requiring subclasses, as the Supreme Court has urged, may reduce conflicts but cannot wholly eliminate them. Although courts can conduct more detailed investigations of possible conflicts and demand greater protections by potential class counsel, judges are poorly situated to identify these problems in advance, much less remedy them. Regulating class action counsel fees, however, is another matter.

4. *Attorneys' fees.* Public indignation about class action settlements that result in enormous legal fees is a major force driving the backlash. This is

particularly true if these fees are part of settlements that produce little or no compensation or genuine relief (as in some secondhand smoking cases), fees that exceed what class members receive (three of RAND's ten case studies), or fees vastly disproportionate to the lawyers' risk, effort, or success (as in some recent asbestos and state tobacco cases). Although no one knows how common these situations are, even plaintiffs' lawyers concede that many abuses occur. Indeed, at times they feel they must accept less merely to appease courts and public opinion. Courts can exercise better control over such abuses. Almost a decade ago, Geoffrey Miller and Jonathan Macey urged courts to auction the right to represent classes, an idea that at least one judge has implemented. Even if quality differences justified the court in rejecting the highest bid and selecting a lower one, an auction would still capture for class members the dollars saved by driving fees down. Other reformers have proposed criteria and procedures to enable judges, after the fact, to tailor fee awards more closely to the value that the lawyers actually added.

5. *Federal and state court class actions.* RAND found a recent surge of class actions in state courts, which often have more liberal class action rules than federal courts. Lawyers' moves to state courts were particularly evident after Congress limited securities class actions in federal courts and after the Fifth Circuit decertified the smokers' class in *Castano v. American Tobacco.* Forum-shopping and judge-shopping are neither surprising nor confined to the plaintiffs' bar. Defense counsel also shop for favorable class action outcomes. They can remove many cases from state court to a more sympathetic federal forum, and as Columbia professor John Coffee emphasizes, they can also decide to negotiate with, or offer favorable terms to, more tractable plaintiffs' lawyers rather than deal with their more recalcitrant adversaries. Legislation pending in Congress would facilitate the removal of class actions from state to federal court, and would bar from federal court "instrastate" class actions (i.e., wherein most of the members reside in the state where the action was originally filed, and that state's law will primarily govern the class's claims) and those of "limited scope" (i.e., the class has fewer than one hundred members or aggregate damages of under $1 million).

Putting aside the delicious irony that many conservative advocates of states' rights and liberal advocates of federal preemption have switched their customary positions on this issue, the proposal has some merit. State judges (as more candid ones sometimes admit) have strong incentives to favor in-state plaintiffs against out-of-state defendants, a form of discrimination that the Framers sought to avoid through the federal courts' diversity jurisdiction and that is even more tempting in class actions. And federal judges are often unfamiliar with the state laws that they must apply in the "intrastate" class actions that they now adjudicate.

6. *Class certification standards.* Much concern goes not to the principle of the class action but to the circumstances under which judges certify it. Federal Rule 23 and analogous state law provisions leave courts with broad discretion; they must apply and balance ambiguous standards such as commonality of issues, superiority of the class action device, and adequacy of class representation. They must do this with little information about the underlying facts or about how the case will change as discovery proceeds, data improve, and settlement pressures grow.

Where class actions are subject to abuse, the law can make it more difficult to certify them. In 1995, for example, Congress found that plaintiffs' lawyers were distorting capital markets by bringing so-called strike suits against issuers whose only offense was that their stock's price had declined. It imposed new conditions on such actions, such as requiring named plaintiffs to have substantial financial stakes in the case. (Predictably, the law simply pushed these cases into the state courts). In mass tort class actions, where the scientific evidence on causation has often proved quite weak, it might be desirable (as Yale's George Priest has urged) to require a court to appraise the merits of plaintiffs' claims before certifying a class, much as it does before issuing a preliminary injunction.

7. *Who should decide?* Perhaps the most important question about class actions is whether certification should be regulated through categorical legislative rules or through judicial decisions that weigh contexts and balance factors. Absent systematic abuse that a rule can control without risk to other values, the law should favor intensive precertification scrutiny by judges who are close to the litigation and must live with the consequences of their decisions. Indeed, given the great variety of situations in which class relief is plausibly sought, we cannot avoid relying on the courts to pick and choose among them. For example, no flat rule should dictate whether a class may be certified for settlement that could not be certified for trial; it depends on the circumstances, as the Supreme Court wisely held in its *Amchem* decision. In regulating class actions, discretion has its place.

~ **15** ~

Punitive Damages: Lawless (In)justice*

Huge punitive damage awards make headlines. Just last month, for example, an Oregon jury awarded almost $80 million in punitive damages to the family of a forty-year smoker who was found to be 50 percent responsible for his own death. In late 1997 a Louisiana jury ordered CSX to pay $3.4 billion for a railroad car fire although CSX merely owned the track and no one was seriously injured. In well-scripted reactions to such awards, plaintiffs lawyers praise the jury's wisdom, defense lawyers vow to appeal its "preposterous" verdict, and insurers liken it to a Powerball lottery. We academics try to put it all in perspective.

The great irony is this: While punitive damages promise to fill an important gap in the law, they are essentially lawless. Some states have recently limited punitive awards, but elsewhere juries remain free to impose them pretty much as they like; appellate courts can review them but lack meaningful standards for doing so. Meanwhile, the punitive damages war, which continues to rage in state capitals, is now joined in Washington, D.C. The weaponry includes constitutional claims, shopworn myths, social science findings, horror stories on both sides, and thinly concealed self-interest gussied up as selfless idealism. Once we clear away the smoke and noise over punitive awards, we reveal them for what they are: demands for justice without law.

First, some facts to supplant the myths. Punitive awards have an ancient pedigree in our law but are nonetheless rare. RAND researchers found in 1997 that punitive damages were awarded in only 7 percent of plaintiffs' verdicts. In product cases where even non-negligent defendants can be liable, only 5 percent of plaintiffs' verdicts included punitive awards. As one might expect, they are most common in cases involving intentional tort (31 percent of plaintiffs' verdicts) and financial injury like insurance or employment disputes (22 percent).

Industry, eyeing public opinion, often exaggerates their frequency. Media reinforce this distortion by reporting only the most unusual cases, usually with a very high ratio of punitive-to-actual damages—1000:1 in both the *CSX* case and *BMW v. Gore*, which was later overturned by the U.S. Supreme Court. Subsequent court reduction of such awards often goes unreported. Most punitive awards are modest, proportionate to actual harm (the median punitive award is only 40 percent above the compensatory one), and almost always for egregiously reprehensible conduct—for example, CSX's perceived callousness during the emergency evacuation.

Generally speaking, then, the punitive awards that juries mete out fit the crimes. But shouldn't punishing social offenders be the job of criminal and regulatory prosecutors, not civil juries that operate under far more permissive rules? The legal safeguards designed (and even constitutionally

*Little has changed since this article was published in 1999. Juries continue to render staggering punitive awards ($160 billion in a case against five tobacco companies, for example), while the Supreme Court has tried to limit the punitive/compensatory damages ratio to single digits.

required) to protect criminal defendants from unjust conviction and undue punishment do not apply to civil actions. In contrast to criminal juries, civil juries in most states are smaller, more error-prone, can reach a verdict by only a preponderance of the evidence, and need not be unanimous. In criminal prosecutions, as in First Amendment cases, the law must clearly define in advance both the standard of conduct and the penalties that might be imposed so that people can approach the line of illegality without inadvertently crossing it. The Constitution does not allow juries to make these things up as they go along.

Standardless punitive damages offend this fundamental principle of justice. Standards for punitive damages are quite vague; with little or no legal guidance, juries can award punitives when the defendant's fault exceeds ordinary negligence but falls short of the greater fault—usually intentional or malicious wrongdoing—that legislatures and courts (and even prosecutors) require before imposing serious criminal sanctions. Even states that regulate punitive damages in other ways may still leave the jury free to assess any amount within very broad limits—or no limits at all.

This is indeterminate sentencing with a vengeance; the only protection is a reviewing court's willingness to second-guess the jury's assessment, which courts are of course reluctant to do. This lawlessness, moreover, is grafted onto a tort system in which juries award even compensatory damages under notoriously ambiguous standards like "pain and suffering." Although some uncertainty is inevitable—tort law defies bright-line rules—it is unacceptable when a single standardless award can bankrupt defendants, leaving subsequent plaintiffs uncompensated.

For example, the strict liability standard for defective products is now more uncertain than ever. It requires juries either to make multifactor balancing judgments about product designs adopted many years earlier, or to apply a difficult test that ascribes consumer expectations about a product's safety that they probably didn't have. The Third Restatement, which is not yet law in most states, would focus the jury on whether a "reasonable alternative design" existed, but would also allow courts to use the other two standards. A manufacturer often cannot tell whether its product meets the test(s) until the jury decides, long after the product was designed and marketed.

Compounding the uncertainty, juries in many states may assess punitive damages against the same manufacturer over and over again for a single design decision on a single product line. This means potentially unlimited liability for a single error in a mass-distributed product. Indeed, juries assessed punitive awards against products like Bendectin and breast implants even when the product was not defective at all, or when a federal safety agency has approved it after years of rigorous testing and regulation. This may be a defensible rule as to compensatory damages, but is truly perverse when it allows punitive damages.

Some states permit plaintiffs to evidence the defendant's wealth so that the jury can decide how high the punitive award should be—this, on the theory that a defendant's wealth measures both its past moral culpability and the sum needed to deter future misconduct. But inviting juries to take wealth into account simply flips Anatole France's sardonic comment that the law allows rich and poor alike to sleep under bridges. Evidence about wealth offends our cherished symbol of blindfolded Justice applying the law equally to all, and encourages juries to redistribute wealth as they see fit, a wholly inappropriate function for a small, ad hoc, unelected group.

In principle, punitive damages can serve useful purposes. In cases where not all victims sue, perhaps because their injuries are hard to detect or link to particular wrongdoers, mere compensatory damages will neither fully compensate the victims nor deter the wrongdoers. If juries know that a substantial part of the damage award go to the plaintiff's lawyer, they may see additional damages as necessary to make her whole. Juries also use punitive awards to "send a clear message" about our collective outrage about morally unacceptable corporate conduct. But if the criminal justice and regulatory systems fail to punish corporate wrongdoers, they should be strengthened and reformed, not circumvented. Class actions, improved health and safety regulation, and other systemic remedies would be more effective than random punitive awards.

Indeed, when juries send messages that are too powerful or arbitrary, they mislead rather than instruct society, multiplying injustice rather than reducing it. Punitive awards that threaten unpredictable, uninsurable, and perhaps ruinous liability for unintentional harm under vaguely defined standards can over deter activity that is socially valuable, like new drug development. As a RAND study notes, "most business decision makers focus on worst-case scenarios, and they will go to great lengths to avoid exposing their companies to [punitive damages]." This extreme risk-aversion causes them to settle even weak claims in the 95 percent of filed cases that never reach trial. When juries awarded punitive windfalls to a few early asbestos plaintiffs, they sent a clear message indeed to the defendants—that they should file for bankruptcy, as scores of them already have. Surely, the prospect of massive compensatory liabilities was a strong and clear enough message.

Bankruptcies precipitated by punitive damages awards compounded the injuries of tens of thousands of equally deserving claimants by preventing those who were later in the queue from recovering even their compensatory damages. Only if companies seek bankruptcy early enough might this first-come, first-served competition be avoided, permitting a fair solution.

The "clear message" rationale also founders on the inherent limitations of juries. They may be satisfactory fact-finders and norm-appliers in ordinary negligence cases, but they are singularly ill-equipped to be philosophers, policymakers, or prosecutors. Unelected, they do not even replicate the demographic diversity of their communities. Disproportionately elderly, they serve in only one case based on a typically atypical set of facts. The little guidance that courts give juries is often confusing, and they are not even asked to justify their judgments publicly. They are kept in the dark about how their case relates to other cases and about the larger, systemic effects of their verdicts.

Standardless punitive damages mock the rule of law. Juries should only impose them under clear legal standards, just as other punitive institutions are obliged to do. Standards for punitives might take many forms—for example, permissible punitive-to-compensatory damage ratios; payment of all compensatory damages before any punitives in limited fund cases; limits on vicarious liability for punitives; rules on their insurability; caps in certain types of cases; limits on multiple awards for single tortious acts; a higher standard of proof; procedures to prevent wealth evidence from contaminating the jury's liability determination; and more precise standards, drawn from experience in earlier cases, for court review of awards. Most states have imposed such standards, and the laggards should now do so. Researchers should evaluate the effects of these changes.

The essential principle, however, is really quite simple: The tougher the jury's sanction, the more law's discipline and authority must constrain it. Only punitive awards that can pass this elementary test should be permitted.

⌒ 16 ⌒

Lying: Law's Ambivalence

Lying is like food, sex, and law; we just can't do without it. Consider some lies people tell each day with hardly a pang of conscience. "You're looking well." "I'm happy to meet you." "Let's get together for lunch." "It's not the money." "This hurts me more than it hurts you." "I'm delighted to be here." "Your cooking is four star." "I would never cheat on my taxes or my spouse." "I shot par on that hole."

As the reader surely knows from personal experience, the list of common lies is very, very long. And, as you might expect, there are even statistics on the point. Thus, a recent study found that 60 percent of strangers lied at least once during a ten-minute get-to-know-you conversation, with the number of lies averaging 2.9, and ranging as high as twelve. (Interestingly, men and women told an equal number of lies, though with somewhat different intents—women to make others feel good, men to build themselves up.)

Our moral precepts and intuitions recognize that lying is not always wrong. We are taught as children to pretend that we are having a good time even when we are unhappy, that we like the food our hosts serve even when it is execrable, that we respect our elders even when they are fools, and that we are willing to share our toys even though this is the last thing we want to do. The Eighth Commandment, for example, prohibits bearing "false witness against thy neighbor," which seems to bar false testimony, defamation, and malicious gossip, perhaps, but not most other kinds of lies. Hypocrisy, Dr. Johnson reminds us, is the tribute that vice pays to virtue. Lies, one might say, are the lubricants that keep our social wheels turning.

These thoughts were provoked by a recent article in the *New York Times* about Jo Hamlett, the mayor of a small town in Iowa, who has proposed—in apparent seriousness—an ordinance that would prohibit residents from lying. "I just feel like it would put a little more Midwestern honesty back in these people," he said, referring particularly to tall tales about hunting and fishing successes in the town. The article did not reveal whether Hamlett is up for reelection.

It is easy to ridicule the mayor's proposal, but it does raise intriguing questions about law's relationship to truth—and thus to lying. The law usually stands up for truth but not always or unequivocally. Consider some legal variations on this theme. Sometimes the law insists that truth is the only thing that matters; other times, it affirms that truth does not matter at all. Even when law demands that a statement be true, it does not always require the strict or full truth. Sometimes it countenances considerable fudging or even what lay people might call "white lies." The law usually demands the most reliable evidence about a fact but then suppresses apparently truthful evidence bearing on that same fact. Indeed, the law sometimes punishes lawyers and others for speaking the truth, as with gag orders.

The law depends on truth the way humans depend on oxygen; both are vital. For law to govern society effectively and enjoy legitimacy, its decisions must correspond to reality with a very high probability. (This is one way to understand the collapse of corrupt regimes like the Soviet Union, whose laws are built on lies.) Nevertheless, important areas of law conspicuously disclaim any interest in whether the assertions that the law regulates are true or false. Religious claims, for example, are protected by the First Amendment, even when they strike most of us as manifestly preposterous. The Supreme Court insists that government may not police truth in this area, even though false religious claims can be very damaging to those who rely on them. Only in the clearest cases of fraud will the Court permit prosecutors to act against religious speech or activity. By the same token, albeit for somewhat different reasons, the Court has created a wide zone of protection for political expression in which people are free

to speak falsely to their hearts' content—especially, and perhaps ironically, with respect to matters of the greatest public importance. The Court in
New York Times v. Sullivan and its progeny has immunized patently false
and defamatory statements of fact against public figures unless they are
published with malice—that is, with actual knowledge of their falsity or
reckless disregard of the truth. This immunity, which extends primarily
but not only to media defendants, protects, if not encourages, sloppy,
even irresponsible reporting.

To the general rule that the law will not protect falsehoods, there are
some exceptions—some of them quite broad. For example, most false statements that are uttered in court under oath and then exposed as lies are nevertheless not punishable as perjury. The common law of deceit provides that
even lies are protected, unless they are material and engender reliance. The
law governing commercial advertising permits many "puffing" statements
("Wheaties, the breakfast of champions") that either cannot be proved or are
flatly false. The law's assumption is that sensible people don't take such
hyperbole too seriously—which amounts to saying that the statements have
little informational value. But if this is so, then it is harder to see why the law
should protect such statements even when (as the seller fully intends) buyers do take them seriously and they are material to the transaction.

The trial and the adversary system are usually justified as a search for
the truth. A more accurate statement would be that they are a search for
truth constrained by other values, which may—and often do—trump
truth-seeking. Some lawyers familiar with European civil law systems find
the adversary system to be, by comparison, scandalously indifferent to the
truth. This dispute, which borders on the theological, is unlikely to be
resolved by either argument or evidence.

Even the staunchest advocates of the adversary system, however, should
recognize that it serves goals other than truth—including some goals that
actually undermine truth-seeking. The most important of these other goals
is to protect individual liberty, especially against state overreaching. To
achieve this goal, the law adopts rules and practices that can interfere with
the search for truth in individual cases and, perhaps, more generally.

Consider some examples. Testimonial (antitestimonial, really) privileges for spouses, confessors, and psychotherapists may prevent the jury
from learning the truth of what happened. Under the hearsay rule (and
subject to many exceptions), an out-of-court statement cannot be introduced to prove the truth of what it asserts if the declarant cannot be cross-
examined before the jury—even if the statement is the best available evidence for the truth of the assertion. Under the exclusionary rule (again,
subject to many exceptions), highly probative evidence is often kept from
the jury merely because it was obtained illegally. Shield laws protect journalists and some others from revealing what they know, even at the cost
of denying courts, juries, and the general public access to the truth.

The code of professional responsibility makes a number of compromises with truth. So long as a lawyer does not consciously avoid learning information from the client or conceal it from the court, the lawyer may zealously represent the client without having or presenting the "whole truth." Even as an officer of the court, a lawyer who suspects (but does not know) that his or her client is lying on the stand may not be obliged to stop the false testimony or inform the court of that suspicion. Lawyers in civil cases need not reveal every fact that might assist their adversaries' case.

The jury—or more precisely, the need to protect its integrity—entails much suppression of truth. I have already noted that the rules of evidence keep much probative evidence from the jury. Judges often impose gag orders on truthful speech by lawyers and jurors. The rule that prohibits lawyers from impeaching jury verdicts protects many erroneous decisions and limits the domain of truth-seeking.

The law, in short, has many fish to fry, and truth is only one of them. If all our law cared about was truth, our society would be organized quite differently than it is—and not necessarily for the better. For one thing, we might well choose a civil law-type inquisitorial system in which, among other differences, lawyers play a less prominent, less exalted role in politics and society, and their clients enjoy less vigorous advocacy and, perhaps, less protection from the state. In addition, political debate would be far less robust, expansive, and critical than it is, as citizens would face greater risks of liability for aggressively challenging public officials and social leaders. A law single-mindedly pursuing truth would constrain religious activity, particularly among unconventional groups that actively recruit by making extravagant claims about salvation.

In principle, one might expect that a law that relentlessly pursues truth would seek to reduce the factual errors—the lies and honest mistakes—made by and to legal decision makers. Since truth negates error, the more law cares about the truth, the fewer errors it should tolerate. In practice, however, we face not one simple choice, but two more complex choices: how much error to accept, and which kinds. To further complicate matters, the "which kind" choice often affects the "how much" choice. Most policy decisions must trade off the risk of "Type 1" errors (false positives), which give a legal benefit or burden to the wrong person, against the risk of "Type 2" errors (false negatives), which fail to give it to the right person. Do we care more about, say, officials giving a disability award to all who are legally eligible for it than we do about preventing ineligible people from receiving it through lies or other errors? Among the factors affecting this trade-off are how costly it would be to reduce each type of error, and how important the benefit is to the individuals seeking it. If it is essential to their well-being, then we are more likely to accept the risk of erroneously giving it to ineligibles. The central points, however, are that the law must choose between the two kinds of errors, and that in choosing, it must often accept (and in effect reward) some level of lying.

Finally, a law concerned only with the truth would also have much less patience with the delays, digressions, and procedures that occur when public and private decision makers look beyond truth to other values. Imagine what life would be like if officials—police wanting to grill a suspect, for example, or zoning boards determined to approve or deny a building permit—could do so without impediment as long as they later turned out to be right on the facts and the law. Mission-driven officials find procedural obstacles frustrating, and citizens assail them as red tape, foot-dragging, and paper-shuffling. Both may be right. But from a broader perspective, these obstacles help protect our liberties. They slow the bureaucratic juggernaut, force it to listen to other views, and oblige it to diversify its portfolio of purposes. And it is not only government that needs this value diversification. Private bureaucracies with immense power over us—health care organizations, insurers, broadcasters, and the like—must be publicly accountable and procedurally fair even when doing so interferes with what they take to be their primary missions.

In a liberal democracy like ours, law must pursue the truth vigorously but not single-mindedly. Errors—and even some lying—are part of the price we pay for our freedom.

∽ 17 ∽

Civil Juries: Here to Stay

The civil jury has changed in many ways throughout the years. Remarkably, however, these changes have seldom been structural. Instead, the social functions of the jury and the context in which it operates have changed. Functionally, the jury has moved from fact reporting to fact finding, from deciding both the law and the facts to deciding only the facts, and from being utterly controlled by judges to being relatively independent. Contextually, it now operates in a milieu of eroding institutional authority, sharpened social divisions, and more complex factual and normative disputes.

The contemporary debate over the jury is one in which the ultimate prize is public opinion ("the thirteenth juror," as some have put it). Law's growing prominence, complexity, and penetration into daily life have galvanized public attention. Articles about the "litigation explosion," bizarre claims, soaring insurance rates, declining availability of insurance, overwhelming judicial caseloads, high legal costs, complex litigation, and interminable trials are common. Some of this commentary is accurate; much of it is false or at least misleading. At the center of the contending arguments is the question of the jury's contribution to these conditions.

Calls to reform the jury persist. Proposals range from limiting or abolishing the jury to enhancing its authority, independence, and influence. Because advocates on both sides often argue from quite different factual and normative premises and do not always articulate or understand these premises and their implications, the issue of reform has seldom been squarely joined in a way that crystallizes the right questions. At a minimum, a coherent debate over jury reform requires agreement on a precise definition of the problem so that relevant evidence can be examined.

DEFINING THE "PROBLEM"

Objections to the use of juries fall into four major categories. One is based on the claim that the jury tends to make irrational decisions. For one reason or another, this argument goes, the jury tends to reach conclusions that are simply erroneous.

Another major category of objections centers on the ways the jury is thought to affect the behavior of six groups of participants in the legal process: insurers, the media, primary actors (that is, people or organizations in general), trial lawyers (of whom insurance lawyers are an important subset), judges, and other policymakers. These objections do not claim that juries are biased or prone to error, but rather that jury decisions by their very nature emit liability signals that are confusing, inconsistent, and arbitrary. In this view, the jury's signals convey little useful information about actual legal norms. Coupled with the largely unregulated, generous system of damage awards, jury decisions generate widespread uncertainty, anxiety, and risk avoidance.

The third major category of objections concerns the administrative costs imposed by the jury system. These include the costs to litigants of waiting for jury trial; the costs associated with the longer duration of jury trials; and the costs of recruiting, screening, selecting, and paying jurors, including opportunity costs to the jurors themselves.

A fourth way to define the "problem" posed by the civil jury constitutes what may be the most fundamental criticism of all. In this view, the jury's most far-reaching consequence relates to its implications for the deeper structure of litigation, particularly the structure of the trial and hence of the pretrial activities of lawyers and adjudicators. Comparative law scholar Arthur von Mehren has argued convincingly that "the presence of a jury makes a discontinuous trial impractical." But as von Mehren also points out, a concentrated trial in turn entails a number of other procedural elements: extensive pretrial proceedings to minimize the problem of surprise, a high degree of lawyer control over the evidentiary and case-shaping processes, a related emphasis on party presentation and party prosecution, and a problem of delay at the pre-trial rather than at the trial stage.

The four types of objections to the civil jury are obviously quite different. Although some appear to be more persuasive than others, none seems clearly sustainable on the basis of the current data. Here, as elsewhere, conclusions about the need for reform may well depend on who one thinks should bear the burden of proof.

Whatever the resolution of this question, these very different critiques call for a wide variety of remedial responses. This essay distinguishes four discrete strategies. Moving from the most incremental to the most radical, they are to reduce administrative costs, restructure the jury, constrain jury discretion, and divert disputes to nonjury forums. (A fifth, improving juror comprehension, is not discussed here.) A number of specific jury reforms to implement each of these strategies is discussed. Some, of course, are consistent with more than one strategy.

REDUCING ADMINISTRATIVE COSTS

Strategies aimed at reducing administrative costs would retain the jury's current functions and structure. One option—directed not so much at reducing the magnitude of these costs as toward changing their distribution—is to raise the fees for parties who demand a jury. As Judge Richard Posner has noted, existing fees for the use of the courts are trivial, far below the level necessary to cover the full social costs and private benefits of even a bench trial, much less a jury trial. If fees were raised, the demand for both jury and bench trials would decline and settlements correspondingly would become more attractive. However, special provision should be made to ensure that low-income disputants enjoy continued access to the courts.

Some reform proposals would also reduce the cost of jury trials by expediting them. These include techniques to streamline voir dire, to present deposition evidence more efficiently, to impose time limits on lawyers, and to narrow the issues before trial. Many of these proposals would expedite trials by improving jury comprehension as well.

The critical question in evaluating reforms aimed at reducing administrative costs is the extent to which they can be instituted without also changing case outcomes. At the margin, of course, every cost change will affect the propensity to litigate (indeed, cheaper jury trials will encourage parties to demand more of them) and is likely to affect the parties differently. The fact that a reform might alter the balance of advantage need not be a decisive objection. But such reforms should be justified in those terms, and not on the supposedly neutral ground of cost reduction.

RESTRUCTURING THE JURY

Two features of the jury's current structure—size and composition—appear to impair jury rationality, to contribute to undesirable behavior by other participants in the legal process, and to affect administrative cost. A restructuring strategy seeks to improve the jury's performance by altering its size, its composition, or both, without necessarily changing the questions that are put to it or the ways it operates.

Commentators have pointed out that the move to smaller civil juries has reduced their representativeness while increasing the likelihood of bias and other sources of irrational behavior. Smaller juries are widely thought to produce somewhat greater variability and thus unpredictability in their verdicts. Some evidence shows that reduced size impairs juries' collective memory. These effects of size may impede the settlement process, which has probably increased the number of trials and led to greater resort to *remittitur* and other techniques for controlling and modifying outlier jury verdicts, perhaps dissipating any administrative savings. An obvious response to these changes would be to increase the jury's size, but this should only result from a process of experimentation that better informs us about the relevant effects and trade-offs of jury panels of different sizes.

The jury's composition also affects the rationality of its decisions and the behavior of actors. In addition to the likelihood that greater diversity among jurors increases the variability of decision outcomes, there is the irony noted by Paul Carrington: Recent developments promoting greater diversity and representativeness, including statutory requirements for more broadly based jury venires and growing judicial control of the voir dire, have occurred at precisely the time that other developments—the reduction in jury size, longer trials, new forms of evidence, and more complex litigation—have rendered representativeness both harder to achieve and more of a barrier to juries capable of rational decisions in certain kinds of cases. This latter concern has led to controversial proposals to select juries in complex disputes from among individuals possessing special expertise in the relevant subject, and for judges to screen scientific testimony more rigorously before it goes to a jury.

CONSTRAINING JURY DISCRETION

The next, more radical strategy moves beyond procedural tinkering and structural changes. It seeks instead (or in addition) to impose significant limitations on jury discretion in the hope of improving rationality, providing clearer liability signals, and reducing administrative costs. These limitations may take at least four different forms.

1. *Ask the jury different substantive questions.* One group of reforms that will constrain discretion appeals to the principle of institutional competence. These reforms emphasize that since jurors can answer some questions more readily than others, the law should only ask jurors the kinds of questions for which they possess the requisite expertise, information, and cognitive capacities. As legal disputes become more complex, the legal doctrines that frame their resolution should be altered to take account of jurors' limited competence.

The effectiveness of reforms that would alter doctrine in order to reformulate jury questions depends on how deeply the critiques of jury rationality cut. If juries are in fact as biased or prone to error as their critics assert, their answers to the new questions may not be much better than their answers to the old ones.

Many jury critics, however, would find more categorical, discretion-constraining doctrines attractive even if such doctrines had little effect on jury bias or rates of error. These critics emphasize that a doctrine's substantive content may be less important than the clarity and determinacy of its rules. This possibility is particularly great in contexts in which potential risk bearers, confronted with a bright line rule, can reallocate risks among themselves at low cost. If people know about a rule, can predict how it will apply to their conduct, and can easily bargain about who should bear the risk under what circumstances and at what cost, they can produce a more efficient risk allocation. Juries can also apply such rules at lower cost and with greater accuracy and predictability.

2. *Increase deference to others' decisions.* We have seen that the jury's discretion can sometimes be constrained by formulating new doctrines that present it with more tractable and, one hopes, more useful questions. But reformers can also limit jury discretion by reinvigorating old doctrines that require the jury to defer to decisions already made by others, especially in tort law. In this category are two important sources of external norms that might be used to confine jury decisions in tort cases: contract and regulation. Both are highly controversial when courts invoke them for this purpose.

Contemporary courts increasingly apply tort principles to transactions and relationships that are also governed—some used to be exclusively governed—by contract principles. Some examples of this extension include liability for pure economic loss, manufacturer and distributor liability to purchasers for defective products, landlord liability to tenants, wrongful discharge, insurer liability for failure to pay claims, and medical malpractice liability even in organized care settings where provider contracts are actually negotiated. Even workplace injuries in settings in which workers' compensation is supposed to be the exclusive remedy against employers have increasingly become the province of tort law.

In tort disputes arising in such situations, courts could bind juries with the norms adopted in these contractual transactions and relationships.

Juries cannot be so easily confined, however, in cases in which defendants cannot rely on an express contract but must instead argue that a risk allocation was implicit in the contract or that the plaintiff made a noncontractual, informed, consensual decision to accept the injury-producing risk. Such cases surely compose the vast majority of those in which the assumed-risk defense is invoked. Juries in product liability cases, for example, must often decide whether the warning accompanying a product adequately informed the user about the risk that resulted in the injury. The only feasible way to constrain jury discretion in cases of this kind is to move the dispute out of the tort system, a strategy discussed below.

The second major source of external norms to which reformers might require juries to defer is administrative regulations. The traditional legal doctrine holds that the jury is the best and ultimate judge of whether a particular course of conduct complies with the standard of reasonableness, nondefectiveness, or normative criteria to which parties in civil liability litigation are held. Even regulations directed at controlling the very same risks that are at issue in the tort case do not bind the jury. Thus, although defendants' *failure* to comply with such regulations almost invariably operates to establish liability, those who *comply* with the regulations may also be held liable.

Commentators have sharply criticized this doctrine. They point to the importance of expert judgment on such technical issues, the advantages of regulatory analysis over ad hoc jury decisions in making the socially relevant trade-offs between risk and benefits, the confusion that tort law's rejection of regulatory standards sows in the private sector, and other problems with the traditional rule. They have called for courts to recognize a regulatory compliance defense that would prevent the jury from second-guessing the regulators and imposing liability on those who comply.

3. *Provide guidance on damage awards.* Jury discretion is at its height in the determination of damages, and the resulting variability of awards in cases that in objective terms seem quite similar is large enough to be disturbing. Quite apart from its unfairness, this variability has undesirable effects on the behavioral incentives of primary actors and on settlement decisions.

A number of reformers have proposed to narrow, though not eliminate, this jury discretion by awarding damages according to established schedules. These schedules could be similar to those used in workers' compensation and similar social insurance programs, but they might be made more flexible by taking into account a variety of factors relevant to measuring the plaintiff's loss. In most such schemes, the jury would make findings that would enable the court to classify the injury according to the damage schedule.

Even a quite flexible system of damage schedules, however, might not gain the necessary public support. Even so, it should be possible to improve the determination of damages by measures short of scheduling. For example, the jury might be informed about a range of previous awards without being confined to that range, or it might be informed about a range but be allowed to award outside that range as long as it gives reasons for doing so. Alternatively, its discretion might be informed by data on the distribution in past cases of the ratios of out-of-pocket losses to total damage awards or of the ratios of compensatory to punitive damages.

4. *Special verdicts*. Another way to control jury discretion would be to require the jury to submit verdicts in a specific form. This approach, authorized by Rule 49 of the Federal Rules of Civil Procedure, seems to have numerous advantages. It would simplify the jury's task by posing specific questions for it to answer, focus the jury's attention on the critical factual issues, obviate the need for the judge to instruct the jury on the law, highlight any inconsistent findings by the jury, and facilitate appellate review by rendering more transparent the factual premises underlying the jury's verdict and animating the judge's application of the law.

These are considerable virtues, making it even more important to know why special verdicts are not used very often. Apparently, the reasons have to do with lawyers' tactical opposition to special verdicts and with judges' fears about erring in the formulation of the questions, calling attention to jury inconsistencies, and inviting more intensive appellate review of jury verdicts.

DIVERSION TO NONJURY FORUMS

Historically, the most far-reaching response to the perceived defects of the civil jury has been to divert disputes to nonjury forums. In most but not all diverted cases, the reallocated fact-finding function remains subject to at least limited judicial review.

Generally speaking, diversion may take three forms. One category consists of alternative dispute resolution techniques. ADR is the least radical of the diversion strategies because most ADR techniques are consensual. They are available to disputants who wish to use them in lieu of a jury trial, but jury trial ordinarily remains as the default option.

A second type of diversion reform—what Jeffrey O'Connell calls the "neo-no-fault" approach—involves somewhat more legal regulation of the parties' access to jury trial. O'Connell has imaginatively crafted a variety of neo-no-fault schemes, tailoring them to address the special characteristics of different areas of tort law and tort litigation. These versions have two pertinent features in common. First, they encourage a potential defendant to make to a potential plaintiff a preaccident offer to defray certain categories of cost (usually out-of-pocket expenses) that the offeree may incur in return for the offeree's waiver of a tort claim. (These plans also encourage postaccident, prelitigation offers.) Second, they provide that if such an offer is rejected, the issues that may be raised in the subsequent litigation, and the burdens of proof that will then apply, will be governed by rules that are more disadvantageous to the offeree than those that would otherwise apply.

A third reform model would partly or completely replace jury trials of particular categories of claims with bench or administrative agency trials. The workers' compensation system, which usually includes exclusive remedy provisions designed to supplant all common law claims by workers against their employers, is perhaps the most important example of the administrative agency model. Environmental protection agencies have displaced some private environmental litigation that would have been tried to juries, although the environmental statutes often preserve damage remedies for nuisance, which may be tried to juries.

Diversion reforms, whatever their merits, probably reached their high-water mark some time ago and may have already begun to retreat. The evidence from some contemporary reform debates indicates strongly that the political obstacles to adopting such reforms are simply enormous, if not insuperable.

LOOKING TO THE FUTURE

If the recent past is prologue, the prospects for reform of the civil jury are not bright. The politics of jury reform are daunting. Virtually all of the important groups with stakes in the system of civil litigation favor retaining the jury. Trial lawyers' veneration of the jury is almost religious in its fervor, and their missionary zeal appears to have won many converts among the general public, which expresses great confidence in the jury. When queried about the value of the jury, judges almost invariably praise it.

Given the broad array of public and special interest support for the jury system, one would not expect politicians to show much interest in jury reform. But the political inertia in favor of the status quo can occasionally be overcome. The insurance crisis of price and availability of the mid-1980s is the most important example. In this spasm of reform activity, unusual for both its intensity and its legislative success, almost all states imposed some restrictions on jury awards—typically with respect to pain and suffering, punitive damages, joint and several liability, or the treatment of collateral sources. For all these changes, this episode in fact demonstrates the political marginality of jury reform efforts. Despite the irresistible political tide propelling tort reform in virtually every state in the 1980s, the changes to the jury that were actually adopted were decidedly incremental. They chipped away at the edges of jury discretion but neither invaded its core nor altered the jury's structure or essential functions.

Two other, more recent developments—the continuing effort to amend the Federal Employers' Liability Act of 1908 (FELA), and the extension of jury trials to claims of sex and disability discrimination—are even more revealing about the current political limits of jury reform. Both developments suggest that public attitudes, far from supporting reforms that would restrict juries, strongly favor preserving and expanding the scope of their authority.

Almost a century ago, FELA established a negligence-based, jury trial liability regime for work-related injuries to railroad workers. Despite years of vigorous campaigning by the railroad industry to convert FELA into a workers' compensation system with awards determined by an administrative agency rather than by juries, this antijury reform has made very little progress.

In 1991, Congress amended Title VII of the Civil Rights Act, partly in order to overrule a series of Supreme Court decisions unfavorable to plaintiffs in employment discrimination cases. The right to jury trial had previously been limited to claims of racial and religious discrimination, but the most controversial of these fiercely contested amendments extended the jury trial to cover claims of sex discrimination.

Additional evidence of the jury's political invulnerability can be seen in the conspicuous failure of no-fault reforms to win enactment. (See essay on auto no-fault later in this part). Federal no-fault legislation is a dead letter, state no-fault plans have made little headway since the 1970s, and all of the plans that have been adopted preserve the option to sue in court, including jury trial. Indeed, the court system is groaning under the unprecedented burden of asbestos-related tort claims, yet only recently has Congress seriously considered legislation to replace jury trials with an administrative compensation scheme. The status quo regarding the civil jury manifestly enjoys powerful political support. Diversion-type reform, in contrast, is a cause without a constituency.

In itself, this may not be particularly troubling. The evidence so far makes both the alleged vices of the jury and the supposed virtues of its alternatives seem exaggerated. No one would suggest, of course, that the jury is an ideal institution; its critics raise many important concerns. If true, the claim that jury unpredictability inhibits settlements even in relatively routine cases should be especially worrisome. But the jury's critics have not yet unequivocally substantiated their claims; still less have they made a compelling case for abolishing the jury.

The case for experimenting with some of the more incremental reforms, however, stands on a much stronger footing. Many of the reform options discussed earlier under the rubric of reducing administrative costs deserve to be tried. States should also consider experimenting with a return to larger juries in the hopes of enhancing their rationality and representativeness. Any additional costs of larger juries might be defrayed by increasing the fees for jury trials to more realistic levels, a reform that can stand on its own merits apart from the issue of jury size.

The strategy of constraining jury discretion is more controversial. Even the most attractive of the reform options entail some genuinely difficult conflicts among values. Of the options for reform, some rationalization of the way in which damages for nonpecuniary losses are assessed probably offers the greatest promise of meeting the legitimate concerns of the jury critics. Such damages are the subject over which the jury's discretion is most unconstrained, the variability of its decisions is most objectionable, and the effects on settlements are most troubling. In this area, moreover, experience with social and private insurance systems, which use such schedules, can provide good information about likely consequences.

Finally, such reforms do not require that the jury be abolished, but demand only that jury decisions on damages be guided, informed, and possibly constrained in the interests of more equal treatment of similar cases and greater predictability of outcomes. On the primacy of these values, at least, the debate on jury reform should be able to reach a firm consensus.

∾ 18 ∾

Impact Litigation: Courts and Institutional Reform

Impact litigation—lawsuits that seek to use the courts to effect widespread social changes—enjoys a very good press. Impact litigation is a weapon brandished primarily by groups on the political left, as in the cases against Big Tobacco and the gun manufacturers. But even conservatives applaud it when their groups are doing the suing, as in challenges to affirmative action programs or environmental regulations.

We need to understand why impact litigation has come to play so central a role in our public life, and also why Americans of all ideological stripes should be wary of it. Reformers, I believe, expect too much from impact litigation, and even its critics often aim at the wrong target. Like war, impact litigation is a continuation of politics by other means, and like war it sometimes accomplishes good things. In the end, however, two practical and closely related concerns provide the strongest grounds for skepticism. First, judges' tools and capacities are not equal to the task, and second, their well-intentioned rulings tend to aggravate the problems they seek to solve and often create new ones.

Two icons of impact litigation are *Brown v. Board of Education*, the 1954 school desegregation decision, and *Roe v. Wade*, the controversial abortion rights decision. Both were carefully designed by advocacy groups to bring an important constitutional issue before the courts that the groups felt the politicians were ignoring or mishandling. Sometimes impact cases are brought as class actions (as in *Brown*), sometimes as individual claims with broad social ramifications (as in *Roe*). Most impact cases seek a judicial order mandating that the defendant do, or refrain from doing, certain things (an "injunction") and rely on the U.S. Constitution. Many, however, seek money damages and invoke state law—for example, the successful challenge to New York's property tax–based school finance system.

WHAT IS IMPACT LITIGATION'S APPEAL?

The mother of all impact litigation, of course, was *Brown*. The NAACP lawyers, led by Thurgood Marshall, launched a long, carefully orchestrated campaign to gain a court order invalidating segregation in the public schools. The ruling's logic encompassed all forms of state-supported discrimination against racial minorities, not just schools. Subsequent decisions enforced this ruling in many ways—by limiting freedom-of-choice plans, by requiring busing, by equalizing expenditures, and so forth—and the political branches and the states fell into line. Many post-*Brown* impact cases—for example, those asserting the rights of women, gays, illegitimates, prisoners, the disabled, the mentally ill and retarded, and undocumented immigrant children—have been squarely based on it. Today, almost fifty years later, only a few hard-line conservatives are willing to say that *Brown* was wrongly decided. The decision is widely hailed as the Warren Court's greatest, most unexceptionable legacy to American social justice, and many aspiring causes have sought to wrap themselves in *Brown*'s mantle.

The appeal of impact litigation, however, goes well beyond *Brown*'s reflected glory. The often stirring social drama it presents lies not simply in the clash of lofty ideals, competing interests, warring parties, and jousting lawyers. Impact cases also enact cherished American myths that ordinary politics often seems to mock: the little guy against the big system, the right to a day in court, principle's triumph over expediency, the taming of corporate power, the shaking up of rogue or heartless bureaucracies, and the possibility of fundamental and structural social change.

Courts, law firms, the American Bar Association, law schools, and the rest of the legal establishment tend to boost impact litigation. It not only generates more high-profile activity and fees for lawyers but also projects an idealized and idealistic image of the profession. Most people view representing the rights of minorities, the downtrodden, and the voiceless (if they are not criminal defendants) as more admirable than the more mundane, common activities of trolling for paying clients and litigating commercial disputes. Lawyers see impact litigation in much the same way athletes see the Olympics—a vivid showcase for their talents and proof of both their social importance and their selfless endeavors.

The mass media increasingly look to litigation for entertainment programming. Impact litigation meets that need while also being genuinely newsworthy. Skilled journalists can turn impact litigation into gripping theater, as exemplified by the many documentaries about *Brown* and civil rights, and by feature films like *Gideon's Trumpet* (on the right to counsel), *Dead Man Walking* (on death penalty litigation), *A Civil Action* (on environmental litigation), and *The Insider* (on tobacco litigation), along with a steady stream of newspaper and magazine articles. Leading foundations on both left and right fund impact cases, hoping to nourish social reform movements that are not yet politically ripe.

None of this could explain impact litigation's appeal unless it seemed effective, which it often does. I discuss many examples below. Indeed, impact litigation can achieve some goals even when the legal merits are weak. Consider the flurry of governmental lawsuits against gun manufacturers. To most legal experts, these cases are nonstarters; most judges will not even submit them to a jury because, among other things, the governmental plaintiffs, unlike shooting victims, have not suffered the kind of direct harm that courts require. These cases, however, are better understood less as solid legal claims than as political ploys—intended to spotlight issues and to embarrass and pressure the industry into adopting safer designs and marketing practices that the government either cannot or will not mandate itself.

In the gun litigation, this tactic has already borne some fruit. Smith & Wesson has agreed to a number of changes as the price of a settlement. This is a common goal and outcome of impact cases—probably 98 percent of all civil cases settle before trial—and one likely result will be more safety locks. What might have led the company to surrender rather than litigate its strong legal position? Embarrassing documents might surface and the adverse publicity ginned up by public agencies and their allies could tarnish its image. It also wanted to minimize the high costs of a protracted litigation against a coalition of deep-pocket governments. The company doubtless thought that, as the first defector from the industry defense, the plaintiffs would reward it with a relatively painless settlement, just as they did with the Brooke Group in the tobacco litigation. Moreover, Smith & Wesson probably hoped to use the plaintiffs as a cat's paw, as Brooke successfully did, to enrich itself and damage its industry rivals as they continued to litigate. (Interestingly, Smith & Wesson, having reaped few of the expected benefits, is now rethinking the deal that it made.)

Legal rules can hobble a case even when the facts seem compelling, but lawsuits need not prevail in order to be politically effective. Consider the tobacco litigation. Although smoking can cause cancer and the industry may have misled regulators and smokers, those facts alone would not suffice to win the case. A government would also have to prove that, like smokers, it was a direct victim of this deception and suffered direct financial harm as a result—a particularly daunting task given that governments may actually have gained a net financial benefit from smoking due to their vast tax revenues from the sale of tobacco products and their reduced pension liabilities from premature smoking-related deaths. Individual smoker-plaintiffs do not face these problems, but face others. For decades, they lost all their cases, as juries penalized them for their choices to smoke, especially after health warnings were mandated in the 1960s. A few individual smokers have still managed to prevail, but this free-choice defense will probably grow stronger as time passes, unless juries accept smokers' claims that the industry addicted them in the prewarning era. Most courts, moreover, have rejected class actions in tobacco cases.*

Even so, tobacco litigation documents succeeded in demonizing the industry, affecting its stock prices and future prospects, and transforming the political landscape. The gun litigation, targeting a much weaker industry, may ultimately do the same. Much of the public, not to mention public-health agencies, favors these outcomes, and it seems beside the point, even churlish, to note how weak the plaintiffs' legal positions are. Impact litigation of this kind seems to vindicate the ironist's axiom that nothing succeeds like failure.

SO WHAT'S THE PROBLEM?

If even legally weak impact litigation helps to make powerful social actors more accountable, reinforces the rule and prestige of law, and produces both educational and entertainment value, what is the problem? Where one stands on this question depends to some extent on where one sits politically. The left tends to favor suits against cigarettes, guns, prison systems, and welfare agencies while the right rallies behind legal challenges to environmental regulation, mandatory school busing, and restrictions on school prayer and abortion. Sometimes even those who claim to oppose impact litigation on principle buy into it, as when conservatives support a balanced-budget amendment to the constitution that would move the most technical, highly politicized fiscal issues into the courts.

Why should a militant moderate worry about using the courts, as impact litigation aims to do, to make large-scale public policy? Begin with a low-visibility problem: the potential for lawyer-client conflicts of interest. Although an ethical lawyer must always subordinate her own interests, including using the case to advance her social or political agenda, to the client's narrow goal of securing a favorable outcome, the special incentives and dynamics of "cause lawyering" encourage such conflicts—over

---

*New cases, some involving "light" cigarettes, have recently been brought under RICO and state consumer fraud statutes. Plaintiffs have won a few preliminary legal rulings and massive verdicts, but the cases are on appeal.

litigation strategy, settlement offers, fees, and other factors. This risk may be smaller in class actions because of the court's legal duty to supervise the conduct and fees of the lawyers representing the class. Even there, however, the risk remains because of judges' limited ability to monitor aggressive lawyers.

This concern helps to explain why the Supreme Court overturned several asbestos class-action settlements that trial judges had approved. Impact litigation on behalf of the mentally retarded engendered conflicts between the lawyers, who sought to close the hospitals and move patients to community facilities, and the desire of many families to keep their relatives institutionalized (albeit under better conditions). A different kind of conflict occurred in the tobacco litigation, where the states that collected billions of settlement dollars must compete with smokers and their lawyers whose recoveries, which might include huge punitive damage awards, could bankrupt the manufacturers before the states can collect.

Two more fundamental critiques often heard in law school classrooms, courtrooms, and legislative chambers go to the legitimacy and institutional competence of judges to decide institutional reform cases. The legitimacy critique notes that the United States is organized constitutionally around separation of powers and majority rule. In such a polity, lawmaking power must be lodged in representative and democratically accountable institutions. Thus the courts, being neither, may not legitimately exercise such lawmaking power and will erode their stock of legitimacy if they seek to do so. By contrast, the institutional competence critique argues that quite apart from any illegitimacy, the courts are poorly equipped to make law because of their training, access to information, the constraints of the adversary process, the limited efficacy of judicial remedies, and other inherent institutional attributes.

JUDICIAL LEGITIMACY

Although the legitimacy critique lends itself to rhetorical flourish, it is far from clear what judicial legitimacy means. I define it as a sense that one is morally obliged to obey a judicial decision because it is law even if one strongly opposes it. A decision that fails to elicit this kind of moral response—or worse, elicits moral revulsion or rebellion—is illegitimate. One may treat a decision as legitimate out of ignorance, indifference, or habitual deference to authority, not just out of a considered moral duty. By the same token, viewing a decision as illegitimate does not necessarily spur one to any particular kind of action.

Consider *Roe v. Wade*, a notorious impact case that many thoughtful Americans denounce as illegitimate and a small number even confront with violence. Even so, the vast majority, including many who oppose it as wrongly decided or bad public policy, still treat it as law and obey it accordingly. Is *Roe* an illegitimate decision? The answer seems to depend on how many people view it not merely as bad law but as usurpation (a distinction not made in public opinion surveys) and how willing they are to act on that conviction.

The legitimacy critique also oversimplifies the nature of our law and politics. As every law student knows, the distinction between interpreting law and making it is a fuzzy one, especially when (as in much impact litigation) the judge must interpret open-ended phrases like "equal protection" and "due process of law." American politics is a remarkably fluid mixture of principle, discretion, pragmatism, competition, and raw power. Legislators who wish to curb "runaway judges" have many levers that, for sound political or other reasons, they often decline to use. By the same token, judges who decide "political" questions (as they often cannot avoid doing in our system) must expect harsh criticism or even reprisals (within constitutional bounds) intended to hold them politically accountable.

The legitimacy critique is also replete with interesting but unintended ironies. First, public esteem for the courts has been remarkably stable (and relative to other government institutions, remarkably high) over a long period during which impact litigation came of age and judicial activism (another ill-defined but rhetorically robust notion) both waxed and waned. Changes in the kinds of cases that the courts hear and how they decide them seem to have little effect on perceived legitimacy.

A second irony is even more striking. The Supreme Court's most controversial decisions, *Brown* included, rested on constitutional arguments that many commentators rejected at the time. In each case, friendly critics strongly warned the Court not to enter what Justice Felix Frankfurter (in one of these cases) called a "political thicket." He was referring to social reform issues disguised as lawsuits, and he thought that courts could not adjudicate such policy disputes and still preserve their legitimacy. Yet these very reform projects—school desegregation, control of police misconduct, legislative reapportionment, limitations of presidential prerogatives, abolition of school prayer, and regulation of abortion, to name just a few—have in fact burnished the Court's public prestige. For different reasons, these cases have helped the Court to prevail at the "bar of politics" (in the phrase of the great constitutional scholar Alexander Bickel), and its political success has buoyed the prestige of lower courts as well.

A final irony: The Court's secure stock of legitimacy from these earlier battles has encouraged attacks on it. Now that we possess the advantages of living in a society in which Jim Crow is dead, legislatures must reapportion themselves, police must warn suspects of their rights, religious groups cannot directly receive government subsidies, and abortions are widely available to women who do not wish to bear children, it is seductively easy to complain that the Court should have left these issues to the politicians, that it went too far, or that (as political scientist Gerald Rosenberg has argued) these important social gains would have occurred anyway had the courts not entered the fray. With these gains firmly entrenched—thanks in part to the Court—we can criticize it now for what it did then without any risk of losing the gains if we err in our counterfactual judgments. Because we can never know if we erred, we can never be refuted.

INSTITUTIONAL COMPETENCE

If the legitimacy critique is overblown, the institutional competence critique is insufficiently appreciated. Impact litigation maximizes the gap between a court's functional disabilities and the demands placed on its capacities. Although these disabilities are numerous, many of the most important can be reduced to three—information, incentives, and rights—which have bedeviled impact cases that were initially considered to be stunning victories for reform.

In our adversary system, a judge must base her decision almost exclusively on admissible evidence proffered by the lawyers and measured against the law. Her task is to resolve specific disputes, not solve social problems. The information she needs is usually quite limited in scope, historical in nature, of a familiar kind, and accessible through conventional evidence. Yet, most institutional reform cases seek to change social structures, practices, and values that are created by a vast number of individuals interacting in intricate, opaque ways with incomplete information. Reforming an urban police department or school system is an exceedingly complex kind of problem in which a change in one relationship or factor will trigger hard-to-predict ripple effects elsewhere in the system, effects that judges cannot anticipate and usually lack authority to control. This is especially true where powerful contrary incentives motivate and constrain the institutions and individuals that the court seeks to reform. Impact litigation to mandate low-income housing, for example, has foundered on market interests (not to mention bureaucratic and political ones) that neutralize and distort the courts' rulings and sometimes make the shortages even worse.

A conscientious judge, working alone with only a generalist's training, must analyze problems like these in all of their technical detail, diagnose them, and fashion solutions that will be effective—not only here and now but over time, and in contexts quite different from the often atypical ones that the lawyers select for their test cases. The judge receives her information from partisan advocates and their hired experts. Within broad ethical limits, each side works to provide incomplete and one-sided (if not misleading) information, depicting both problems and solutions as far simpler than they really are. Unlike a legislature, a judge has very few tools for shaping the behavior of the numerous actors who must be induced to comply with her solution.

Indeed, a judge wields only two tools, both of them coercive: She can issue an injunction and then punish violators, and she can order wrong-doers to pay money. These tools, although ostensibly strong, are in reality pathetically weak; they affect only a narrow band on the broad spectrum of human motivation—and only the litigants at that. In contrast, legisla-tures and agencies can coerce everyone in society. More important, they can gain compliance through a variety of more flexible and positive inducements such as subsidies, bargaining, coalition building, informa-tion, public education, insurance, bureaucracies, and many more. The *Brown* decision alone produced little school desegregation until more than a decade later when Congress passed a statute providing federal agencies with a variety of fiscal and administrative sanctions to imple-ment it. (Whether the desegregation that was ultimately achieved actually improved black children's education is a complex question that is hotly debated everywhere, including in black communities.)

Impact litigation seeks a judicial declaration of new legal rights. But although rights are among the most precious of human endowments, they are crude instruments for accomplishing most of what a complex society attempts to do collectively. A right is binary; one either has it or one doesn't. In contrast, sound social policy is a matter of finding the right point along a continuum; it is a matter of degree, of more or less, and of striking a nuanced balance. Once rights are recognized, they are difficult to change, whereas effective policy demands constant flexible adjustment in light of changing conditions. Rights are costly to define, defend, and challenge, yet policy needs to minimize the social costs of getting things done. Rights magnify the role of judges and lawyers but successful policy largely depends on nonlegal institutions and competencies.

Under these conditions, one would expect judicial solutions to the kinds of problems that impact litigation takes on to be misconceived, impractical, or even perverse—and they often are. Consider *Brown*, the paradigm of successful impact litigation. Although desegregation has helped to achieve a more balanced racial mix in some school districts, in many communities, public schools—especially those in the largest cities outside the South—remain at least as racially segregated as they were before *Brown*, though no longer by force of law.

No wonder, then, that some leading civil rights figures like Derrick Bell and former congressman (now minister) Floyd Flake have conclud-ed, sadly, that the great courtroom victory in *Brown* ill-served most black schoolchildren. Despite the Supreme Court's best efforts, it could neither understand nor control the complex social dynamics driving Americans' residential decisions and schooling choices. In a vicious cycle of frustra-tion all too often unleashed by impact cases, a determined federal judge relied on *Brown* to order the Missouri legislature to enact a tax to support his decrees to reform the Kansas City school system. Two decades and $2 billion of judicially mandated and supervised reforms later, the city's schools are an utter shambles—without accreditation, only 25 percent white, and draining scarce state funds from other needy districts. When the Supreme Court eventually reversed the unfortunate decision, it was too late; the damage had already been done.

Countless other examples could be cited, each with its unique and complex story and its surprising, often unhappy ending. Deinstitutionalization of the mentally ill, hailed by reformers as a triumph of enlightened judicial policy, has contributed to much homelessness, substance abuse, and menacing disorder in the public spaces in which ordinary citizens, including the poor, must often live. Decades after the landmark *Mount Laurel* and *Yonkers* decisions mandated affordable housing for the poor, the affected communities have built little of it. Common Cause's litigation effort to bolster campaign finance reform produced a Supreme Court decision, *Buckley v. Valeo,* that the group has been fighting ever since because it granted First Amendment protection to the very campaign expenditures that Common Cause had hoped to restrict. Litigation to guarantee black representatives in Congress by drawing district lines helped to reduce the number of black members and fortified conservative control of surrounding districts. By most accounts, court victories by civil rights groups demanding single-member (rather than at-large) districts in state and local assemblies have in fact reduced black voter influence in those assemblies. Successful litigation on behalf of undocumented aliens helped fuel a political and bureaucratic backlash that in 1996 produced a much harsher, unfair enforcement system.

Many experts now view the Warren Court's *Gault* decision, once celebrated as a victory by juvenile justice reformers, as misguided and itself in need of fundamental reform. Shortly after the litigation campaign against the death penalty succeeded, the states enacted new laws further entrenching it. Litigators are now reduced to trying to delay executions in the hope that exculpatory DNA evidence will turn up or governors will issue pardons, both rare events. Conservative groups cheered when courts invalidated some forms of affirmative action in public universities, failing to anticipate that this would simply spawn new forms of preference, such as automatically admitting the top tier from all secondary schools in the state, that many conservatives may find even more objectionable because the new preferences will force the admission of more ill-prepared students.

OCCASIONALLY GOOD NEWS

The story of impact litigation, of course, is by no means a uniformly bleak one. The civil rights revolution, a precondition for social justice, would not have occurred when it did without some judicial prodding and protection.

School busing has worked better in smaller communities than in large metropolitan areas. The courts forced some prison and community mental health systems to be far more humane and eliminated their worst abuses. By most accounts (though not all), court-driven reapportionment has been a valuable and enduring reform. A structural challenge to the New York City foster care system produced worthwhile changes, and other cases have prompted desirable reforms in some other public services.

Even when impact litigation fails to gain its explicit ends through the courts, moreover, it can ease gridlock and invigorate social processes that produce desirable changes. Litigation against the tobacco industry, although so far unsuccessful in legal terms, unearthed documents that have galvanized antismoking efforts. Similarly, gun litigation has improved the prospects for sensible regulatory controls and new technological fixes. Death penalty litigation has focused public attention on previously obscure patterns of enforcement that profoundly trouble even capital punishment advocates. As a result, the public debate is taking a new turn. Litigation has forced Swiss banks to restore funds to Holocaust survivors and their descendants. Judicial judgments against individuals who have committed atrocities have not yet produced compensation for the victims but have succeeded in making life much more difficult for the perpetrators, hopefully deterring future violations.

HISTORY LESSONS

The history of impact litigation suggests some recurrent features. First, these and other examples suggest that impact litigation is likely to be most effective in seizing media and public attention at least momentarily, moving certain issues higher on the policy agenda, turning up evidence of abuses that policymakers have not pursued, and casting a lurid but revealing spotlight on corners of social life that the rest of us might otherwise ignore. Whether such litigation can frame workable, flexible, and politically sustainable remedies to complex problems, however, is far more doubtful.

Second, it is difficult to trace the actual effect of a case beyond the court decision (or settlement) itself. After all, the same forces that propel a case onto a court's docket also operate in other social domains where those forces might have produced the change anyway. (One can always say this, of course, but that does not mean it is necessarily wrong.) For impact litigation enthusiasts, it is enough that the case seemed to achieve its goal or even that one cannot prove the contrary, while skeptics can point to other possible causes and to unanticipated effects. In the case of *Brown*, for example, Rosenberg argues that evolving public attitudes, civil rights protests, economic growth, and other causal factors were already in motion, and that *Brown* in itself contributed little to the changes that ensued a decade later.

Indeed, impact litigation may undermine its successes by strengthening the hands of its opponents—another recurrent feature. Although *Roe v. Wade*'s survival seems secure for the time being, the decision clearly galvanized a conservative movement that ever since has stymied liberal reforms in many policy areas far beyond abortion. Even Justice Ruth Bader Ginsburg, perhaps the leading women's rights litigator at the time, now believes that *Roe* derailed the movement to liberalize abortion. By generating an immediate and powerful political backlash, *Roe* prompted more restrictive state laws, reversing a strong pre-*Roe* trend toward more liberal access to abortion. Congress responded to the judicial supervision of prison systems with a law limiting the continuing court supervision of those systems.

Although we cannot clearly delineate all the impacts of a complex litigation, numerous case studies establish that a decision's consequences will almost always differ both from what the plaintiffs originally sought and from what the court envisioned. *Brown*'s social and educational effects are warning enough that impact litigation often produces unexpected and perverse results. This is especially likely in the institutional reform line of impact cases where a court's order is directed at, and must be implemented by, large bureaucracies such as school systems and police departments whose incentives and behaviors are opaque and whose operating routines are shaped by realities on the ground that are hard to grasp, much less change. An endemic feature of such cases is that a legal success here simply creates or aggravates problems over there, just as pushing against a pillow at one point simply causes it to puff out elsewhere.

A common and well-documented example is prison litigation. When courts order states to spend more to improve prison conditions—often with the connivance of the defendant prison officials who can use the lawsuit as leverage to pry more funds, staff, and authority from the state legislature—states usually allocate less to public schools, hospitals, or police, or must raise taxes that are already regressive.

More generally, impact litigation's fragmented first-come-first-served approach to resource allocation and policy effectively empowers unelected advocates and judges to set the public priorities that the citizenry elected officials to determine, and then to deflect criticism by saying that a disembodied law required this. In our political system, accountability is already elusive precisely because responsibility is so hard to locate. Impact litigation makes it that much easier for everyone—legislators, bureaucrats, judges, lawyers, and litigants—to disclaim it. The buck stops nowhere; impact litigation keeps it moving.

Finally, experience with impact litigation confirms the limited effectiveness of top-down legal rules in regulating complex social behavior. Much top-down law, of course, is unavoidable—criminal and tax law, for example. But reformers could often achieve their goals more effectively by relying more on other techniques such as decentralized rules (as in allocating scarce organs), rights trading (as in environmental protection), auctions (as in allocating valuable broadcast spectrum), moving public funds from providers to citizens (as with vouchers), self-regulation (as with some Internet policies), and improved information (as with hospital malpractice).

These alternative forms, however, can only succeed if reformers repose less confidence in the problem-solving capacity of judges and more in that of politicians, bureaucrats, and private actors—a confidence that many reformers think has not yet been earned. So long as impact litigation remains a valuable political resource—one that moves issues onto and up the public agenda, intimidates and even co-opts opponents, unearths documents that gain media attention, and does all of this in the still-prestigious name of law—it will be part of the reformer's arsenal. For better *and* for worse, impact litigation has become an entrenched part of our rights-oriented, individualistic, legal-political culture.

～ 19 ～

Gun Control: Keeping Tort Law in Its Place

The legal culture has recently propagated a new genus: the mass tort subrogation action in which an entity that has incurred costs on behalf of a tort victim seeks to recover those costs from the wrongdoer. Government agencies are the plaintiffs in the most notorious of these cases, but some have also been brought by health and welfare pension funds, insurers, tort victim compensation trusts, and other entities. Although the law of mass tort subrogation is still in flux, we already know enough to predict that this latest creature spells trouble for the legal system and not just for the defendants. It is costly to entertain even when it is unavailing.

It all began in the mid-1990s, when a number of entrepreneurial private and government lawyers convinced state politicians to sue the tobacco industry. The plaintiffs advanced a number of legal theories, but almost all of them relied directly or indirectly on the fact that the state governments, through their Medicaid and other programs, had taken an enormous fiscal hit in providing health and disability benefits to smokers, and that these costs were caused by the industry's fraud and other intentional and unintentional wrongdoing. Eventually, all of the states joined this litigation and, after an earlier settlement fell apart, they finally came to terms with the industry in 1997 for a total of $246 billion to be paid out over twenty-five years.

These cases were only the beginning. Slow off the mark for tactical reasons, the Clinton administration sued the industry under a similar theory under subrogation. Because the settlement in the state cases did not bar individual and class actions by nonstate plaintiffs, a number of these were brought. Some have won stunning jury verdicts. Brown & Williamson paid $750,000 to a smoker after trial, the first time this had ever happened. A Florida jury dropped a nuclear bomb in the *Engle* class action, awarding $160 billion in punitive damages; this is on appeal to the state supreme court. An Oregon jury levied almost $30 million, virtually all punitive damages. A new generation of litigation—against "light" cigarettes, usually under consumer fraud statutes that downplay the smokers' role—threatens to impose even more massive liabilities.

In the wake of Big Tobacco's settlement with the states, a number of union pension funds and insurers sued the industry, invoking subrogation theories. In addition, Owens Corning and the trust created in 1988 by the court administering the Johns-Manville bankruptcy sued the industry under a similar theory, seeking to recover amounts they had previously paid to asbestos victims who had been smokers. States and cities have brought other subrogation claims against manufacturers of lead-based paint for health care and cleanup costs.

Although the courts have allowed some of these subrogation claims to proceed (e.g., Rhode Island's lead paint case), they have dismissed most of them usually on the ground that the government's financial harm is too remote from the tortious conduct. The big exception is U.S. district court judge Jack Weinstein in the Eastern District of New York, who refused to dismiss the claims in either the Manville Trust case (now dropped by the plaintiffs) or the union pension fund cases. (Although these claims have been rejected by all circuits, including Weinstein's own Second Circuit, he allowed a jury to award Empire Blue Cross $17.8 million against tobacco companies.) Because these claims usually allege not only common-law tort damages but RICO violations subject to treble damages, a lot rides on their outcomes.

This brings us to the most tenuous mass tort subrogation claims of all, those against the gun manufacturers. Emboldened by the success of the state tobacco cases, at least thirty-two cities and New York State have sued dozens of gun manufacturers. They hope to recover crime-related expenditures supposedly linked to unlawful gun use, and in some cases to recover health and disability outlays as well, while avoiding the shoals that have wrecked most subrogation cases. The manufacturers, government plaintiffs say, use distribution systems that make it easy for criminals to buy guns. Some cities also claim that this constitutes a public nuisance. Some of these theories are plausible, others are fanciful.

The gun litigation was showcased by *Hamilton v. Beretta*, which was brought (not coincidentally) in Judge Weinstein's court in Brooklyn early in 1995. Although not itself a subrogation case, the plaintiffs, who are relatives of people killed by handguns, are conventional wrongful death claimants. *Hamilton* has developed most of the substantive theories that the government plaintiffs in the subrogation cases have invoked. For this reason, it merits attention. In *Hamilton*, the plaintiffs sued numerous manufacturers under a variety of theories, alleging that the guns used in the killings were negligently and fraudulently marketed and defectively designed, and that manufacturing them was an "ultrahazardous" activity for which the producers were strictly liable.

Judge Weinstein dismissed the product liability and fraud claims, and seven plaintiffs including Stephen Fox, a surviving but permanently disabled handgun victim, proceeded to trial against twenty-five manufacturers on the negligent marketing theory. This theory asserted that the firms had distributed their products so carelessly as to create and bolster an illegal, underground market enabling minors and criminals to obtain the guns that killed (or in Fox's case, injured) the plaintiffs. The identities of the miscreant manufacturers were unknown because only one of the guns was recovered. Nevertheless, Judge Weinstein allowed plaintiffs to use a "market share" theory, adopted during the 1980s litigation over DES, the carcinogenic antimiscarriage drug. Under this theory, all of the manufacturers of a fungible product could be held liable for these negligent practices under certain limited circumstances. After a four-week trial in 1999, the jury found fifteen manufacturers liable for negligent distribution and awarded Fox almost $4 million, to be apportioned on a market share basis among three of them.

The manufacturers appealed to the U.S. Court of Appeals for the Second Circuit, which then certified two questions to the New York Court of Appeals, the state's highest court: whether the manufacturers owed plaintiffs a duty to avoid negligent marketing and distribution of the guns, and, if so, whether and how the market share allocation theory applied in this case. The state court of appeals unanimously answered these questions in the negative; it rejected Fox's claims and sent the case back to the Second Circuit, presumably ending it. But the court left open a possible claim in future cases against manufacturers who have reason to know that particular distributors consistently supply guns to the illegal market and perhaps against those that willfully avert their eyes.

With that sensible caveat, dismissal of *Hamilton* was the correct decision; the California Supreme Court later dismissed a similar claim. Judge Weinstein wasted more than six years of the parties' and courts' time and money by nurturing this case and thus encouraging lawyers to file others like it. This waste will increase as cities and states struggle to distinguish

Hamilton in a desperate and probably vain attempt to justify their (tax-payers') litigation investments.

These claims are likely losers for many reasons: doctrine, fairness, institutional competence, public policy, and politics. As every first-year torts student knows, plaintiffs must establish that the defendant owes a legal duty to the plaintiff. Is a gun manufacturer under a legal duty to protect all victims of criminals who intentionally misuse its product? Begin with the fact that the gun is not defective in any conventional sense (would that it were!), so traditional strict product liability does not apply. In addition, the courts have rejected any duty to protect strangers unless the defendant has a "special relationship" with either the injurer or the victim, a relationship that also places the defendant in a good position to prevent the harm.

The leading "special relationship" case, *Tarasoff v. Regents of University of California*, has been widely criticized and limited on the ground that it extends legal duty too far. There, the California Supreme Court imposed a duty on a psychiatrist to take reasonable steps to protect a named individual whom his patient had threatened to kill. In the gun cases, by contrast, the potential victims are both numerous and nameless insofar as the manufacturer is concerned. Judge Weinstein tried to circumvent this problem, however, by ruling that manufacturers could control the sales practices of downstream sellers and thus had a duty to entrust the guns only to distributors and retailers who would sell them to responsible buyers. But entrustment liability is premised on a level of knowledge about the risks posed by specific users that gun manufacturers lack and could only acquire at great cost.

Even if gun plaintiffs can overcome these hurdles, they would have to prove that the negligent entrustment actually and proximately caused plaintiffs' harms, obstacles magnified in the subrogation cases where the cities' claims are even more indirect. How could they do so? There are many links in the causal chain between a manufacturer's sale of a gun to a wholesale distributor and the gun's use by the criminal, and the manufacturer controls few if any of them. An estimated half-million guns are stolen each year, and many of these are presumably used by criminals. Other guns are purchased after they have passed through many hands, sometimes including those of legitimate gun owners.

Fairness considerations also militate against liability for a manufacturer that lacks specific knowledge about downstream transfers. Guns, after all, are a legal product with social value when used properly. In addition to having many legitimate uses, including sporting and private collecting, guns may deter many criminals who fear that their victims are armed. One can easily sympathize with victims whose assailants are judgment-proof, but why should a manufacturer of a socially desired product have to pay for a crime that it could not foresee or control, committed by a criminal it could not identify especially when it may not even have manufactured the gun in question? Fairness dictates that if anyone should pay—an open question—it should perhaps be the local government that failed to prevent the crime or the federal government that extensively regulates and licenses gun dealers for this very purpose. (Where the plaintiff is a city, its own potential liability creates a special irony.)

Which institution—the court or the legislature—is best equipped to resolve the problem of gun-related injuries? The doctrinal problems only hint at the difficulties courts face in dealing with these cases. Causal proof on how guns come into the possession of criminals and on the costs and benefits of various control alternatives depends on the careful analysis of social science data that do not yet exist and that obviously will be difficult to obtain. When the gun cannot be recovered, as is often the case, courts cannot determine which of the many manufacturers made it; nor can they use the market share liability theory that has enabled them to finesse this question in the DES cases, where the products in question were fungible. The gun plaintiffs contend that legislatures play politics with the gun issue and cannot be relied upon to enact adequate controls, so the courts must intervene if the problem is to be solved.

But this, of course, begs the very questions at issue: whether judges should be the engineers of gun control policy, and whether tort liability is an effective policy instrument in this area. The answers to both questions are plainly no. Gun control is not a stealth issue but a highly visible one in which interests from all sides have engaged. Politicians at all levels of government are obliged to address it. Voters are manifestly capable of holding them accountable in ways that, for sound constitutional reasons, do not apply to life-tenured judges like Weinstein.

We live in a polity that values individual freedom, has a long and respected tradition of private gun ownership, and delegates much of the policymaking responsibility in this area to the fifty states. More than 250 million guns are already in circulation and easily accessible by criminals. No consensus yet exists on how to reconcile the competing values of individual freedom, public safety, and regulatory costs, nor is there agreement on how legal and moral responsibility should be divided among gun manufacturers, distributors, retailers, buyers, criminals, and government agencies. Many of the empirical issues on which a sound policy depends remain murky—for example, the effectiveness of different control strategies, the possible deterrent value of guns, the possibilities of proposed technological fixes, and the cost-absorbing capacities of a fragmented and declining industry that bears little resemblance to Big Tobacco.

Under these conditions, it is not at all obvious what the best solutions are or indeed that there is any solution other than better crime control and perhaps social insurance of crime victims' injuries. What seems clear is that tort law devised by generalist judges, deployed by government plaintiffs, and applied by lay juries with neither technical expertise nor public accountability is one of the last places we can expect to solve this vitally important puzzle. Judge Weinstein, however, evidently disagrees. In April 2004, he allowed New York City to proceed with its suit against gun manufacturers, now on a public nuisance theory. Stay tuned.

〜 20 〜

Tort Reform: A Mixed Bag*

The Contract with America is about to be breached. Major civil litigation proposals just passed the House and now go to the Senate. If enacted, they will transform tort law, including the laws governing product liability and other personal injury claims. For those damaged by corporate wrongdoing, this new legal order will not be a pretty sight.

While the pending legislation contains some promising ideas, most of it flagrantly violates the contract's three central assumptions: that the dead hand of federal uniformity is stifling innovation and local choice; that middle-class and low-income consumers and accident victims need greater legal protection; and that the law must be based on "common sense"—cheap, simple, predictable, and less lawyer-friendly. These violations should seriously trouble not only liberals but also the conservatives and neoliberals who subscribe to the contract's tenets.

Ever since colonial times, tort law has been governed almost exclusively by state law. State courts and legislatures have gradually refined this law, in some cases even eliminating it and substituting no-fault systems, as with workplace and auto accidents. The new legislation would change much of this by making products liability law federal, and for no good reason. (The contract's commitment to preserving states' diversity against "one size fits all" federal rules evidently does not apply to those federal rules that Newt Gingrich favors.) While objective experts have rightly criticized much of tort law, they have seldom objected to torts' state law status. Quite the contrary.

The Republicans, however, claim that state-to-state differences in product liability threaten the financial and competitive well-being of U.S.

---

*This essay, published in 1995 during the era of Newt Gingrich's "Contract with America," is still timely. The legislation discussed here never passed and remains a top priority for the second Bush administration, whose proposals will surely differ in some details.

firms. They maintain that uniform interstate rules are needed. For two decades, Congress has rejected such pleas. In the single instance when it ventured into the field—regulating claims against some vaccine manufacturers—it decided to use existing state law rules almost entirely rather than adopting a new set of federal ones.

Besides, since the 1960s, states' laws have tended to converge. Many states have adopted strict product liability principles that do not require plaintiffs to prove that a manufacturer was negligent. Of course, product liability plaintiffs still take home bigger awards for a given injury in some states than others. Notoriously, plaintiffs' lawyers like to try cases in front of generous juries in East Texas and the Bronx, while defendants prefer the more parsimonious juries of New England. But it is not the rules that cause interstate variation in the size of the awards juries hand down; it is the jurors. Uniform rules would have little effect on jury awards within a state, since both federal and state juries in any given state are drawn from roughly similar pools of potential jurors.

The case for a federal products liability law, then, cannot rest on the inherent value of uniform state laws. It must rest, if at all, on the superior content of the rules that Congress would impose on the states. Would the newly mandated rules be sufficiently better than existing state rules to justify preempting them? For the most part, the answer is no.

To be sure, several of the new rules are designed to deal with real weaknesses in state tort law. Some states' punitive damage rules, for example, allow juries to add exorbitant monetary penalties on top of compensatory damages. Using the relaxed standards of civil law rather than the more rigorous ones of criminal law, they can impose severe financial punishment simply by finding that the defendant was reckless.

Until recently, demands for punitive damages were rare in tort cases. Evidently, they are now the norm. Yale professor George Priest, studying two Alabama counties, found that almost all tort plaintiffs now seek punitive damages. Although awards are far less common, juries eager to "send a message" can render outlandish awards that the courts often uphold. In an Alabama case last year, for example, a life insurance company's agent committed fraud on a $25,000 policy, causing the policyholders two weeks of sleeplessness but no real economic losses; yet the court upheld a $25 million award. The new bill is right to address this issue.

The new legislation also rightly zeroes in on some states' joint liability rules. These rules allow plaintiffs in many multidefendant cases to hold one defendant liable for all of the damages—including those it did not cause—so long as the jury cannot readily distinguish its causal contribution from those of the other defendants. This rule is unjust when the most culpable defendants are insolvent (or otherwise immune from paying), while the fault of the one who must pay was relatively minor.

Unfortunately, the House's solutions to these real problems are flawed. The bill offers two solutions to the issues of punitive damages and joint liability: capping punitives at either $250,000 or three times the compensatory damages; and limiting joint liability to the plaintiff's economic damages (damages for pain and suffering would be paid only by those clearly at fault). Although these reforms are steps in the right direction, they need further refinement. The punitives formula is too rigid for the extraordinary range of tort cases. The new joint liability rule will simply replace one injustice with another by making a wholly innocent victim rather than a partly guilty defendant bear the risk of some defendants' inability to pay.

Another reform would alter litigation in federal court cases in which state law controls the dispute. The most far-reaching change would impose a "loser pays" rule. A party who rejects another party's settlement offer and then fails to obtain an outcome more favorable than the rejected offer would pay a price for his intransigence: Specifically, he would foot his adversary's postoffer expenses, including attorneys' fees. This amounts to a radical reversal of the traditional American rule, under which each party bears his own expenses. It betrays the contract's commitment to make the law protect middle-class and poor people. This reform would effectively bar them from the federal courts by threatening them with ruinous costs if their suits turned out to be unsuccessful—a risk that only the wealthy could afford. If Congress really wants to help ordinary tort victims, it should support a proposal advanced by University of Virginia law professor Jeffrey O'Connell and others that would tie plaintiffs' lawyers' compensation more closely to the work and value they actually produce when cases settle quickly.

"Loser pays" would either wreak great injustice or be ineffectual. A person of modest means could sue only on a fairly sure thing, when he might find a contingency fee lawyer to take his case. But since the new rule would apply only to certain federal court cases, plaintiffs could readily avoid its bite; they would need only to file their claims in state court (rather than federal), where the traditional rule would apply. There are good arguments for keeping such cases in state courts, but this is surely a roundabout way to do it.

A third goal of the contract is to simplify the law so that it is cheaper, more predictable and makes "common sense." But, again, the proposed legislation will do just the opposite, creating make-work for lawyers. The new law will give rise to endless legal uncertainties. Under the "loser pays" reform, courts will have to determine the cost of a certain species of fee (known as a "noncontingent" fee) that simply does not exist for most personal injury claims. The reform also permits a judge to avoid "loser pays" if the rule would be "manifestly unjust." This term, however, is open-ended, and the provision would probably require courts to compare the parties' wealth—an action that violates traditional notions of legal equality.

Perhaps the greatest confusion will be sown as courts attempt to integrate ill-defined new federal rules with whatever parts of state tort law Congress meant to preserve (a matter left unclear). An entirely new body of statutory interpretation will be necessary: State courts will be trying to figure out which parts of their long-evolved tort jurisprudence remain viable, while federal judges, who must often rely entirely on state law, will be more confused than ever about what that law is. To Joe Six-pack, this new jurisprudence will be even more technical and opaque than the old one.

So much for "common sense" reforms to reduce legal complexity and protect ordinary Americans from federal overreaching. In an act of legal contortion worthy of the most cunning Wall Street lawyer, the Contract with America has managed to breach itself.

⌁ 21 ⌁

Surrogate Motherhood: Reflections on Baby M*

I come to the *Baby M* case with little knowledge of family law. The twists and turns of its doctrines, the fine distinctions developed by those who must solve its dauntingly difficult problems, and its intricate technical apparatus are all matters about which I possess no expertise. Still, the untutored, "commonsense" view may be valuable when the experts are sharply divided, as they are here.

Even if family lawyers had forged a consensus about *Baby M* and its larger implications, the public might well look elsewhere for solutions. Disputes implicating new technologies or social arrangements mark the "frontier," the "cutting edge," of legal and social change. This suggests that we are operating in a relatively open-ended normative environment where deeply held values clash with new social facts, and legal uncertainty and popular anxiety are endemic. In this "new ball game" (to use another cliché), the old rules seem anachronistic and everything is up for grabs. Even generalists may have something to contribute.

I shall say little about the legal doctrines applicable to *Baby M*. It is, of course, a custody dispute seeking to resolve the conflicting claims of idiosyncratic, all-too-human individuals. Everyone might have been better served had the New Jersey courts confined their pronouncements to the custody issue, but judges too are human. They succumbed to an understandable temptation to reach out and explore the case's fascinating social

*In this essay, published in 1988, I have updated the data on adoption and infertility, not on surrogacy.

meaning, a weakness for which law professors and pundits, for whom discursiveness is a sacred vocation, should be grateful.

In this spirit, I shall make three principal arguments. In part I, "Morality," I maintain that surrogacy is not intrinsically immoral; indeed, one can properly view it as a praiseworthy act of generosity and commitment to the creation of a wanted life. In part II, "Consequences," I make a rough, quite conservative assessment of surrogacy's consequences and conclude that it will generate very large, widely distributed private and social benefits. Unless surrogacy's risks are comparable to these benefits, I argue, the law should uphold surrogacy contracts, not categorically condemn them as the Supreme Court of New Jersey did. In part III, "Regulation," I consider the risks associated with surrogacy, show how a combination of familiar legal techniques can substantially eliminate these risks, and discuss the question of specific enforcement of surrogacy contracts.

MORALITY

The labeling of surrogacy as "baby selling" was utterly predictable. That phrase, like a rhetorical guillotine, sharply cuts off serious debate. Once that dread imputation attaches to the practice, people are understandably reluctant to advocate it. Yet there is some truth to the "baby selling" charge. Surrogacy does involve an exchange that in any other context would be viewed as a sale, and this remains true even if the surrogate performs without fee and possesses no legal rights to the child that she surrenders. Having carried a healthy baby to term, she has received something of great, perhaps inestimable value, in return for her exertions: the sublime pleasure of the gestational and perinatal processes. These pleasures, of course, are unique; they can be enjoyed in no other way. Polemical labels, however, do little to advance understanding of a complex phenomenon such as surrogacy. Surrogacy is a special kind of baby selling, and examination of its special character shows that the "baby selling" epithet should stimulate—not end—the moral and policy debate. The important questions are whether, when, and under what terms, the law ought to permit the practice.

The reasons why surrogacy should be viewed as "baby selling with a difference" are most evident when we examine the dimensions of the infertility problem to which surrogacy responds, and then compare surrogacy to adoption, an alternative infertility remedy whose moral legitimacy is unquestioned. Infertility has been viewed as a personal and social calamity by most societies and linked to surrogacy since ancient times. In 1995, an estimated 7.1 percent of married couples were considered infertile; 15 percent of women of childbearing age had used some kind of infertility service.

Adoption of U.S.-born children, the traditional solution to infertility, has become far less available due to abortion, improved contraception, the reduced social stigma of retaining a child born out of wedlock, declining teen pregnancy, and other factors. In 1995, an estimated 500,000 women were seeking to adopt, yet the number of such children available for adoption was far lower; the number of adoptions declined from 175,000 in 1970 to 127,000 in 1992. (International adoption, however, has risen to more than 19,000 in 2001, mostly from China and Russia.) More than half of private adoptions are now independent rather than through more closely regulated private agencies, and the cost now exceeds $25,000, particularly for healthy white babies for whom the waiting time can be five years. Supply and demand factors dictate lower costs and waiting times for biracial babies and even lower for black ones.

But some infertile couples look to surrogacy for reasons going beyond the vast unmet demand for adoptive children. Surrogacy enjoys certain advantages over adoption. The child ends up not with an adoptive couple but with the child's own biological father. The father and his spouse are in a position to learn considerably more about the surrogate's background than adoptive parents can about that of an adopted child. In addition, the surrogate should know from the very outset—even before she becomes pregnant—that she can have no legitimate expectation of keeping the child. There is some empirical evidence that most surrogates know this emotionally as well as cognitively. This knowledge, of course, does not always prevent the growth of the kind of possessory feelings about the child that the revocability-of-consent doctrine in adoption law is designed to protect. But it will probably inhibit those feelings from flourishing as fully as they do in a mother who decides later in the process to place her child for adoption. Finally, surrogacy, unlike adoption, does not simply reallocate rights to a living child; it has the additional, infinitely precious virtue of generating new, ardently desired life. These differences between surrogacy and adoption strongly suggest that the proscription of baby selling in the adoption context does not necessarily condemn surrogacy. Indeed, surrogacy actually advances some of the values that the ban seeks to protect.

Broadly speaking, critics oppose the practice of surrogacy on only two grounds. One is an overriding principled objection, an argumentative "trump" that takes the question out of the realm of prudential interest-balancing and puts it in the realm of nonutilitarian morality, such as natural law. Alternatively, one might object to surrogacy because, all things considered, its consequences are undesirable. On the current state of the record, neither objection seems persuasive. In the remainder of this part, I consider natural law objections, and in the next part, I discuss the consequentialist critique.

Generally speaking, natural law objections to surrogacy focus on the nature of surrogacy, the nature of the surrogate's consent, and the failure to consider the child's interests. Opponents often point out that the essence of surrogacy is the surrogate's use of her body to produce a child for a stranger, which they consider a profoundly alienating, unnatural act. But if that action is a moral vice, then the venerable practice of wet-nursing and the more recent practices of donating eggs or sperm to the gestational mother are likewise condemned. Surrogacy, of course, involves a longer, more intense involvement than these other practices, but it seems odd to view this difference, important as it may be, as the difference between moral and immoral behavior.

The more common objection emphasizes that the surrogate (usually) performs this service for a fee rather than for purely altruistic reasons. Yet it is not at all clear why this feature of surrogacy is morally objectionable in itself, especially if (as I speculate below) the service is actually available to a wide range of would-be parents. If paying money to obtain the child is wrong, then adoption and sperm and egg donation, which often involve such payments, must join surrogacy in the dock. In addition, of course, society often permits individuals to provide at a profit many services that we rightly regard as precious, like health and child care.

Opponents sometimes argue that surrogacy cannot really be voluntary and thus lacks the quality of autonomous will that imparts moral legitimacy to human choices. The existing data, however, suggest that women who offer themselves as surrogates do so for straightforward reasons ranging from altruism to a desire for money. The moral argument from involuntariness usually emphasizes that economic circumstances impel some women to choose surrogacy. Some surrogates are financially insecure and have had limited education; again, Baby M's surrogate seems typical. Such women may view surrogacy as a compelling solution to an inadequate income. Surrogacy often involves a transaction between men and women of different social status; most surrogates need money and the potential father must be in a financial position to pay substantial fees to the surrogate and to intermediaries. Perhaps it is this combination of factors that prompted the New Jersey Supreme Court to describe surrogate motherhood—in the second paragraph of its opinion—as "potentially degrading to women."

These contentions, however, prove too much. The available data contradict the view that surrogates are members of an "underclass." Surrogates are not desperate because they are usually less wealthy than the men with whom they contract. Indeed, almost all seem to have satisfying emotional support networks; over 85 percent of their husbands and lovers endorse their surrogacy decision. Moreover, second thoughts following difficult choices are ubiquitous in life. The risk of subsequent regret is the price we pay for our commitment to personal autonomy and responsibility in the face of uncertainty. Thus, a surrogate's decision does not become involuntary in any meaningful sense simply because she later regrets the decision. Morally speaking, it should be enough for society to ensure that she is reasonably well-informed about the risks that may later befall her, including possible feelings of shame and sorrow. Sound regulation of surrogacy contracts, which I discuss below, can achieve this.

Nor, morally speaking, is a constrained choice necessarily equivalent to no real choice. Circumstantial limitations on choice are seldom distributed equally or fairly in society. But a community that cherishes a woman's freedom and individuality should accord a high degree of respect to her choices, and should override them only when her decision is plainly uninformed or offends deeply and widely held social values. Surrogacy has little in common with prostitution in this respect. No choice is morally unacceptable, then, simply because it is constrained or even because some choosers are more constrained than others. Indeed, constraint is what makes choices problematic—and thus morally relevant—in the first place.

We should be especially reluctant to censure as immoral a choice that produces a universally blessed gift—the creation of a new human life that is wanted by its parents. When opponents characterize surrogacy as "degradation" or as "exploitation," they abuse ordinary language and mock surrogates' claims to autonomy and respect. One may wish to prohibit surrogacy on policy grounds, but one cannot coherently condemn it as inherently immoral.

The interests of surrogate-born children are plainly central to an appraisal of surrogacy's morality. Objection to a practice on behalf of individuals who would not even exist in its absence, and who are fervently wanted by their future parents, seems odd, to say the least. A complaint of this kind might be morally intelligible if one could confidently predict that surrogate-born children, their parents, or the larger society would suffer dire consequences. Yet a priori, there is no reason to predict anything but a normal life for such children. Available evidence also suggests that most other individuals directly affected by surrogacy rarely have problems. It cannot be immoral for society to accept risks, especially when they are quite small and are borne in pursuit of a great good. Were this not true, our most praiseworthy actions would be condemned. In saying this, however, I certainly do not mean to disparage the deep concerns expressed by virtually all commentators that something might go awry. In particular, the surrogate, the father, or both might change their minds after impregnation or birth occurs, and they or the child may suffer as a result. I share these concerns and discuss later on how the law should deal with them. My purpose up to this point, however, has been more limited—to show that the mere existence of these risks does not render surrogacy morally objectionable.

CONSEQUENCES

If surrogacy is not morally objectionable per se, we must then consider the second species of objection to the practice, a consequentialist argument that surrogacy's effects are, on balance, undesirable. The difficulty with this kind of argument is that surrogacy's consequences do not exist in a vacuum; they must be appraised in context. The relevant context, I maintain, is a legal regime in which the state regulates surrogacy contracts, using the law to shape the consequences of surrogacy by enhancing its benefits and reducing its risks.

Consider the advantages of surrogacy. According to the trial judge's findings, an estimated ten to fifteen percent of married couples are childless involuntarily (a proportion that has increased rapidly in recent decades), and between 500,000 and one million married women are now thought to be unable to have a genetically or gestationally related child without some fertilization assistance or uterine implant. The judge in *Baby M* found that in 1984, two million couples contended for the 58,000 children placed for adoption; these couples experienced a waiting period of three to seven years. Adoption costs as much as $20,000 per child, and sometimes more. According to one survey, the average private domestic adoption averaged almost $8,000.

These data permit us to evaluate the worth of surrogacy to married couples with infertility problems. Lest this exercise be misunderstood, I emphasize that it is neither an attempt to place a dollar value on human life nor an assertion that society can somehow achieve the benefits of surrogacy without running some risks. It is simply a crude effort to estimate what infertile couples would willingly pay for the service.

The data indicate that the private benefits would be high indeed; they could total hundreds of millions of dollars, depending on how many of the 2.1 million infertile married couples engaged surrogates. This estimate is conservative in some respects. It does not reflect the desire of many infertile couples to pay more—presumably much more—for a child who is genetically related to one of them, whose biological mother can be selected by the father, and whose gestation can be monitored by him. Nor does it impute any value to the greater speed of surrogacy, as compared with adoption.

The distribution of these benefits, and not simply their magnitude, is an important consideration. Although the New Jersey Supreme Court insinuated that surrogacy is available only to high-income couples, there is little reason to credit this view. Although the cost is often substantial ($20,000 plus expenses is common), such a sum—which is far less than the down payment on a very modest home—is surely within the reach of millions of couples for whom a prospective child is well worth saving and borrowing for. Enforcing surrogacy contracts, moreover, would immediately lower the cost by reducing uncertainty and increasing supply.

Even if surrogacy services are less widely accessible than I suppose, it would by no means follow that they should be denied to those who can afford them. We generally believe that some goods, such as minimum education, nutrition, and health care, should not be available to some individuals unless they are available to all. It is inconceivable, however, that the opportunity to create wanted life is one of them. This opportunity is infinitely precious, but it is not a scarce resource in quite the same sense as education, nutrition, and health care. Allowing some persons to avail themselves of surrogacy does not limit the parental options of others, and the surrogate's act, unlike certain organ donations, does not reduce her own parental opportunities. To deny individuals access to surrogacy just because all cannot enjoy it would not promote the ideal of equality but would pervert it to no legitimate purpose.

My analysis of surrogacy's benefits, as is obvious from the qualifications and uncertain data, cannot yield an "accurate" or "reliable" estimate. Even an "accurate" estimate would not necessarily conclude the question of whether and under what circumstances society should permit surrogacy. The analysis does show, however, that the benefits of surrogacy are likely to be great indeed, and this showing should suffice to accomplish two limited purposes. First, it should shift the burden of persuasion to those who oppose surrogacy; if they believe that society should prevent consenting individuals from obtaining benefits of that magnitude, opponents should provide compelling justifications. Second, the magnitude of these benefits suggests that the appropriate social policy response to surrogacy is not to prohibit the practice but to regulate it. A decision to bar surrogacy would be a decision to forego those benefits (or to drive them underground). By regulating the practice, we may capture the value while minimizing the risk.

REGULATION

Surrogacy, like most good things, is not an unmitigated blessing. Indeed, if advances in the science and technology of fertility eventually solve the dilemmas of infertile couples, the arguments for permitting surrogacy will be far weaker. Until that halcyon day, however, a social decision balancing the risks of surrogacy against its benefits seems morally inescapable unless we are prepared to consign most such couples to many years, and perhaps lives, of childlessness.

Surrogacy contracts entail two principal kinds of risks. First, the parties may not be fully informed about the risks of the transaction. Second, even if fully informed when they make the contract, they may change their minds later and try to avoid their legal obligations. When this occurs (as in *Baby M*), it attracts media attention, which can play on public fears (and curiosity) and obscure the large, less visible benefits of surrogacy to infertile couples and society. But on a more objective view (and especially in relation to the benefits), these risks seem small. More to the present point, effective regulation of surrogacy contracts can largely eliminate them.

Generally speaking, private surrogacy arrangements are beneficial and worthy of society's respect. For this reason, the law should facilitate them while safeguarding those public values that the participants cannot be expected to protect. This is particularly true of society's deep concern about the support and custody of surrogate-born children if one or both parents renounce their contractual obligations. While permitting participants to structure surrogate arrangements largely as they wish, the law can play an important role in minimizing the risk that disputes implicating society's interests will arise.

The process of surrogate contracting should be regulated in four respects. First, legislators should prescribe the authoritative norms that will govern these arrangements and perhaps standardize the contract provisions that are necessary to implement these social norms. For example, it might mandate psychological and other testing of the surrogate, genetic testing of the father, in vivo testing of the fetus, and timely dissemination of test results to all relevant parties. Second, the law should reduce uncertainty about how it will deal with certain contingencies that may arise, especially the risk that either or both parties will change their minds. Third, it should ensure that the parties are as fully informed as is reasonably possible about their contractual obligations and about how these obligations will be enforced. Finally, it should vindicate the crucial public values at stake by protecting children from the risk of abandonment, by ensuring custody, if possible, by at least one biologically related parent, by enforcing the father's support obligations, and by removing unnecessary impediments to surrogacy contracts that satisfy these conditions.

To fulfill these aims, the content, implications, and risks of surrogacy contracts must be made as salient and visible as possible. The signing should be a solemn event which highlights the responsibilities undertaken. The state might require, for example, that the parties sign the contract in the presence of a designated public official or private agency only after the designee has counseled the parties and satisfied herself that they fully appreciate the contract's significance and contingencies. Failure to comply with these minimally intrusive formal requirements would render the contract unenforceable. The law may also mandate public filing of surrogacy contracts.

In this connection, the law should state (and the counselor should reiterate) that a surrogacy contract will be construed strictly according to its original terms, regardless of the parties' subsequent decisions for or among themselves, subject to certain carefully specified exceptions (for example, the death of the father prior to birth). The law should be particularly clear that the surrogate must surrender the child at birth and will enjoy no parental rights not provided by the contract, a restriction most state laws impose on sperm donors. Regulations should prescribe a post-signing, pre-impregnation "cooling off" period at the end of which either party may renounce the contract. If unscrupulous intermediaries pose significant risks, the law can adopt any number of familiar controls, ranging from simple registration requirements through premarket licensing schemes to criminal sanctions, just as it has done for adoption agencies and marriage and family counselors.

Duly regulated surrogacy contracts weaken considerably the case for prolonging the mother's right to revoke her consent beyond a pre-impregnation cooling-off period. Although state law would permit her to do so were she placing the child for adoption, the differences between surrogacy and adoption, discussed earlier justify limiting surrogates' revocability rights.

The revocability problem, however, raises a related question: Should contractual obligations be subject to judicially imposed specific perform-ance? Surrogacy is unique, of course, and money damages are obviously an inadequate remedy for the disappointed parent. Moreover, to the extent that contractual obligations—especially those requiring the surro-gate to surrender the child at birth—are not specifically enforceable, would-be parents may be reluctant to enter such contracts. On the other hand, society may not want judges sending marshals to wrench infants from the arms of their mothers, compelling pregnant women to submit to abortions that they refuse to have, or restraining pregnant women from having abortions that they firmly want. Disputes of this kind, of course, are not unique to surrogacy.

The specific performance issue deserves considerably more thought precisely because a simple, categorical answer is certain to be wrong. At present, I favor a discriminating approach to requests for specific per-formance, one that takes into account the competing values at stake. I believe, for example, that specific performance of a mother's contractual obligation to abort or to refrain from aborting should not be available. The state's coercive power should not—and perhaps as a constitutional matter, may not—intrude in this fashion upon such private decisions. On the other hand, certain other contractual obligations that are central to the integrity of the arrangement, such as a mother's duty to submit to in vivo testing of the fetus, should probably be subject to specific performance. If the surrogate tenders the child, the father's contractual obligation to take it should be specifically enforceable, subject to the usual defenses. In such cases, the surrogate's claim for money damages against the father cannot vindicate the child's and society's interests in encouraging custody with at least one biological parent. But as soon as the father indicates, by inac-tion or otherwise, that he does not want or will not care for the child, the state must move swiftly to take custody and place the child for adoption. In any event, the father's obligation to pay for the child's support should survive any of these contingencies.

I am less certain about compelling specific performance of the mother's contractual obligation to surrender the child to the father. In searching for an answer, however, I am struck by the fact that virtually all surrogates to date have surrendered the child without court intervention. If this is true, I am strongly inclined to allow fathers to get specific performance in the rare cases in which a dispute of this kind arises.

Although I am well aware of the long catalog of regulatory failures, surrogacy contracts appear to satisfy many of the preconditions for effective regulation that analysts have identified. Surrogacy, unlike toxic chemicals or narcotics distribution, is difficult to conceal. It usually requires advertising, a protracted gestation period that becomes progressively more notorious, the involvement of doctors, hospitals, and public agencies, recordkeeping, and the protections (under my approach) of a highly regulated, judicially enforceable contract. Although stringent regulation could spawn a black market in surrogate-mothered babies, it would be more vulnerable to detection and disruption than most black markets.

In addition to its visibility, surrogacy requires the cooperation of a number of people who are likely to have strong motives to comply with the contract, as regulated by law. The father and intermediary will have strong stakes in its enforcement, and health care providers will demand a clear delineation of their legal rights and obligations. Compared to many other human relationships (including familial ones), the individuals involved in surrogacy tend to have limited interactions, the kinds of contingencies that may arise can be cataloged, and the possible responses are predictable. Surrogacy involves no complex technologies (such as nuclear power generation) or transactions (such as securities trading) that the regulator must understand and control. Indeed, family law provides a rich source of norms, experience, and institutional guidance upon which the law can draw in attempting to predict behavior and regulate contracts dealing with surrogacy.

The incentive structure surrounding surrogacy also supports effective regulation. In contrast to the regulation of campaign finance, for example, there is no powerful, well-defined constituency with a strong interest in weakening the enforcement of surrogacy contracts and regulations. Purchasers of surrogacy services are well situated to identify and protect their rights without much governmental intervention. Even if one assumes (as many opponents of surrogacy do) that surrogates are especially vulnerable to exploitation, the regulatory measures that I propose can amply protect their legitimate interests.

Under these conditions, little additional bureaucratic apparatus should be needed to keep the risks associated with surrogacy to a socially tolerable level. Instead, a regime of private contract, constrained and modified by a small number of legislated rules and enforceable in the courts or other arbitral fora, should protect the relevant private and social values implicated by surrogacy. I have sketched the general contours of the regulatory system needed; for the most part, it can be relatively simple, procedural, and suppletive in nature. Regulation's crucial role here should be to shape and facilitate, rather than to deform or stifle, the thousands of life-creating, life-enhancing surrogacy contracts that individuals wish to make. The principal obstacle to attaining this social bounty is the law's uncertain treatment of surrogacy. Fortunately, that is one problem we can do something about.

– PART IV –

DEALING WITH TERRORISM
AND VICTIMS

That the terrorist strikes at the World Trade Center on September 11, 2001, transformed many of our ways of thinking about America's role in the world has become a cliché—but remains true nonetheless. Urgent issues of war and peace, national and local security, the legal rights of suspected terrorists, and the just treatment of victims have been at the fore of public debates ever since. The essays in this part address a number of moral, legal, political, and policy aspects of this evolving crisis.

I first take up the question of American policy toward Iraq, particularly the possible justifications for preemptive war. This essay, written in late 2002 well before the United States decided to seek United Nations Security Council approval of its possible invasion of Iraq, contends that the United Nations Charter's provisions regarding nations' right to wage war have been rendered somewhat anachronistic in an age in which the greatest threats to national security are posed not by traditional armies that mass and then cross borders to strike at their enemies but by clandestine terrorist organizations enjoying sanctuary in failed states. The next essay analyzes another practice to which 9/11 has given increased salience: ethnoracial profiling. Here, I explain why profiling through stereotypes is a regrettable but unavoidable response to the necessity of screening large numbers of people in short periods of time with virtually no information about them or the risks that they might pose, and a strong preference for certain kinds of errors relative to others. At the same time, I suggest how profiling can under certain conditions be made somewhat more palatable and less unjust.

The next two essays concern the compensation of innocent victims of misfortunes of various kinds. The first of these raises hard questions about when government should assume a public obligation to compensate victims, given the vast range of circumstances that may have brought about their injuries, the disputed role of government in our society, and the different ways of thinking about government responsibility for different types of misfortune. I offer some tentative answers, including the suggestion that public programs for the victims of terrorist attacks may be hard to justify in any principled way. The second moves from these general considerations to a particularized assessment of the 9/11 Compensation Fund, which lavished benefits on the victims that were far more generous than anything provided by other public programs or by the tort system. Here, I argue that the recipients of these benefits, while of course entitled to our deepest sympathy and charitable support, no more deserved special government compensation than any number of other innocent victims of cruel misfortune who can look for succor only to private charity, private insurance (if any), and perhaps a smattering of minimal public benefits.

The final essay in this part discusses the difficult problems associated with adjudicating the innocence or guilt of people accused of terrorist-related crimes. Such adjudications can raise many due process concerns, particularly when the government seeks to rely upon classified evidence, anonymous witnesses, and proceedings to which public—and perhaps even defense lawyer—access must be limited for asserted national security reasons. I present one possible model for a form of hearing that might strike an acceptable balance among the conflicting public and private values, a hearing that is already authorized by statute but has never yet been used.

ꙮ 22 ꙮ

Preemptive Strikes: Revising the UN Charter

Rule of law. The very phrase stirs the heart and makes the blood race, and not just for lawyers. In our legal tradition, this ideal runs in a direct line all the way back to Magna Carta. Our Declaration of Independence invoked "the Laws of Nature and of Nature's God," and also celebrated English law. The Constitution built a larger legal framework on this common law foundation, affirming principles that we still struggle to fulfill.

Nothing tests the rule of law more than war. Both our crusade against terrorism and the idea of invading Iraq have lent urgency to the question of how compatible these wars are with the rule of law. My answer is, "It depends." Fighting terrorism obliges us to rethink and redesign parts of our domestic criminal, national security, immigration, and procedural law. Although difficult, the adjustments can be made without abandoning bedrock constitutional principles. But terrorism and the proliferation of weapons of mass destruction have more radical implications for international law, particularly the United Nations Charter. New geopolitical realities have rendered anachronistic some of the Charter's limits on our right to

defend vital national interests. If the Charter effectively weakens our consti-
tutional order and national security, it must be reinterpreted or changed.
U.S. Supreme Court justice Robert Jackson's observation about the
Constitution more than fifty years ago applies at least as much to the
Charter today: It "is not a suicide pact."

War may be incompatible with the rule of law if the stakes in military
victory are high enough and other values pale in comparison. Indeed, if
an enemy truly threatens the survival of the nation or its way of life, it follows that the rule of law cannot survive without victory; any law that
impedes victory will be (literally) self-defeating. This was Justice Jackson's
point, of course, and it applies when a nation seeks total conquest and
extermination, as with the Arab states' invasion of Israel in 1948 and
Hitler's war against the Jews. But even less exigent wars—Vietnam, for
example—may compromise legal protections. Justice Oliver Wendell
Holmes noted this in the wake of World War I: "When a nation is at war
many things that might be said in time of peace are such a hindrance to
its effort that their utterance will not be endured so long as men fight and
. . . no court could regard them as protected by any constitutional right."
Holmes was discussing speech, but his point extends to other civil liberties threatened by war.

Fortunately, most law does not impede military victory, and some law
actually facilitates it. The "law of war," then, is not an oxymoron. Almost
all states endorse the law of war and bind themselves to observe it. The
Geneva Conventions, for example, require belligerent states to treat prisoners of war humanely and to refrain from acts of war against civilians.
States enter into these treaties less out of idealistic commitment to the rule
of law or international solidarity than with the hope of protecting their
own captured soldiers and vulnerable populations. Especially when such
legal restraints are viewed before the fact—that is, before a nation is at
war and is tempted to violate them—they seem to make all states and
societies better off.

Law also has ample breathing space where the danger to national
security is significant but not imminent. After all, the threat may never
materialize, and if it does, it may still permit a militarily effective
response. Even a law that could impair military effectiveness during a
genuine security crisis—for example, a law allowing work stoppages in
critical industries or barring interrogation of suspected terrorists without Miranda warnings—may not have the feared impact until the crisis
actually arises. If a hostile state stockpiles weapons and seeks the capacity to destroy our homeland or allies, enough time may remain to prepare an adequate deterrent. Although the law's risk to security during
this hiatus is more worrisome than before the crisis, this risk may still
be acceptable, all things considered.

Many thoughtful Americans (and even more Europeans) describe the Iraqi threat in just these terms. The danger that Saddam Hussein poses, they say, is neither serious nor imminent. They claim that intelligence data do not establish that he now possesses weapons of mass destruction; that even if he had them, it would be irrational for him to use them; that we will still have time enough to respond if this situation changes; that an invasion would deflect attention from, and perhaps even aggravate, the more urgent Al Qaeda threat; that the risks and costs of invasion are too great; and that both the predictable and unforeseeable difficulties following even a successful invasion would only make matters worse.

All of these claims are plausible. They may even be correct—although I find the case for invasion much stronger if Iraq thwarts the UN inspections. But my point is not about the wisdom of war with Iraq or about the rule of law generally. It is about the appropriate role for a particular law, the UN Charter, in managing this kind of conflict. I maintain not only that this law's role in Iraq is in fact limited, but that this limitation is a good thing—for the United States and for the larger international order.

For centuries, "realists" have emphasized that there is no international sovereign to regulate the interactions of states, no morality common to all states, and thus no "international community" for law to constitute and represent. In this view, there is only a multitude of states, each of which follows a simple rule: Use national power to pursue the national interest. This rule, of course, often prompts states to take actions that seem to be enlightened and promote peace. They may observe comity, provide foreign aid, compromise with other states, comply with the laws of war, protect other human rights, enter into bilateral and multilateral treaties, accept the rulings of international tribunals, and support the UN. But these actions simply reflect a longer, broader view of their national interests. The notion that a particular international law regime is more than the pursuit of these interests by the most powerful states at that moment in time is just a serviceable fiction. When international law strays too far from geopolitical reality, it will and should be changed—de facto, if not de jure.

This is what is now occurring in the debate over Iraq. The "legalists" (for want of a better term) and other opponents of American intervention invoke the Charter and other rules that ordain respect for Iraq's sovereignty, narrow the right of self-defense to situations of armed attack, require Security Council authorization of force, necessitate multilateral implementation of resolutions, and so forth. This legal regime, however, was adopted almost sixty years ago in an altogether different world when the great powers, exhausted by war and still clinging to their restive and far-flung empires, competed for hegemony. Future wars were expected to be (as many are) localized conflicts waged by states through uniformed armies across conventional borders and terminating in peace treaties or formal cessation of hostilities.

Today, however, we know better. The United States is now the sole hegemon. Its economic, military, political, cultural, and ideological powers utterly dwarf those of other states. As analyst Fareed Zakaria has noted, our military expenditures exceed those of the next fifteen states combined, yet these outlays constitute only 4 percent of the U.S. gross domestic product. Our vast economic superiority is likely to persist. The single greatest present threat to peace is a shadowy, stealthy, nimble congeries of nonuniformed terrorist groups, sometimes but not always state-sponsored, who view the United States as their main target. These groups strike without warning and often without provocation, and can wreak massive destruction on civilian population centers. Enemy troops massing at borders or threatening military assets are no longer the only forms of imminent threat.

The UN is not equipped—politically, legally, or militarily—to deal effectively with this new threat. The General Assembly consists of almost two hundred states, each with an equal vote, but relatively few of them are democracies in any meaningful sense. As for the Security Council, national self-interest often causes its permanent members to appease or even support autocratic state sponsors of terrorism. The United States has sometimes supported such regimes as the lesser evil—for example, Iraq and then the Taliban during the 1980s.

Is it conceivable that the United States would have agreed to the current UN decision-making system under today's geopolitical conditions? I think not. That being so, we should either insist that this system be changed or treat it as having been effectively altered by the subsequent transformation of the international order. Just as the Supreme Court overthrew the old Constitution during the New Deal without benefit of amendment—a legal revolution that my colleague Bruce Ackerman describes approvingly as a "constitutional moment" akin to the one during Reconstruction—the United States should now protect our vital security interests as best we can. We should do this with the UN's imprimatur if possible, but without it if necessary.

I am not suggesting that an invasion of Iraq, much less a unilateral one, would necessarily be wise. Indeed, I have already listed respectable arguments to the contrary whose tenor is to question whether our vital security interests are truly at risk. If the UN can succeed in disarming Iraq—an action ordered by many Security Council resolutions since 1991—this would surely be the best course. And even if invasion should prove to be necessary, sound reasons of statecraft argue for assembling as broad an international coalition as possible.

What I *am* arguing is that the United States can no longer treat as legally binding those provisions of the UN Charter that would prevent us from taking military action, including invasion, to repel genuine threats to our homeland and other vital interests, as we properly define them, before it is too late. Preemptive strikes are warranted if, but only if, diplomacy has failed, conflict seems inevitable, the enemy would wreak great damage, and further delay would strengthen it by weakening our deterrence and defense. No great power can renounce this right of anticipatory self-defense against grave threats that are imminent in this sense, and the United States has never done so. To the extent that international law is understood to deny us this right, those (like me) who support international law should seek to change it.

The status of domestic law after September 11 is very different. More than two centuries of experience under the Constitution, much of it during periods of war and other threats to national security, demonstrate several reassuring conclusions. First, as legal scholar Geoffrey Stone shows, we do seem to learn from our mistakes. War often prompts us to restrict civil liberties in ways that in peacetime we then regret and repeal. Consequently, each new episode of wartime restriction is less arbitrary and repressive than the last. Second, we may need to adjust the balance between procedural protections for individuals and groups accused of supporting terrorism and the government's national security imperatives, but this adjustment need not mean abandoning our basic civil liberties.

The issues that September 11 is bringing to the courts are novel in some respects but familiar in others. When the government labels U.S. citizens as "unlawful combatants" who can be detained and sequestered until they are no longer of interest, or when it designates groups as "terrorist organizations" and their supporters as possible criminals, its factual and legal predicates must be subjected to close legislative, administrative, and ultimately judicial scrutiny under rigorous standards of evidentiary reliability. When the government seeks to withhold from suspects' lawyers the information needed for a fair and effective defense, the courts must test its claims against the flexible but demanding principles of due process and "least restrictive alternative." To be sure, legislators and judges will often feel obliged to defer to Justice Department officials who earnestly invoke national security exigencies, but they can still ask hard questions, demand good answers, and search for better procedural solutions. The same Constitution that prevents social suicide also protects the liberties that sustain and legitimate democratic life.

～ 23 ～

Profiling: The Uses of Stereotypes

Racial profiling has become the hottest civil rights issue of the day, but it deserves cooler reflection than it has received. Politicians and pundits, regardless of their politics, reflexively denounce it; nary a word is raised in its defense. Many states have already barred it, and Congress is likely to do so. Some police chiefs resist Justice Department interrogation policies they think entail profiling. Yet September 11, as Dr. Johnson said of the gallows, concentrates the mind wonderfully. The disaster that befell us then and might recur in some form necessitates a profiling debate that is clear-eyed and hardheaded, not demagogic.

The furor about racial profiling is easy to understand. "Driving while black" and "flying while Arab" are emblems of the indignities that law enforcement officials are said to inflict on minorities on the basis of demeaning stereotypes and racial prejudice. This is no laughing matter. Respect for the rule of law means that people must not be singled out for enforcement scrutiny simply because of their race or ethnicity.

Or does it? Much turns on the meaning of "simply" in the last sentence. Profiling is not only inevitable but sensible public policy under certain conditions and with appropriate safeguards against abuse. After September 11, the stakes in deciding when and how profiling may be used and how to remedy abuses when they occur could not be higher.

A fruitful debate on profiling properly begins with our values as a society. The most important of these, of course, is self-defense, without which no other values can be realized. But we should be wary of claims that we must sacrifice our ideals in the name of national security; this means that other ideals remain central to the inquiry. The one most threatened by profiling is the principle that all individuals are equal before the law by reason of their membership in a political community committed to formal equality. In most but not all respects, we extend the same entitlement to aliens who are present in the polity legally or illegally. Differential treatment must meet a burden of justification—in the case of racial classifications, a very high one.

This ideal has a corollary: Government may not treat individuals arbitrarily. To put this principle another way, it must base its action on information that is reliable enough to justify its exercise of power over free individuals. How good must the information be? The law's answer is that it depends. Criminal punishment requires proof beyond a reasonable doubt, while a tort judgment demands only the preponderance of the evidence. Health agencies can often act with little more than a rational suspicion that a substance might be dangerous. A consular official can deny a visa if in her "opinion" the applicant is likely to become a public charge and unlike the previous examples, courts may not review this decision. Information good enough for one kind of decision, then, is not nearly good enough for others. Context is everything.

This brings us to profiling by law enforcement officials. Consider the context in which an FBI agent must search for the September 11 terrorists, or a security officer at a railroad and airline terminal must screen for new ones. Vast numbers of individuals pass through the officer's line of vision, and they do so only fleetingly, for a few seconds at most. As a result, the official must make a decision about each of them within those few seconds, unless she is prepared to hold all of them up for the time it will take to interrogate each, one by one. She knows absolutely nothing about these individuals, other than the physical characteristics that she can immediately observe, and learning more about them through interrogation will take a lot of time. The time this would take is costly to her task; each question she stops to ask will either allow others to pass by unnoticed or prolong the wait of those in the already long, steadily lengthening line. The time is even more costly to those waiting in line; for them, more than for her, time is money and opportunity. Politicians know how their constituents hate lines and constantly press her, along with customs, immigration, and toll officials, to shorten them.

At the same time, her risks of being wrong are dramatically asymmetrical. If she stops everyone, she will cause all of the problems just described and all of the people (except one, perhaps) will turn out to be perfectly innocent. On the other hand, if she fails to stop the one person among them who is in fact a terrorist, she causes a social calamity of incalculable proportions (not to mention losing her job). In choosing, as she must, between these competing risks, her self-interest and the social interest will drive her in the direction of avoiding calamity. The fact that society also tells her to be even-handed only adds to her dilemma, while providing no useful guidance as to what to do, given these incentives.

So what should she do? We can get at this question by asking what we would do were we in her place. To answer this question, we need not engage in moral speculation but can look to our own daily experiences. Each day, we all face choices that are very similar in structure, albeit far less consequential. We must make decisions very rapidly about things that matter to us. We know that our information is inadequate to the choice, but we also know that we cannot in the time available get information that is sufficiently better to improve our decision significantly. We consider our risks of error, which are often asymmetrical. Because we must momentarily integrate all this uncertainty into a concrete choice, we resort to shortcuts to decision making. (Psychologists call these "heuristics.")

The most important and universal of these tactical shortcuts is the stereotype. The advantage of stereotypes is that they economize on information, enabling us to choose quickly when our information is inadequate. This is a great, indeed indispensable virtue, precisely because this problem is ubiquitous in daily life, so ubiquitous that we scarcely notice it, nor do we notice how often we use stereotypes to solve it. Indeed, we could not live without stereotypes. We use them in order to predict how others will behave, as when we assume that blacks will vote Democratic (though many do not), and to anticipate others' desires, needs, or expectations, as when we offer help to disabled people (though some of them find this presumptuous). We use them when we take safety precautions when a large, unkempt, angry-looking man approaches us on a dark street (though he may simply be asking directions), and when we assume that higher-status schools are better (though they often prove to be unsuitable). Such assumptions are especially important in a mass society where people know less and less about one another.

Stereotypes, of course, have an obvious downside: They are sometimes wrong, almost by definition. After all, if they were wrong all the time, no rational person would use them, and if they were never wrong, they would be indisputable facts, not stereotypes. Stereotypes fall somewhere in between these extremes, but it is hard to know precisely where because we seldom know precisely how accurate they are. Although all stereotypes are over-broad, most are probably correct much more often than they are wrong; that is why they are useful. But when a stereotype *is* wrong, those who are exceptions to it naturally feel that they have not been treated equally as individuals, and they are right. Their uniqueness is being overlooked so that others can use stereotypes for the much larger universe of cases where the stereotypes are true and valuable. In this way, the palpable claims of discrete individuals are sacrificed to a disembodied social interest. This sacrifice offends not just them but others among us who identify with their sense of injustice, and when their indignation is compounded by the discourtesy or bias of bag checkers or law enforcement agents, the wound is even more deeply felt.

This is where the law comes in. When we view these stereotype-based injustices as sufficiently grave, we prohibit them. Even then, however, we do so only in a qualified way that expresses our ambivalence. Civil rights law, for example, proscribes racial, gender, disability, and age stereotyping. At the same time, it allows government, employers, and others to adduce a public interest or business reason strong enough to justify using them. The law allows religious groups to hire only coreligionists. Officials drawing legislative districts may to some extent treat all members of a minority group as if they all had the same political interests. The military can bar women from certain combat roles. Employers can assume that women are usually less suitable for jobs requiring very heavy lifting. Such practices reflect stereotypes that are thought to be reasonable in general, though false as to particular individuals.

Can the same be said of racial or ethnic profiling? Again, context is everything. We would object to a public college that categorically admitted women rather than men on the theory that women tend to be better students—not because the stereotype is false but because the school can readily ascertain academic promise on an individualized basis when reviewing applicants' files, which it must do anyway. On the other hand, no one would think it unjust for our officer to screen for Osama bin Laden, who is a very tall man with a beard and turban, by stopping all men meeting that general description. This is so not only because the stakes in apprehending him are immense but also because in making instantaneous decisions about whom to stop, the official can use gender, size, physiognomy, and dress as valuable clues. She would be irresponsible and incompetent not to do so even though every man she stopped was likely to be a false positive and thus to feel unjustly treated for having been singled out.

Racial profiling in more typical law enforcement settings can raise difficult moral questions. Suppose that society views drug dealing as a serious vice, and that a disproportionate number of drug dealers are black men although of course many are not. Would this stereotype justify stopping black men simply because of their color? Clearly not. The law properly requires more particularized evidence of wrongdoing. Suppose further, however, that police were to observe a black man engaging in the ostensibly furtive behavior that characterizes most but not all drug dealers, behavior also engaged in by some innocent men. Here, the behavioral stereotype would legally justify stopping the man. But what if the officer relied on both stereotypes in some impossible-to-parse combination? What if the behavioral stereotype alone had produced a very close call, and the racial one pushed it over the line?

Although I cannot answer all these questions, most critics of racial profiling do not even ask them. A wise policy will insist that the justice of profiling depends on a number of variables. How serious is the crime risk? How do we feel about the relative costs of false positives and false negatives? How accurate is the stereotype? How practicable is it to pursue the facts through an individualized inquiry rather than through stereotypes? If stereotypes must be used, are there some that rely on less incendiary and objectionable factors?

A sensible profiling policy will also recognize that safeguards become more essential as the enforcement process progresses. Stereotypes that are reasonable at the stage of deciding whom to screen for questioning may be unacceptable at the later stages of arrest and prosecution, when official decisions should be based on more individualized information and when lawyers and other procedural safeguards can be made available. Screening officials can be taught about the many exceptions to even serviceable stereotypes, to recognize them when they appear, and to behave in ways that encourage those being screened not to take it personally.

It is now a cliché that September 11 changed our world. Profiling is bound to be part of the new dispensation. Clearer thinking and greater sensitivity to its potential uses and abuses can help produce both a safer and a more just America.

∾ **24** ∾

Compensating Victims: Some Hard Questions

From the earliest civilizations to the present day, the law has demanded that victims be compensated. Principles governing compensation can be found in the Code of Hammurabi, the Bible, the Talmud, the Koran, and every body of secular law on earth. Even acknowledging the great antiquity of victim compensation, however, the subject's prominence in contemporary public debates is striking. Pick up a newspaper today and one is likely to read about lawsuits or legislation seeking reparations for a catalog of past and continuing injuries. The individuals and groups seeking compensation, moreover, are exceedingly diverse. They range from people harmed by accidents ("torts"), to the targets of conventional fraud or crime, to broad classes of individuals victimized by socially inflicted, large-scale wrongs or atrocities. These last include, for example, the families of Holocaust victims, the descendants of slaves, comfort women, *braceros* (Mexican agricultural workers in the United States), indigenous peoples, subjects of tyrannical regimes across the globe, sweatshop workers for multinational employers, and many others.

This vast expansion of compensation claimants in the United States is noteworthy in itself, but it is even more remarkable in light of several notable social and demographic developments that might seem to cut the other way. For example, we are a much wealthier society than ever before, and as the late political scientist Aaron Wildavsky famously put it, "wealthier is safer." The rates of violent crimes, as well as many nonviolent ones, have declined sharply in most American communities during the last decade or two. Private and social insurance coverage for victims' pecuniary costs has increased significantly over time, although it remains far from universal or comprehensive. This expansion of insurance might be expected to reduce the need to turn to noninsurance sources for compensation.

Indeed, given these salutary changes, the continuing growth in compensation claims may even seem paradoxical. The paradox resolves, however, when one considers some other attitudinal and institutional developments. As American society has become safer and less violent, we have also come to regard the dangers that remain as that much more intolerable. The source of this insistent demand for what legal historian Lawrence Friedman calls "perfect justice" is doubtless complicated. Part of the explanation for this demand is surely the ever-higher social expectations generated by our higher levels of education and income. Two other developments, moreover, shape these public expectations—and are in turn shaped by them. A highly competitive mass media has emerged whose ambition (among others) is to communicate real and imagined injustices to the public in the most dramatic, compelling, and disturbing forms. A second change, partly responding to the media and partly fueling it, is institutional in nature. Our contemporary legal and governmental systems have greatly extended the remedial structures of compensation in both private law (primarily through the tort system) and public law (primarily through civil rights and compensation statutes).

I have been asked to say whether I favor compensating the victims of crime. My answer is to ask what I think is the right question: Compared to what? In order to answer this question coherently, one would have to consider many different possible risk management and compensation systems implicating controversial empirical claims, conflicting values, and complex institutional arrangements. I cannot begin to do this question justice in a short think piece intended to raise questions rather than to resolve them.

THE PURPOSES OF COMPENSATION

In American society—indeed in all societies—compensating victims can serve a number of different public goals. As an analytical matter, we can usefully distinguish four such goals. These are (1) corrective justice, (2) deterrence of wrongdoing, (3) moral affirmation, and (4) distributive justice. Each of these compensatory purposes rests upon particular conceptions that desperately need clarification precisely because we use them so frequently and so loosely.

In addition to these analytical distinctions, there are others that do and should shape how we think about compensation. For example, one's claim for compensation may be as a matter of legal right (e.g., through tort law, social insurance, or private insurance contract), or may instead be a claim to the exercise of discretion, either by a discretionary public program or by a private philanthropy. Empirical questions also abound, including how well, along a variety of dimensions, victims are compensated by tort law as compared with insurance and (in the case of crime victims) special state compensation programs. RAND has conducted extensive studies to answer these empirical questions.

Government can pursue the four purposes—corrective justice, deterrence, moral affirmation, and distributive justice—through different policy instruments. But because each of these policy instruments entails distinctive moral, political, and administrative tradeoffs, government's choices are inevitably controversial. In addition, the analysis of these purposes and of their policy implications may be affected by whether the victim in question was injured by a crime, by a noncriminal tort (all crimes are torts but not vice-versa), or by a nontortious accident or illness (i.e., one for which there is no injurer who is liable for compensation).

1. *Corrective justice.* The ancient ideal of corrective justice, which was most famously advanced by Aristotle in his Nichomachean Ethics, has attracted great interest in recent years among scholars and policymakers.

Moral and legal philosophers like Ernest Weinrib and Jules Coleman have sought to explicate the distinctive claims that corrective justice makes, as well as the doctrinal and institutional features that a system of corrective justice must exhibit in order to vindicate those claims. Legislators routinely invoke the goal of corrective justice in advocating new compensatory arrangements for victims of crimes or of civil wrongs.

In its dominant formulation, corrective justice entails an intervention in the relationship between a wrongdoer and his victim, compelling the former to repair the harm that he has wrongfully imposed on the latter. In this sense, corrective justice is fundamentally backward-looking and restorative. It is a closed moral system that defines a victim as one who has been wrongfully harmed by another and the injurer as one who has caused this harm. Responsibility for corrective justice inheres in this relationship. Corrective justice imaginatively reconstructs the victim's situation before the wrong was committed, and seeks to recreate the status quo ante by restoring the victim, as much as possible, to the position that he would have occupied absent the wrong.

In our legal system, tort law is the main instrument for formally pursuing corrective justice. Tort law is a system of compensation administered by the courts in private litigation that is conducted largely according to common law principles subject to an adversary process. In tort law, the ideal of corrective justice requires wrongful injurers to compensate innocent victims. The two forms of wrongfulness are negligence (i.e., the creation of unreasonable risks of harm to others) and intentional harm. (Indeed, injurers who intentionally harm others or engage in aggravated forms of negligence may be liable for punitive damages (i.e., damages above and beyond what is needed to compensate for losses).

In several respects, however, the link between tort law and corrective justice—and hence compensation—has been broken, or at least attenuated. First, most accident victims do not seek compensation through the tort system at all because they are unaware of their rights, cannot convince a lawyer to take their case, or for other reasons. Second, many of those who do sue in tort do not recover anything. This may be because they cannot prove the facts on which their legal claim depends, or because of certain "technical" rules of tort law that can prevent compensation of otherwise deserving victims. For example, tort law provides for immunities that categorically protect some injurers from any liability to their victims. Immunities enjoyed by charitable organizations, spouses, or other family members are disappearing but others—particularly governmental immunity for many wrongs committed by public officials—remain and constitute serious limitations on victim compensation. Another compensation-limiting doctrine is "contributory negligence," under which a victim who negligently contributes to his own injury may be barred from recovering some or all of his losses.

A third disconnect between tort law and corrective justice is the fact that even those who are entitled to tort compensation for their injuries are typically paid not by the wrongdoers who injured them but by innocent third parties: the victim's own insurer, the injurer's liability insurer, or a social insurer (government). Fourth, even successful tort claimants must incur legal fees and other transaction costs that amount to one-third or more of their award, leaving them with significant uncompensated losses.

Finally—and most relevant to victims of crime—relatively few criminals are in a position to pay the victim damages, so any significant compensation must come instead from public and private sources. Private insurance is likely to cover certain out-of-pocket costs like health care, rehabilitative services, and disability-related wage loss, but will not cover pain-and-suffering, demoralization, and other nonpecuniary costs that crime victims often suffer. The same is true of social insurance. Only special programs for crime victims can compensate for such nonpecuniary costs.

The disconnect between tort law and corrective justice is not unique. Government compensation programs also break that link at many points. Disability compensation under Social Security, for example, is available only if the claimant has worked the requisite number of qualifying quarters and meets certain other criteria. Eligibility for Medicaid depends in some states on whether the structure of the claimant's family, such as whether both parents reside with the claimant. In some states, unemployment insurance is not available to seasonal workers. These examples could easily be multiplied. Government programs that compensate victims only compensate *some* victims; the excluded, moreover, are often similarly situated to the included with respect to their need for assistance.

2. *Deterrence.* Victim compensation serves not only the ideal of corrective justice but the social goal of deterring wrongdoing. By forcing injurers to bear the costs of their victims' losses—in economistic terms, to "internalize the externalities" and thus price their misconduct efficiently—the duty to compensate creates an incentive for potential actors to consider in advance the harms their actions might cause, since those harms, should they occur, will now be chargeable to the injurer. Unlike corrective justice, the deterrence rationale for compensation looks forward to future decisions by future actors rather than to restoring an earlier state of affairs. Deterrence, then, is intended to create socially desirable incentives for future conduct—what economists call ex ante incentives.

Deterrence constitutes a vital function of victim compensation, for several reasons. If the deterrence is effective, it will reduce (indeed, in economic theory, it should eliminate) the amount of wrongdoing before harm is inflicted, rather than simply shifting the losses after they occur. But this is a very big "if." For several reasons, deterrence is often weak or incomplete. Potential wrongdoers, like all of us, are sometimes irrational in the economic sense that they do not calculate the probabilities either of injuring someone or of being called to account. Even if they tried to calculate in this fashion, they would usually lack the necessary information about the state of the law and the expected harm (magnitude of the risk times the magnitude of the harm if it occurs) of their action. Deterrence would fail even with a perfectly informed, wholly rational wrongdoer (if such exists) so long as he knows that the penalty discounted by the probability of being held liable is low enough relative to the benefits to him from his misconduct.

Compensation of victims is not the only way to achieve deterrence, and may not be the best way. In the tort system, the wrongdoer pays damages measured by the victim's harm, but this amount may not be the level of damages that will produce the socially optimal level of deterrence. Where the wrongdoing is a crime subject to fines or imprisonment, these criminal sanctions may (or may not) produce more effective deterrence than victim compensation. (This is especially true where the criminal, being insolvent, cannot pay damages and no governmental compensation exists). Other noncompensation deterrents to wrongdoing include administrative regulation of the risk, social ostracism of and adverse publicity about wrongdoers, public education about the conduct in question, etc. Indeed, depending on who is paying the compensation, it may actually weaken deterrence, as I discuss below in the section on distributive justice.

3. *Moral affirmation.* Compensation does not merely help to restore the victim to the status quo ante (corrective justice) and to create incentives for socially desirable conduct in the future (deterrence). It also affirms certain moral facts about the incident: the wrongfulness of what the injurer did, and the total or relative innocence of the victim. Absent a duty to pay and a right to receive compensation, this moral accounting might be merely abstract. In contrast, the specific transfer entailed by compensation makes both the moral failure of the injurer and the moral claim of the victim unmistakably clear. The clarity of this moral signal, however, partly depends on the source of compensation. If the payment comes from a government insurance fund, the signal is likely to be more muted and ambiguous than if it comes from the wrongdoer. The suggestion will be that the payment is simply the government's cost of doing business—the business of loss-spreading.

Compensation (or the lack of it) may also affirm other values. As Jack Rosenthal has noted, philanthropy instantiates the moral commitments of its donors. In some cases, private giving may exceed whatever remedies the government or the law provides, and may be actuated in part by a belief or fear that those remedies are inadequate. The interaction between public and private compensation is a complicated and important subject, worthy of far more attention than it ordinarily receives.

These private moral commitments may include not only empathy but what Rosenthal calls (in the context of the 9/11 charities) the donors' "vengeful philanthropy." That this was a unique response to a particularly detestable crime (i.e., terrorism) committed on American soil is further suggested by the observation that the American victims of terror committed overseas have elicited much less generous donations. Compensation may also affirm donors' conception of moral community. For example, compensation to the 9/11 victims by private charities and government programs reflect a sense of national community, while most other crimes and torts do not.

4. *Distributive justice.* Compensation can do more than establish a just and moral relationship between injurer and victim, as in corrective justice. When it is the community that compensates a victim—ordinarily through government-administered social insurance—the compensation also establishes a relationship of justice between community and victim. And when the community condemns the wrongdoer for the harm he inflicted on the victim—through imposition of tort damages, regulatory penalties, or criminal sanctions—it likewise establishes a justice relationship with the wrongdoer.

The community's relationship to the victim requires additional comment. When the community uses public funds to compensate victims, it is deciding that the victim's loss is one that should be spread among all of its members (i.e., taxpayers). The justification for governmental loss-spreading rests on some or all of a set of conventional but contestable assumptions. First, it assumes that people are risk-averse—that is, they would prefer to incur a small, certain cost now (in the form of increased taxes) in order to avoid the risk of a large loss to themselves in the future (an uncompensated injury). Second, it assumes that the loss of a dollar imposes greater unhappiness on a poor person than on a rich one. Third, it assumes that people will not (and perhaps should not) privately insure against these losses (or at least all of them). Finally, it assumes that government should bear the responsibility of spreading the loss. I now consider some of the most important arguments for and against requiring government to do so.

COMPENSATION BY GOVERNMENT

A liberal society presumes that government's role should generally be limited to doing for people what they cannot do for themselves. People can insure themselves privately against most losses from crime and other misfortunes, and most people do so. Although modern governments in fact manage risks in a multitude of ways, some special justification is needed before society assigns government this function. This justification, moreover, must go beyond the fact that victims would think themselves better off if the government did so; after all, those who are favored by government almost always think this. Three main justifications can be plausibly advanced: efficiency, redistribution, and special responsibility.

1. *Efficiency*. Government can be an efficient risk spreader. Government can exploit the "law of large numbers" in designing insurance pools, which tends to reduce unit administrative costs and enhance the statistical predictability of its underwriting decisions. This also enables it to identify some statistical risks that potential victims are less likely to appreciate and insure against. Government can also use law to coerce people into the insurance pool, which helps to overcome adverse selection, an important insurance market imperfection.

These strengths in government compensation, however, also entail some characteristic weaknesses. Mandated participation may be unfair to some who would prefer private insurance arrangements. Depending on whether and to what extent the compensation fund is financed by requiring risk-rated payments from wrongdoers, government insurance programs may offer little in the way of deterrence. Lacking a profit motive, government compensation funds often suffer from certain administrative inefficiencies, and their policies are often shaped by political factors.

2. *Redistribution*. It is just such political factors, of course, that make redistribution through government compensation possible and perhaps desirable. Such redistribution-through-compensation is especially attractive when victims are too poor to be able to self-insure against their losses or to insure through private insurance markets. On the other hand, this approach may be less justified where many of the program's beneficiaries are not poor and could self- or market-insure more efficiently than government can insure them.

3. *Special responsibility*. One may argue that government is responsible in some moral sense for the victim's loss. The government's responsibility for crimes committed by others is a complex matter, involving questions about the nature of victimization, causality, and the scope of public duty. Is there any set of coherent and consistent principles, for example, that can explain why some victims of misfortunes are compensated while most others—those born with congenital defects, low intelligence, susceptibility to grave diseases, or incompetent or abusive parents—are not? Even if we focus our attention on the victims of crimes, why are the victims of the 9/11 attacks compensated (most of them quite generously, I might add) while the victims of uninsured drunk drivers are not? (See "The 9/11 Compensation Fund" essay.) Why do many state laws compensate the victims of street crime but not the victims of economic crimes or medical malpractice who are unable to persuade lawyers to take their costly to litigate cases?

One answer might be that the compensable losses from crimes in these examples are due to wrongs that the government should have prevented. But this explanation only raises a host of other difficult questions. To begin with, government obviously cannot prevent all crimes, nor should it attempt to do so—any more than we should try to prevent all accidents.

Although we do not like to say it, some crimes—like many accidents—
are simply not worth preventing, given the prevention costs, scarce
enforcement resources, and other social priorities. As in tort law more
generally, governmental liability typically requires the victim to show
that the government was negligent—as where government owns property
on which injuries occur or has failed to exercise adequate supervision of
the use of weapons by the police. Can we say that a failure to prevent the
crimes for which compensation programs pay constitutes negligence?

In certain specific cases, this is surely so. The law, however, holds that
the police have no duty to protect specific individuals and thus that
police inaction is not tortious except under unusual conditions—for
example, when the police specifically told the victim that it would protect
him, the victim relied on this assurance, and the crime would not have
occurred had the police done so. As this last requirement (what lawyers
call "cause-in-fact") suggests, many crimes would occur even if the police
did what they are supposed to do.

Certain kinds of victims, moreover, are arguably in a better position to
prevent their harms than are the police. The distinction between "deserving" and "undeserving" victims, while often hard to draw, is nevertheless
drawn constantly by legislatures, politicians, juries, private institutions,
and public opinion. Some examples might include those who do not lock
their cars or apartments, or who walk in notoriously dangerous neighborhoods without taking reasonable precautions, or who drink themselves into oblivion in situations that leave them defenseless to predators.
To recognize the possibility that some victims are the best crime avoiders
is not to "blame the victim." Instead, it merely calls attention to an important but often-ignored fact: Crime prevention is the responsibility not
only of the government but of all of us.

Even in the strongest cases for compensation—where government
actually caused the victim's loss, as with illegal police actions—the law
often precludes government liability for damages even when it has clearly
violated the Constitution or a statute. Indeed, the Federal Tort Claims Act
expressly immunizes from governmental liability many *intentional* torts
(a category that includes some criminal acts) committed by federal officials. State laws confer a roughly similar set of immunities on state agencies and officials.

My point is not to defend these rules but to show that a program to compensate victims of crime constitutes an exception to a widespread, long-
standing pattern of noncompensation for governmental negligence or illegality. One can certainly criticize this traditional pattern—indeed, I wrote a
book, *Suing Government*, doing just that—but serious criticism demands
that we seriously consider the arguments that have supported noncompensation for so long. These arguments emphasize a number of factors more
or less peculiar to government, which I can only summarize here.

Government owes a legal duty to protect the general public, not individuals. Proving cause-in-fact in cases of governmental inaction is more problematic and error-prone than in cases of government action. Juries should not have the power to second-guess politically accountable officials. Government, as the ultimate "deep pocket" defendant, tends to attract spurious claims that will often be decided by juries who tend, as we all tend, to be more generous with what appears to be other people's money. Compensation will only take resources away from vital public functions. The prospect of officials' liability tends to distort their decision making in ways that are especially harmful to the public interest.

One might argue that terrorism is a special kind of crime such that the case for compensating victims of terrorism is stronger than that for compensating the victims of other kinds of crimes. Terrorism, one might say, is a relatively indiscriminate assault on the government or on the society as a whole, part of a premeditated ideological program seeking to create a climate of generalized fear, suspicion, and profound disorientation in which public and private life are utterly convulsed and deformed. Other crimes, in this view, are usually targeted on particular individuals and are motivated by more familiar reasons like greed, passion, revenge, and sociopathy. Terrorism is usually sponsored by a state or a network of organizations like Al Qaeda that is tantamount to a state-within-states, while conventional crime is primarily the work of individuals.

The important question for our purposes is whether victims of terror are more (or less) deserving of government compensation than victims of ordinary crime. The differences in the two categories are easily exaggerated. Organized crime entities, for example, resemble terrorist groups in many of these respects, although they tend to be nonideological; the Mafia, at least, focuses obsessively on economic gain and views some government officials (those whom it can corrupt) as allies. Terrorists sometimes operate without organizational support and often target individual victims. These overlaps help to explain certain similarities in legal techniques found in the RICO statute and the antiterrorism laws enacted in the wake of the Oklahoma City and 9/11 catastrophes. And in both cases, of course, the victims are equally innocent and suffer the same kinds of injuries.

But these similarities and differences do not really resolve the question of whether government should compensate victims of either category qua crime victims. (I add this qualification—qua crime victims—to remind us that government already pays for (or subsidizes) certain losses suffered by victims of both kinds, through other public programs like Social Security disability, Medicaid, Medicare, unemployment insurance, and the like). In my view, the differences do not justify treating the two categories differently for compensation purposes.

Compensation of victims can take many forms. Different rationales for compensation imply different legal techniques and constraints.

Compensation paid by injurers to victims through the tort system most directly advances the ideal of corrective justice, but this system exhibits many shortcomings. Government compensation avoids certain of these shortcomings but entails others. One of the most challenging is the need to justify compensating some victims but not others. To say that the government is "responsible" for compensation is to beg all of the difficult normative and empirical questions raised by the concept of responsibility. These questions are particularly important in a liberal society that limits the role of government in dealing with the many kinds of misfortunes that befall us.

If the experience of the 9/11 compensation program teaches us anything, it is that once the government fashions a special compensation program for one set of victims, it will find it difficult to deny such favorable treatment to others—at least as a logical and moral matter. When the line-drawing occurs, it is likely to be on political grounds, not logical or moral ones. Pending legislation that would extend the 9/11 program to the victims of Oklahoma City, Khobar Towers, the U.S.S. *Cole*, and other highly visible terrorist attacks may gain traction in part because the victims' claims are logically and morally indistinguishable from those of the 9/11 victims. In the end, however, the decisive factor will be political. The victim groups that will fare best are those that are easily identifiable, concentrated in important legislative districts, members of influential groups, suffer large losses in circumstances that are mediagenic and evoke widespread sympathy, and can more readily link those losses to government policy.

These factors help to explain why Congress has established special federal compensation programs for some occupational groups (e.g., veterans, uranium workers, and coal miners with black lung) and not for others (e.g., textile workers with brown lung), and for children with vaccine-related injuries but not for those with birth defects. (As I write, Congress is considering a compensation program for victims of asbestos exposure.)

Another lesson of the 9/11 program is that most people who sustain enormous emotional, economic, and personal losses and who receive government compensation for these losses will always approach their awards with a mixture of relief and resentment—relief because the money is a welcome balm for their suffering, and resentment because it can never replace what they have lost. Indeed, the very effort to attach a monetary value to their most precious relationships will affront many survivors, even as they feel obliged to accept it. The compensation will never be enough—not because they are greedy but because they are human and thus to a degree are inconsolable.

What this means, at a minimum, is that victim compensation programs will always be a source of contention and bitterness even as they are a source of assistance to those whom they serve. These programs, moreover, inevitably draw lines that will strike many others as arbitrary and unfair, excluding claimants who seem equally worthy from a logical and moral point of view. Finally, they create incentives for ("reward" would be an accurate but inflammatory synonym) people to define themselves as victims—as indeed they are—since only by doing so can they qualify for compensation. Whether this self-definition helps them to get beyond their losses or instead retards their recovery is an important question best left to psychologists.

⌁ 25 ⌁

The 9/11 Compensation Fund: A Bad Precedent

The window for filing applications to the 9/11 Victims Compensation Fund closed in December 2003. After vigorous, eleventh-hour efforts by fund administrators to persuade the remaining eligibles to enter the program, approximately 97 percent of the death claimants and more than four thousand personal injury claimants did so. Of the nonfilers, some took the tort option and are suing the airlines and others whom they deem responsible for their losses. Some did not press their claims in either forum, perhaps out of grief or fear of the daunting processes. In all, the fund paid some $7 billion to victims.

It is not too early to begin assessing the fund as a unique policy tool, as a model of a distinctive technique for compensating personal injury and death victims. This preliminary assessment can also shed light on how well the fund has performed the specific duties that Congress mandated in the Airline Transportation Safety and System Stabilization Act, a statute enacted with great haste and little deliberation less than two weeks after 9/11.

The law's chief aim was to keep the airlines aloft in an unprecedented crisis consisting of new terrorist threats, severely reduced traffic, potentially ruinous liability exposure, and skittish insurance markets. Several provisions addressed liability and insurance threats. First, the law limited airlines' tort exposure to the amount of liability insurance already in force on 9/11 ($6 billion). Second, the law provided a remedial alternative to the tort system for victims of physical harm or death caused by the crashes. Creating the fund in the U.S. Department of Justice, it authorized administrators to compensate victims under a number of rules, including requiring them to waive their tort claims in order to be eligible for compensation. Some rules are statutory, others have been adopted by regulation, and the act vests the fund's special master, Kenneth Feinberg, with enormous discretion to interpret the statute and frame regulations.

Some of these rules are consistent with the tort system, and the statute uses many terms taken from tort law. Other rules might be considered "tort-plus." For example, the law defines economic loss very broadly to include not only the usual out-of-pocket costs but "loss of business or employment opportunities" (presumably meaning future income or profit) if allowed under state law. It also pays for "nonpecuniary losses of any kind or nature," apparently even where state law does not allow it. Still other fund rules depart from tort system principles. Thus, awards are reduced by "all" collateral sources, even including life insurance (but not including private charity). The fund must make awards within 120 days after the claim application is substantially complete. No judicial review is permitted. In death cases, a $250,000 minimum award for pain-and-suffering applies.

Finally, some of the fund's features deviate sharply from tort law. Unlike tort (but like some social insurance schemes), the act decouples the goals of compensation and deterrence. Many lawyers are representing claimants without fee. The fund's administrator and staff view themselves as victims' advocates; they have vigorously encouraged claims, revised their rules in response to victims' criticisms, and sought to humanize an irreducibly bureaucratic process.

By almost all accounts, the fund has succeeded admirably in the difficult, morbid task that Congress assigned it. From its inception, the fund raised a host of important questions about our society's most fundamental notions of corrective and distributive justice, questions that are worth revisiting now that the claims period has ended. Perhaps the most basic is the question of what policy analysts call horizontal equity, constitutional theorists call equal protection, and common lawyers call analogical reasoning: whether the system treats like cases alike. On this important criterion, I would give Congress a failing grade. It is not simply that the fund compensates the victims of one set of terrorist attacks (9/11) but not victims of other terrorist attacks on American and foreign soil (Oklahoma City, Khobar Towers, and others). It is also that the fund pays the 9/11 victims while most other innocent victims of crime, intentional wrongdoing, or negligence must suffer without remedy unless they are "lucky" enough to have been injured by someone who can be held liable under the tort system's peculiar, often arbitrary rules and who is also sufficiently insured or secure financially to pay the judgment. And as already noted, the fund's awards are far more generous and quickly and easily obtained than a tort remedy in most cases. This is particularly true where, as in the 9/11 litigation against the airlines and the World Trade Center, any fault-based liability is highly doubtful and would in any event take many years to establish, and where a third of any recovery would probably go to the lawyers.

As a political matter, of course, Congress's vastly superior treatment of the 9/11 victims is perfectly intelligible. After all, Congress wanted to protect the airlines against potentially massive liability. It also saw the 9/11 victims as a symbol of a unique trauma inflicted on the nation's collective psyche, trauma that had to be repaired as swiftly as possible. But as a matter of fair and equal treatment of other equally innocent victims of misfortune, the fund's scheme seems morally obtuse and impossible to justify. Special master Feinberg is keenly aware of this dilemma. He wonders how he should be expected to reply to the family whose equally innocent loved one died in any accident other than 9/11, including a terrorist incident, and who were to ask, "Why not us?"

One possible reply to at least some of them—the family of a soldier killed in Iraq, for example—is that compensation for such a loss is already available under social insurance programs such as workers' compensation or Social Security (or its military equivalent). These programs, like the fund, pay victims on a no-fault basis and usually with little delay. Again, however, such programs are far less generous than the tortlike awards that the fund provides to the families of 9/11 victims.

This difference between tort and the fund in turn highlights one of the most important questions concerning the approach of American society to misfortune. Under what conditions should society (1) provide victims with an individually tailored, full compensation remedy, (2) provide them with one that treats them more as members of broad victim categories receiving awards addressed only to their basic needs, or (3) leave them to private charity, self-insurance, or other forms of self-protection?

This is not the place to answer such immensely difficult and controversial questions; here are just a few of the complications. First, the concept of "misfortune" is highly contested in courtrooms, legislatures, and private discourse among citizens. Are smokers who die of lung cancer victims of misfortune? What about unbelted drivers or passengers who suffer injuries that would have been prevented? Or people whose genetic endowment makes them more vulnerable to certain illnesses? A second and related point is that we disagree sharply about the roles that government and private entities or individuals should play in bearing risks, even of those losses widely viewed as misfortunes. Examples include health care costs, sudden declines in property values, and inadequate public schools. Third, there is little consensus on the nature, extent, and merits of tort law as a background, rights-oriented, fault-based system for compensating certain types of injuries.

Small wonder, then, that American society has deployed such a messy, ostensibly incoherent, if not unprincipled, mixture of institutions and approaches—tort, social insurance, private insurance, contract, charity, private savings, categorical programs—for remedying misfortunes of one kind or another. The 9/11 fund well reflects this characteristically American eclecticism and the extraordinary circumstances of its sudden birth. As I discussed earlier, the fund creates a remedy that combines many features of tort law with some elements that are more characteristic of social insurance and, at least in the collateral source deduction rule, private insurance. The result is what Stanford Law School's Robert Rabin aptly calls a "hybrid" system in which claimants seek individualized, case-by-case determinations leading to compensation at tort (or tort-plus) levels, while also having the benefits—and some constraints—of collective, more categorical compensation at lower levels through a relatively inexpensive and riskless administrative process. It is doubtful, however, whether a future administrative program for victims of a large-scale catastrophe would be as flexible, personalized, and antibureaucratic as the 9/11 fund has been.

This is hardly the first time that American society has confronted the question of how the government should approach private misfortune. Conventional wisdom dates this confrontation to the New Deal era, when the federal government responded to the economic and psychological crisis caused by the Great Depression with a congeries of programs that put all levels of government into the business of bearing and spreading risks of misfortune previously borne by individual citizens and families. Harvard sociologist Theda Skocpol takes this story back further in time to the Civil War veterans' pensions at the federal level and an array of social welfare programs at the state level in the early decades of the twentieth century.

An intriguing footnote to the decision to create the 9/11 fund is the research of Michele Landis Dauber, a lawyer-sociologist at Stanford Law School. Dauber has already unearthed a surprising number of relevant federal laws going back to the early days of the Republic, laws that, mutatis mutandis, grew out of analogous social misfortunes and in some ways prefigured the 9/11 fund. In her telling, both the nature of the crisis and the political-legal response that led to the fund (and the kinds of criticisms the fund has aroused) have historical antecedents. Although many of the early compensation laws were private bills to relieve a relatively small number of individuals, compensation was also sometimes provided on a more categorical basis through administrative mechanisms that she contends foreshadowed the modern welfare state. The triggering events were often fires, floods, storms, earthquakes, and similar disasters, but some of them involved foreign raids on American communities, the early nineteenth-century equivalent of the terrorist attacks of 9/11.

A particularly arresting example was a law enacted by Congress in 1816 to compensate citizens for property lost, captured, or destroyed by the British troops and their Indian allies during the unpopular War of 1812 in a category of cases defined, albeit ambiguously, in the law. As Dauber shows, the public justifications advanced for this compensation program were similar to those advanced for compensating the 9/11 victims. Even more interesting from today's vantage point, the administrator ("commissioner") of the 1816 law, Richard Bland Lee, had to make numerous eligibility decisions of a kind all too familiar to Ken Feinberg. Lee's decisions, moreover, generated a furious backlash in Congress strikingly reminiscent of the contemporary politics of welfare entitlement programs. In 1817 Lee's authority under the increasingly unpopular law was severely curtailed.

Feinberg's political and administrative skills evidently exceed Lee's. Although Feinberg has been criticized and was sued by some high-income families angry at both the life insurance offsets and the fund's informal cap on high-end compensation, he and the fund have benefited from the strong bipartisan political and judicial support for the program. The prospect for similar programs in a future where terrorist attacks may become all too common is unclear. Perhaps 9/11 will continue to be seen as sui generis, limiting the power of the next victims' "Why not us?" lament to obtain a similar remedy. We must pray that there will be few of them.

∽ 26 ∽

Adjudicating Terrorism: A Hybrid Model Court

The Supreme Court in its recent rulings has given U.S. citizens who are captives in the war on terror, as well as noncitizen Guantánamo detainees, the right to hearings. Now comes the hard part: what kinds of hearings, in which courts, by what process? The Court wisely refrained from answering these questions in detail. Arguments on the specifics had not been presented to the Court, and the limited guidance that the justices did offer was more intuitive than analytical. Wisdom aside, this sort of self-restraint is constitutionally required: Article 1, Section 8, Clause 14 gives Congress—not the judicial or the executive branch—the authority to make rules for the armed forces, including the initial design of hearings for the prisoners. This is a task of the utmost delicacy, affected at almost every step by imperatives of due process, separation of powers, and military effectiveness. Striking the optimal balance is not simply a matter of defining justice, liberty, and security and then trading them off against one another when they conflict. Congress must also make difficult judgments about the facts "on the ground"—literally, on the unmarked and constantly changing battlefields of this war—facts that are not accessible to ordinary citizens or even to most public officials or lawyers defending suspected terrorists. Obviously, a political consensus on fair procedures under these unusual conditions is bound to be elusive.

As it happens, Congress confronted and solved a quite similar problem only eight years ago. In 1996, after the Oklahoma City bombing (by citizen terrorists) raised concerns over further attacks, it created a special Alien Terrorist Removal Court (ATRC) to adjudicate the deportation of noncitizens charged with terrorism on the basis of classified information. The ATRC consists of five federal trial judges. The government applies to one of them in secret, asserting probable cause to believe that a particular person is a noncitizen terrorist in the United States and that an ordinary public proceeding would pose a risk to national security. If the judge agrees, he commences a proceeding that mixes secrecy and openness. There is a public hearing, and the accused can attend, be represented by counsel, offer evidence, and examine and challenge the government's unclassified evidence.

Classified evidence, however, must be reviewed by the judge in private. He then has the duty to preserve its classification while giving the accused access to as much evidence as possible. If the government wants to rely on the secret evidence, it must prepare an adequate declassified summary of it for the accused. But if the judge decides such a summary would threaten a person's life or health, the hearing can go forward without it. Either way, the judge adjudicates the case based on all the evidence—classified and unclassified. If it shows the accused to be a terrorist, the judge must order deportation; if it doesn't, he must release the accused (except if the judge finds that release would seriously harm national security, in which case he can still order deportation).

The delicate balance of rights and security is most favorable to an accused who is a legal permanent resident because he is entitled to an attorney with a special security clearance, who is authorized to examine and challenge the classified evidence. The ATRC has never been used to deport suspects (mostly because the government has been able to use standard procedures), but Congress could apply its methods—its balance of national security and due process—to the hearings newly mandated by the Supreme Court. The hearings could be used to test the government's underlying factual claims against detainees. Are they enemy combatants or were they merely in the wrong place at the wrong time? Are we still in such a state of war that continued detentions are required? Would defense lawyers really impede interrogation? Congress could also modify the hearings process within the limits set by the Supreme Court, varying the rules when applied to citizens and various categories of noncitizens, to those held abroad or in the United States, to emergency and nonemergency situations, to different levels of defense lawyer involvement, and to particular governmental purposes—deportation, interrogation, preventive detention, or criminal prosecution.

New due-process models like these are essential because none of the traditional categories for the accused—citizen enemy, prisoner of war under the Geneva Convention, deportable alien, criminal defendant—fully captures the character and status of many terrorists. Fortunately, Congress's creation of the ATRC shows not just that useful hybrids can be fashioned but that they are also politically feasible.

– PART V –

A NATION OF IMMIGRANTS

America has always been a nation of immigrants, and never more than today. During the 1990s and early years of the new century, the level of more or less permanent immigration, legal and illegal, has reached the highest levels in American history—probably more than fifteen million during this period. This influx has brought the percentage of foreign-born in the population to more than 12 percent, approaching the record percentage set early in the last century at the height of the migration from Europe. The demographics of the new immigrants are also unprecedented, with the vast majority being people of color migrating from Latin America and Asia, many on the wrong side of a large education gap separating them from the rest of the population. (Owing to those admitted under the skills-based preferences—fewer than 12 percent of legal admissions in 2003—many other newcomers are better educated than the average American.) Immigration now accounts for about 40 percent of the nation's population growth. All signs point to a long-term continuation of this expansive flow—I have described it as a one-way ratchet upward—which has been slowed, perhaps only temporarily, by the processing delays occasioned by post-9/11 security concerns.

What, then, does immigration portend for America's future? Five essays shed light on this compelling question. The first discusses whether immigration seriously threatens the nation's coherence and cohesion, as many commentators fear, and I explain the reasons for my optimistic conclusion that it does not. In the second, a *New York Times* op-ed piece drawn from a much longer journal article, I analyze our moral and legal obligation to provide sanctuary to refugees. I propose an innovative market-based mechanism to distribute refugee protection burdens more widely, thereby increasing the number who can be protected and reducing the costs of doing so. The third essay, written shortly after President Bush's election in 2000, argues that the immigration reform legislation enacted in 1996, while addressing a genuine enforcement problem in removing criminal aliens, is seriously flawed and should be amended to deal more justly with the many cases of individual inequity and hardship. The next essay explores whether and how our conception of citizenship may be altered by the war on terror, particularly in light of the prosecution of some American citizens with only tenuous connections to American society. The final essay, written as a comment for the *Los Angeles Times* on a November 2004 referendum proposal to permit noncitizens to vote in San Francisco school board elections, canvasses the arguments for and against such a change. It concludes that the proposal, which was defeated, was not in the best interests of either immigrants or the larger society, although some legal changes to promote greater participation might be warranted.

↔ **27** ↔

Immigration, Diversity, and Nationhood: The Formula Still Works

America is a nation of immigrants. This hackneyed truth, however, raises a paradoxical question: Can we be a nation when we are so diverse?

A century ago, the confident, affirmative answer to this question was expressed in another cliché: the melting pot. Today, however, many Americans prefer other images—a stew, a salad, a mosaic—in which the many parts do not fully merge into the whole but instead retain their distinctive identities. To some Americans, this metaphorical shift calls for celebration; to others it is a source of profound anxiety. Although the jury is still out, I believe that the ultimate verdict will vindicate the optimists.

Immigration law has always mirrored the tensions among these competing images. In the beginning, there wasn't much law. Local communities actively recruited immigrants to work in their high-growth economies or else to join them as coreligionists. The few legal restrictions newcomers faced were imposed by states and localities concerned with revenue, public health, and the control of indigents. (Slaves, of course, were not voluntary immigrants and were intricately regulated.) Federal immigration restrictions, which would largely supplant state regulation, were not adopted until 1875 and did not significantly limit entry (except by Asians) until the 1920s.

Until recently, the constitutional law of immigration was remarkably simple and straightforward. The "plenary power doctrine" left Congress free to treat aliens pretty much as it liked, both procedurally and substantively. The Supreme Court in a 1953 case defined aliens' due process rights as whatever process Congress chose to provide. Congress delegated enormous administrative discretion to the Immigration and Naturalization Service (INS), and although aliens could challenge their deportation orders, the scope of review was usually narrow.

Even during the 1960s and 1970s, when the courts expanded constitutional rights and often overturned agency decisions in environmental, consumer, and other regulatory cases, immigration law remained anomalous, resisting the dominant rights-oriented trends in public law. While the courts occasionally read statutes creatively to protect aliens, the more typical pattern was one of abject judicial deference, producing a strikingly simple rule of decision: Unless the INS erred egregiously, the government won. Immigration law practice remained something of a backwater.

The first persistent signs of change occurred in the early 1980s, when political and doctrinal developments began to propel immigration law into the mainstream. An unprecedented surge of illegal migration to the United States, along with the new asylum process established under the Refugee Act of 1980, provided even undocumented aliens who were bound to lose on the merits with a fragile procedural foothold in the country. As a result of the new law, even a weak asylum claim could delay their removal for months or years. Not surprisingly, hundreds of thousands of undocumented aliens invoked the new process.

The courts now faced a host of new and difficult legal issues. They had to define the legal standards—substantive, procedural, and evidentiary—governing asylum claims, standards derived from both domestic and international law. Moreover, many hard constitutional issues were raised by the government's efforts to interdict aliens on the high seas or at the border, discourage them from applying for asylum, deny them social services and work permits, and detain (i.e., imprison) them pending completion of their proceedings (or indefinitely, if their countries refused to repatriate them).

An increasingly sophisticated, resourceful, and well-organized immigration bar litigated these complex issues. In addition to private firms, enterprising, imaginative young public interest lawyers funded by foundation grants, public subsidies, and statutory fee awards, and sometimes allied with pro bono private practitioners and law school clinics, won many important cases against an overburdened, often out-lawyered INS. To be sure, most of these victories were won in the lower federal courts, while the U.S. Supreme Court continued to defer to Congress and the INS, citing the old plenary power chestnuts. But even the Court renovated immigration law during the 1980s, liberally interpreting the procedural rights of returning resident aliens, the statutory rights of asylum claimants under the Refugee Act, and the constitutional rights of undocumented alien children to attend public schools at taxpayers' expense.

Meanwhile, legal immigration was steadily rising to near-record levels. Many lawyers prospered by serving corporate clients, which routinely sought green cards, nonimmigrant (i.e., temporary) visas, status adjustments, and other immigration benefits needed for their existing and future employees. Family-based immigration practice, often overlapping with the business side, also grew. By 1990, business immigration law was a recognized boutique specialty in many large, diversified, full-service private firms. And as labor shortages developed during the mid- and late 1990s, this area of practice boomed. (Indeed, Congress later authorized employers in the computer industry to import still more skilled workers, before cutting back during the post-bubble recession.) Immigration law and practice had finally come of age.

Ironically, even the rise of illegal immigration has fueled business immigration practice. Congress's enactment of employer sanctions in 1986, although aimed at illegal aliens, has given immigration lawyers new corporate counseling and litigation opportunities. Moreover, almost half of the illegal aliens entered the United States legally but overstayed or otherwise violated their visa conditions. Their employers must often hire lawyers to prevent the INS from removing them.

While many of the recent changes target immigration lawyers' domestic and foreign business clients, other reforms primarily affect individual immigrants and their families. In 1996, Congress passed three statutes—the Antiterrorism and Effective Death Penalty Act (AEDPA), the Illegal Immigration Reform and Immigrant Responsibility Act (IIRIRA), and the landmark welfare reform law—that profoundly altered the balance that Congress and the courts had previously struck between law enforcement interests and immigrant rights.

AEDPA and IIRIRA impose harsh restrictions on the procedures available to determine aliens' legal status. (See "Reforming the 1996 Immigration Reform" essay.) IIRIRA creates a process to summarily exclude aliens who arrive at the U.S. border without documents or with papers deemed fraudulent by INS inspectors, an error-prone process that may impede legitimate asylum claims. It also severely limits judicial review of INS decisions. And both the new laws impose particularly tough sanctions on aliens who committed crimes even long ago, requiring the INS to detain and remove them swiftly. At the same time, Congress also eliminated most of the INS's traditional discretion to waive exclusion, deportation, and detention for humanitarian, administrative, or other compelling reasons.

Many of the new provisions, such as one barring out-of-status aliens from receiving a legal visa for many years, target illegal aliens. Some, however, restrict even law-abiding, long-term legal immigrants. For example, IIRIRA makes it harder for low-income families to bring their relatives to the United States, and the welfare reform law, even after some liberalizing amendments, leaves many legal immigrants ineligible for most federally funded and state funded benefits, including SSI, AFDC, and food stamps. The 1996 laws together constitute the most radical reform of immigration law in decades—or perhaps ever. They responded to some genuinely difficult law enforcement problems. Congress, for example, was properly concerned about the endless procedural delays that many immigration lawyers and their clients have used to prolong their stays while they work and try to remain permanently through marriage, employment, amnesty, the visa lottery, or going underground if necessary. Congress was also concerned about the soaring criminal alien population. In 1980, fewer than one thousand federal inmates were foreign born, 3.6 percent of the total. By 1996, the number had grown to almost 31,000, or 29 percent of the total. Much the same was true of state prisons; the foreign born accounted for an estimated 21 percent of California's prisoners and 13 percent of New York's. Nationwide, 300,000 or more deportable criminal aliens were in custody or under other legal supervision—almost ten times as many as in 1980—at an estimated cost of $6 billion per year. Yet despite a high-priority INS effort to deport these criminals, the agency managed to remove only 55,000 of them in 1998. (And even that low number represented a major improvement for the agency.)

Still, some of the new provisions are so extreme, misguided, or perverse that even the INS leadership considers them arbitrary, unfair, and unadministrable. Precluding the INS from granting aliens discretionary relief from deportation in hardship cases prevents the agency from making the humane, prudent adjustments that are often needed. Discretionary relief can also enable the agency to use its scarce enforcement resources more effectively and avoid public censure and embarrassment when its absurdly and cruelly inflexible decisions are brought to light, as they frequently are. The law's summary removal procedure for undocumented asylum claimants gives even the lowest-level inspector practically final say over such life-and-death issues as whether the individual will face persecution if returned to his country of origin. And the new restrictions on judicial review may well be unconstitutional if interpreted to preclude access to habeas corpus.

There is much to criticize in these measures, and Congress should revise them accordingly. Many immigrant advocates view these provisions as proof of a racist, xenophobic public backlash against recent immigrants, most of whom now come from underdeveloped countries in Latin America and Asia, not Europe. These advocates also point to California voters' approval of ballot propositions in 1994 and 1998. The former, which was largely struck down by a federal court, would bar illegal aliens from access to many public services—an approach also adopted by Arizona in 2004. The latter, later echoed in some other states, limits bilingual education programs.

Public attitudes toward immigration, however, are far more complicated—and intriguing. Consider the following facts. First, challenges to the historically high levels of legal immigration set by the 1990 law have consistently failed. Congress has shown little interest even in the restrictions recommended by its own blue-ribbon Commission on

Immigration Reform. Second, even illegal aliens have fared well in Congress, which not only legalized 2.7 million of them, mostly Mexicans, in the late 1980s but also, a decade later, enacted a new amnesty for some 400,000 more from elsewhere in Central America. In the wake of Hurricane Mitch, even more received "temporary" amnesty. Congress also grandfathered in other illegal aliens under a now-lapsed provision allowing them to gain permanent residence simply by paying a $1,000 fee and filing their green cards in the United States, thus relieving them even of the inconvenience of going home to apply for U.S. admission. President Bush favors a large new amnesty for Mexican guestworkers. Third, Congress and the states restored many of the SSI and food stamp benefits for low-income immigrants that Congress had eliminated in 1996, although recent and new immigrants often remain ineligible. Finally, the kind of xenophobic violence and politics that have become so chillingly common in Europe and Asia are relatively rare here. Many Republican Party leaders strongly support immigration, seeing that the social conservatism, upward mobility, and entrepreneurial spirit of many newcomers could attract them to a more immigrant-friendly GOP, a point underscored by the influential role Hispanic voters played during the 2004 elections in battleground states like California, Texas, and Florida as well as a growing number of others.

These recent gains for immigrants, however, have aroused some public concerns. Illegal immigration continues at very high levels, and even new legal immigrants are less white, English-speaking, and Protestant than their predecessors. Nor is California the only state where bilingual education has become a major curricular and fiscal battleground, as evidence mounts that many costly programs retard English fluency. About half the states have now established English as their official language. The increasingly politicized debate over ethnicity and language, coupled with attacks by some immigrant advocates on the traditional assimilative ideal, have aggravated old anxieties about what Arthur Schlesinger calls the "disuniting of America." Indeed, the affirmative action debate has been sharpened by the anomaly that newcomers who never suffered discrimination in the United States compete for preferences with the already beleaguered descendants of enslaved African Americans. Even citizenship has come under a cloud. Federal prosecutors claimed that over 13,000 naturalization exams were falsified in the late 1990s. Growing numbers of new Americans hold dual nationality and may be able to vote in their old countries. Some U.S. cities plan to allow noncitizens to vote. A number of American citizens have been held (and one convicted) in connection with post-9/11 terrorism investigations. (I focus on citizenship-related developments in the other essays in this part.)

Despite these challenges, public support for legal, ethnically diverse immigration remains strong, most legal immigrants appear to be assimilating as quickly as their predecessors did, and the strength of the American polity and economy remains the envy of the world. More than ever, we are the nation of immigrants that our political myths and rhetoric proclaim us to be. Although diversity poses an unprecedented test of our national unity, the evidence so far suggests that we are passing it with flying colors.

∽ **28** ∽

Refugees: Protecting More by Sharing the Burden

As the worldwide tide of refugees swells remorselessly—Sudan is only the latest in a long list of recent catastrophes—the international community seems paralyzed. The UN High Commissioner on Refugees admits that he cannot cope; individual nations make only token contributions, though some, like the United States and some Nordic countries, are more dutiful than others. Forced repatriation is an unpalatable option; it simply returns refugees to their persecutors. Meanwhile, millions of refugees languish for months or years in squalid camps, prey to disease, famine and continued displacement.

These failures demand a new approach. Clearly, the family of nations has an obligation to share the burden; the question is how to overcome each nation's tendency to sit back and hope someone else will pay the freight. Such an effort must begin by recognizing that nations differ greatly in their willingness and ability to absorb refugees. Some are wealthy, others poor. Some are thinly settled, others overcrowded. Some have docile populations; others cannot protect refugees from violence.

Why not use these differences to promote international burden-sharing? Usually, people with diverse preferences and resources turn those differences to mutual advantage by trading. When a buyer values a car more than cash, and a seller prefers cash to her car, they cut a deal and both benefit. Now apply the principle to refugees. Suppose that the U.N. or a regional body established a yearly refugee protection quota for each participating nation, set up trading rules, and then allowed nations to trade protection duties. If these duties and bargains could be made enforceable, what would happen? Very likely, a rich but crowded country like Japan would discharge its obligation by paying a poor but thinly settled one like Russia to accept its quota. Russia in turn might pay even more receptive nations to take on part of its quota.

Why might nations join such a system? Most countries are vulnerable to refugee crises. Tradeable quotas would offer them a form of disaster insurance: They would assume a certain small burden (their quota) to avoid the risk of an uncertain larger one (a sudden refugee flood). For the recalcitrant ones, powerful members like the United States and Canada could impose foreign aid, trade, and immigration sanctions. By assuring each nation that it would bear only its fair share of the burden, the system could attract more takers.

This kind of enforced burden-sharing has shown promise in other areas. The Clean Air Act reduces pollution more effectively and cheaply by letting polluters trade a limited number of air pollution rights. New Jersey municipalities must provide their fair share of affordable housing, but they may buy and sell their obligations to do so; as a result, wealthy suburbs pay cities like Newark to build housing for poor people. The Kyoto Treaty, which has just gone into effect without our participation, allocates responsibility for curbing greenhouse gases among nations according to pollution levels, wealth, and other criteria. The agency allocating the refugee quotas could give special consideration to factors like language; for example, French-speaking countries might be encouraged to accept Haitians. It could prohibit refugee-receiving nations from discriminating against ethnic minorities, and monitor human rights conditions in the refugees' countries of origin so that they could eventually be repatriated.

Many will find the notion of trading refugees repugnant to humanitarian ideals, but the contrary is true. Relying only on the altruism of a few nations to protect refugees simply means that most receive no protection at all. But by using the self-interest of all nations to drive refugee burden-sharing, we might advance human rights better than the present broken system.

~ **29** ~

Reforming the 1996 Immigration Reform: Advice to President Bush

Now that you are about to be safely ensconced in the White House, it is time to vindicate your campaign promise to clean up the mess in Washington. Although you surely were most concerned about the messes perpetrated by your opponents, a few of them were bipartisan. Those are often the hardest to rectify. After all, both parties invested political capital in creating them, and neither wants to admit that a mistake was made, much less that it was partly responsible for it.

The 1996 immigration law is an example, and its reform presents an unusual opportunity for bipartisan progress. In the Illegal Immigration Reform and Immigrant Responsibility Act (IIRIRA), Congress virtually rewrote the immigration statute's enforcement provisions to accelerate the deportation of unsuccessful asylum seekers, convicted criminals, and other aliens who have no right to remain in the United States; Congress also sought to ensure that the Immigration and Naturalization Service effectively controlled those aliens, so that they would definitely be removed when their time came.

Although few people would seriously disagree with these goals, some of the means chosen to implement them are unjust, inefficient, and unworkable. In order to speed up and ensure the removals, Congress mandated ninety-day, and possibly indefinite, detention (i.e., imprisonment) of almost all deportable aliens, and imposed harsh, new, and retroactively applied grounds for deportation. It severely restricted judicial review and many other procedural rights long enjoyed by aliens. It also narrowed the discretion the INS had been able to use to provide relief in hardship cases or to temper the letter of the law when its rigid application would be unjust to U.S. citizens or legal resident aliens.

Such injustices have multiplied under IIRIRA. Most involve long-term resident aliens whom the INS now wants to deport for a minor crime committed long ago and never repeated and which may not even have been a ground for deportation at that time. Other injustices involve people facing indefinite detention not because they have committed crimes but because they are here illegally and come from countries that refuse to take them back. Many have U.S. citizen spouses and children who will either have to live apart from their deported family member or join him in what amounts to permanent exile from the only home he has ever known. Until 1996, INS could have considered equitable relief in hardship cases. Now the law ties its hands, or at least that has been the agency's position.

You and the Congress can readily clean up this particular mess without impeding the swift removal of serious criminals. You should restore INS discretion to deal flexibly and fairly with these cases and provide more guidance as to the appropriate criteria. You should make detention of asylum seekers pending removal only presumptive, not automatic, and you should limit deportable offenses to serious crimes not defined retroactively. You should reinstate judicial review not just to the constitutional minimum (which the Supreme Court may order anyway) but to the level necessary to ensure INS compliance with the law, which is a chronic problem.

Admittedly, some will attack these proposals as being soft on crime, limiting our national sovereignty, encouraging illegal migration, and helping immigration lawyers. Sometimes, however, making a tough law fairer is not only good policy but good politics—the same reason that many states are now reforming an unfair death penalty process. Isn't that what a compassionate conservative is supposed to do?

∽ 30 ∽

Citizenship after 9/11: Continuity and Change

The U.S. Supreme Court's recent decisions in *Rasul v. Bush* and *Hamdi v. Rumsfeld* concerning the hearing rights of terrorism suspects detained at Guantánamo and in the United States have received much public attention, and deservedly so. By anyone's definition, these are landmark decisions—both for their holdings and for their supporting rhetoric about constitutional limits on the commander-in-chief during wartime. Less obvious but equally important, the decisions cast a spotlight on the status of American citizenship in the post-9/11 world.

One little-noted feature of the Court's analysis was its differential treatment of the U.S. citizen detainee, Hamdi, and the noncitizen detainees in Guantánamo. Although the Court did not prescribe in detail the kinds of hearings to which the two groups are entitled (and was especially cryptic about the nature of the Guantánamo hearings), it seems clear that citizens like Hamdi will be able to claim more procedural protections than noncitizens can. This may be true, moreover, whether the detainees are held onshore or abroad—although this is less certain. Also left open is the role that defense lawyers will be allowed to play in pre-hearing interrogations. Here too, however, citizens are likely to have more extensive rights than noncitizens.

This difference raises basic questions about the nature and meaning of citizenship. Why does the law distinguish between citizens and noncitizens at all? For which purposes should it do so, and with what legal consequences? More specifically, should detainees' procedural rights turn on their citizenship? And most fundamentally, who should answer these questions—the U.S. Congress? The courts? The military? International tribunals?

Questions like these are particularly vexing in the case of a citizen such as Hamdi. Born in the United States, Hamdi left with his family for Saudi Arabia as a child, never (so far as we know) to return until seized on the battlefield in Afghanistan and brought here for interrogation and processing as an enemy combatant. Assuming that citizens can claim greater rights than noncitizens, is Hamdi—a man with no apparent links to the United States other than the accident of birth here—the kind of citizen who should receive them? The Constitution's answer appears to be yes.

Four aspects of citizenship are most relevant to cases like Hamdi: acquisition, duality, loss, and differential rights:

Acquisition. Most countries today base their citizenship, at least in part, on the jus soli (or birthright) principle—the idea that with very minor exceptions, anyone born on its territory is, simply by virtue of that fact, a citizen. Even some nations like Germany that traditionally limited citizenship to those with a common ethnicity have recently added some jus soli elements. The United States, however, has the most expansive version of jus soli citizenship, extending it even to the native-born children of illegal aliens and temporary visitors, however briefly either the mother or the native-born child is here—in Hamdi's case, not very long. For those not born here, naturalization is also relatively simple, requiring only five years' legal residency (three, if married to a citizen), good moral character, and the most rudimentary knowledge of the English language and American government. Under the principle of jus sanguinis (law of descent), foreign-born children of an American parent can often acquire citizenship without meeting even these standards.

Dual citizenship. Easy acquisition of U.S. citizenship, combined with nationality laws of other countries and cross-national intermarriage, makes dual or even triple citizenship increasingly common. The children of such marriages who are born in the United States often enjoy both American citizenship through birth and their parents' citizenship(s) by descent. Hamdi, for example, was an American citizen by birth in the United States and a Saudi citizen by descent from his parents. In addition, although immigrants naturalizing here must renounce their earlier allegiances, their countries of origin may decide to treat such renunciations as legally ineffective, in which case they retain their original (renounced) nationalities as well as their new American one. In the past, the U.S. government discouraged dual nationality, seeing it as a potential source of conflicts of loyalty, diplomatic disputes, and other problems. Today, however, the government is resigned to it.

Loss of citizenship. If American citizenship is easy to acquire, it is also difficult to lose—unless the citizen intentionally expatriates himself in a formal document before a government official. Beginning in 1907, Congress enacted provisions that denationalized U.S. citizens who committed specified acts. (A woman's acquiring a foreign nationality through marriage was one such act, an egregiously discriminatory provision upheld by the Supreme Court but later repealed by Congress.) Expatriating acts included such conduct as naturalizing in or declaring allegiance to a foreign country, voting in a foreign election, deserting the U.S. military in a time of war, avoiding military service during wartime by leaving or remaining outside the country, returning to and living in one's country of origin for a certain period after having naturalized in the United States, serving in a foreign government, and, of course, treason. In a zigzag series of denationalization decisions culminating in the 1967 case of *Afroyim v. Rusk*, the Court developed a rule that denies Congress any power to deprive a citizen of his citizenship without his consent. This rule, now codified in statute, limits denationalization to the rare situation in which one commits a legally defined expatriating act specifically intending to relinquish citizenship.

Differential rights. Traditionally, federal and much state law allowed government and employers to favor citizens over noncitizens in the allocation of public benefits and jobs. This was justified on the theory (to the extent one was articulated) that these were discretionary privileges, not rights, and that visitors had weaker claims on them than citizens did. Supreme Court decisions, however, gradually limited the states' power to discriminate against noncitizens; in 1971, the Court rejected a state law denying noncitizens otherwise available welfare benefits. Thereafter, the law tended to minimize the differences between the legal rights (and duties, which are minimal in both cases) of citizens and noncitizens. I have termed this a "devaluation" of citizenship and argued that, although this reduced immigrants' incentives to naturalize, it was on balance desirable that the law treated citizens and noncitizens largely the same. (The main exceptions were the citizens' right to vote, their higher priority in bringing close relative immigrants to the United States, and their eligibility for some public jobs barred to noncitizens.) In 1996, Congress seemed to "revalue" citizenship by enacting a welfare reform law that limited noncitizens' access to a number of federally funded benefit programs—a discrimination later upheld by the courts. Within a few years, however, Congress restored some of these benefits, and most of the high-immigration states used their own funds to replace some of the withdrawn support, so that most (though not all) legal immigrants can now claim much the same basic benefits that their citizen counterparts enjoy.

For almost all Americans, the idea of an exclusive national citizenship, one that draws a sharp line between members and nonmembers and treats the latter unequally in certain respects, is unexceptionable. To many, this idea is part of what it means to be an American. Fairness, in this conventional view, requires only that U.S. citizenship be available on easy terms to all long-term immigrants on a nondiscriminatory basis.

In contrast, however, many intellectuals who write about citizenship take a different view: They oppose pretty much any discrimination against noncitizens. The big exception is the right to vote, but even here many academics propose that noncitizens be allowed to vote, particularly in local or special-purpose (e.g., school board) elections, as permitted in many European and some American communities (see "Immigrant Voting" essay). The intellectual critique of traditional citizenship is of three types: egalitarian, functional, and transnational.

Egalitarian. In the egalitarian view, very common among academics, status differentials are presumptively illegitimate, especially when government mandates them. Even more objectionable are differentials that correlate with and disadvantage racial and ethnic minorities, as is the case with the citizen/noncitizen distinction. These inequalities, the argument runs, are like suspect classifications in equal protection jurisprudence; they must be narrowly tailored and can be justified, if at all, only by compelling reasons. In addition, many egalitarians, drawing on the work of the English social theorist T. H. Marshall, maintain that the legal-political conception of citizenship is radically incomplete. In this view, a robust citizenship requires a level of economic and social equality necessary for full participation in public and private life.

Functional. Another critique of traditional citizenship emphasizes that noncitizens are hardworking, pay taxes, and obey the laws (at least those in legal status do), just as citizens do. Given this functional equality, the argument goes, noncitizens should enjoy the same rights as citizens. Academics often extend this argument to undocumented workers, noting the unfairness of the fact that these workers pay the same payroll, sales, and indirect taxes as others do but are not in a position, because of their illegal status, to claim Social Security and other benefits that their taxes help finance.

Transnational. To many commentators, the traditional notion of citizenship, organized around the nation-state, is increasingly anachronistic. Human rights advocates cite the growing number of international conventions that recognize universal rights—for example, protections against torture, persecution, discrimination, and environmental insults—that individuals can claim as human beings rather than as members of a particular national polity. Others point to the growth of supranational institutions such as the European Union, World Trade Organization, United Nations, International Criminal Court, and many regional groupings such as NAFTA that exercise real power over individuals and nations. Multinational corporations and international nongovernmental organizations transcend national borders and allegiances. Today, people are educated, work, invest, and consume in a global market that is increasingly shaped by forces over which any single nation, even the United States, has relatively little control. In this environment, many academics think, it makes little sense for people's basic rights to vary simply by virtue of their nationality.

How, then, should we think about the nature and law of citizenship after 9/11? The most important fact in our new world is that the main risk to our national security, which until 9/11 seemed to exist only abroad, is now domestic, indeed local (especially for New York and Washington, D.C.). This risk can be contained only by intensive intelligence gathering and by screening of people in public places, often on the basis of statistical profiles that inevitably produce some false positives (see "Profiling," in part IV).

Should all U.S. citizens be automatically exempted from this screening, just as they can now avoid long lines and interrogation at airports and other ports of entry? Does the fact that the Oklahoma City bombers turned out to be U.S. citizens mean that citizenship is not a good screening criterion, that noncitizen status is a poor proxy for the risk of terrorism? These questions are complicated by legal rules that confer full citizenship on people like Hamdi who were born here but have no other ties to or stake in the United States, and that give noncitizens fewer rights, both procedural (as *Hamdi* and *Rasul* seem to imply) and substantive (as the 1996 welfare law provides).

Citizenship is a broad legal category bearing rights that Congress may not constitutionally subdivide. In a 1964 decision, *Schneider v. Rusk*, the Court overturned a law that treated birthright and naturalized citizens differently, and under this principle, Congress may lack power to disadvantage birthright citizens like Hamdi just because they moved abroad at an early age and became strangers. (Interestingly, Hamdi has renounced his U.S. citizenship in order to be deported to Saudi Arabia.)

In contrast, Congress has broad discretion to regulate naturalization standards. Would it increase the nation's security or unity by requiring applicants for post-9/11 citizenship to demonstrate greater knowledge about, and loyalty and commitment to, American life than the law required in the past?

This is an important question for us to debate. In my view, we should resist the temptation to toughen naturalization by imposing new tests of loyalty and commitment. For birthright citizens like Hamdi who lived among us only briefly and long ago severed any ties to our society, membership should perhaps lapse at some point. But any individual whom our government holds in custody, whether citizen or stranger, should be able to test the legality of that custody as a matter of human rights, not citizenship.

31

Immigrant Voting: Wrong Response to a Genuine Need

In November 2004, San Francisco narrowly defeated a proposal to allow noncitizens to vote in school board elections. This is a complicated, controversial issue that merits substantial discussion. Although it is important to encourage immigrants to involve themselves in their children's schools, giving them voting rights is more doubtful.

San Francisco's proposal targeted a genuine problem. Many immigrant children attend schools that are shockingly inadequate, and their parents face many obstacles in improving them. The parents' lack of English fluency is a major disability. Many of them work several jobs, have long commutes, and are left with little time to supervise homework, much less participate in school governance. The stakes are high not only for the immigrants themselves but for the rest of America. Their U.S.-born children, after all, are automatically citizens even if the parents are not, and these children will constitute a steadily growing share of the electorate that will shape our future. Fairness and equality concerns might also justify giving the vote to noncitizens. After all, they are taxpayers; even the undocumented pay sales taxes and often payroll taxes. Since noncitizens, like everyone else, are vitally affected by official decisions, the argument goes, they should also be able to choose those who govern them.

History might also reinforce noncitizens' claim to the franchise. Until the 1920s, some states allowed noncitizens to vote in state and local elections. (None allows it today, although states still have the power to do so; voting rules in localities like San Francisco depend on state law). Even now, some municipalities permit noncitizens to vote for school board members; a few extend the vote to all local elections. Some European nations allow noncitizens to vote in municipal elections, although not national ones.

To these arguments favoring noncitizen voting, however, there are serious responses. On the evidence, voting is a low priority for most immigrants, just as it is for the eighteen year olds enfranchised by the 26th Amendment. Only a small fraction of the immigrants eligible for citizenship seek it quickly; they wait more than eight years on average, and Mexicans, the largest group by far, wait much longer. Relatively few immigrants are likely to vote for the school board even if they can; indeed, only a small fraction of eligible citizen voters now vote in these elections.

This is not, in itself, a conclusive reason to deny them the vote. It would be wrong to withhold such a fundamental right solely on the ground that people are unlikely to exercise it. Why not give noncitizens the same choice that citizens possess? But this is precisely the point. Recently arrived immigrants, and others who are eligible to naturalize but have chosen not to do so, are not yet citizens—and may never be. In a self-governing democracy, it is not unfair to recognize and maintain this distinction so long as legal immigrants are offered the opportunity to become citizens on an equal basis without undue obstacles or unreasonable delay. Current naturalization law meets these conditions.

Today, the vote is one of the few significant remaining differences between the status of citizen and noncitizen. (Another is that citizens enjoy higher priority in gaining admission for immigrant relatives. Not all immigrants receive the same welfare benefits that citizens do. Noncitizens can be deported but this is very rare except for criminals and the undocumented.) Should voting continue to be limited to citizens? In my view, the right to vote should be predicated on citizenship, and the right to citizenship should continue to require a significant period of legal residence. (Illegal immigrants would not qualify, even though many have children in the schools.) Newcomers need time to acquire the very minimal political knowledge conducive to rational voting.

But some legal changes might make the distinction easier to justify. Our five-year waiting period for citizenship, which goes back to the nineteenth century, may not be optimal. (The period is three years in Canada and also here for those with a U.S. citizen spouse; Australia's period is even shorter.) Our naturalization tests, now being revised, may not measure political knowledge effectively. We should also consider extending the vote to immigrants who have met the naturalization requirements but are delayed by long bureaucratic backlogs; their vote should not have to wait until the government gets around to scheduling their ceremonies.

That said, however, the line between citizen and noncitizen defined by the right to vote is worth preserving. Before newcomers receive full political equality, they should have to make the basic commitment to American democracy that our minimal, nondiscriminatory preconditions for naturalization now require. My guess is that the vast majority of immigrants would agree.

PART VI

DEVELOPING GIANTS

The United States is no longer the center of the world, if it ever was. Two megasocieties, China and India, dwarf us in population (together they constitute more than a third of the world's people) and in economic growth rates (China's annual growth rate has exceeded 9 percent for more than a decade; India's has averaged about 6 percent in the same period). To be sure, their impressive economic gains have been distributed very unevenly between urban and rural areas and still leave them with very low living standards. Nevertheless, these advances by China and India are largely responsible for the significant reduction in world poverty in the last decade, and both countries are poised for further gains. In 2004, India installed a prime minister who is a renowned pro-growth economist, while China's economy expanded at its now-customary torrid pace while managing to keep inflation at a moderate level.

Americans must learn more about these two countries than their dizzying numbers. In particular, they need to learn how these societies work—culturally, socially, religiously, legally, and politically. I hope that the two essays in this part will help to begin filling this knowledge gap. I wrote the one on China after a short visit in which I studied its legal and political development. The essay on India reflects two much longer stays totaling four months during which I traveled to all corners of India learning about that vast, diverse country while lecturing to academic and professional audiences about American institutions.

ᢌ **32** ᢌ

China: Forward and Backward

Only a ninety-minute drive from the teeming streets of Beijing, the Great Wall traces its sinuous course across the stark Chinese landscape. Zigging and zagging up the mountainsides, down into valleys, and across plains, the 3,500-year-old fortification winds like a snake, often doubling back on itself, only to thrust forward once again whenever its surroundings permit.

The progress of the rule of law in China seems much the same, at least to this first-time visitor. Like the Great Wall, the Chinese legal system advances slowly, indirectly, uncertainly as it explores the contours of the rugged, rather hostile environment. And like the Great Wall, legal change confronts threats from both sides—not just the predictable assaults from traditional enemies but also the insidious challenges from its supposed friends.

I went to China under the auspices of the China Law Center, a program at Yale Law School that promotes Chinese legal reform and increases understanding of China's legal system. Our hosts, a group of law professors, legislative staff, and judges at the national, provincial, and local levels, as well as other government personnel, are seeking to develop firmer legal foundations for their embryonic system of administrative litigation. This system is based on a 1989 statute passed by the National People's Congress.

These worthies desperately need someone's help. Imagine what it is like for individuals, organizations, and business firms to operate in a centralized, bureaucratically guided economy without anything that resembles our notions of administrative law. Imagine a society of 1.2 billion individuals, whose conduct is always subject to the close scrutiny and traditionally unquestioned authority of state officials. Their power is legitimated by almost three millennia of Confucian teachings about the cultural superiority of bureaucratic elites and about citizens' sacred duty to obey their decrees. Imagine a political system in which all major decisions are made by a Communist Party whose opaque power structure parallels the formal government apparatus but is accountable neither to that government nor to the rule of law. Imagine a university system in which the government can suddenly close all of the Internet cafes in Beijing in order to stifle foreign criticism of its human rights record and prevent its students from gaining access to outside sources of information. Finally, imagine a civil society without independent churches, private groups, or other intermediate institutions to stand between the individual and the state.

Such imaginings, of course, have not prevented law firms and businesses from flocking to China. The Tiananmen Square massacre briefly chilled their ardor, but it soon returned with even greater intensity as the pace of China's economic activity has accelerated, along with its demand for lawyers and the urgency of legal reform. Even more lawyers will be needed to help deal with a growing crisis in China's banking system that is concentrated in four immense, state-owned commercial banks. According to Standard & Poor's, perhaps half of all their loans should be classified as nonperforming—a problem several times as severe as Japan's and getting steadily worse. The banking system's collapse, of course, would choke off China's long-running economic growth.

The growth prospects for law are more robust. This is an extraordinary moment in China's legal development. Chinese lawyers are only now coming of age professionally. When the Communist Party took power in 1949, it denounced bourgeois law as an instrument of oppression, disparaged lawyers as enemies of the people, made their judiciary a tool of state policy, and closed the law schools. Two immense social upheavals—the Great Leap Forward (1958–1960) and the Cultural Revolution (1966–1976)—retarded China's economic, political, and legal development, resulting in a lost generation of lawyers, law professors, and legally trained judges and administrators. As a result, today's lawyers constitute China's first legally trained professionals since 1949. Equally important, their views about law, government, private property, and much else were shaped by the hardships they endured during those convulsions. These views reflect their own bitter experiences in growing up under an arbitrary, corrupt regime with little use for administrative law—or indeed, for any law at all.

Another reason that the law has gained new prominence in China is the remarkable pace of economic development. The country has managed to sustain average GDP growth rates of 8–9 percent since 1979, when the great reformer Deng Xiaoping introduced market reforms. During the 1990s, the growth rate was often in double digits. Today China has the third largest economy in the world (after the United States and Japan) and the fastest growing one. This economy can no longer do without lawyers and a legal culture to encourage transactions, protect property rights, assure personal security, limit governmental power, and foster predictability.

The immediate cause of China's new legal consciousness, however, is obviously its entry into the World Trade Organization (WTO). Every lawyer and judge I met emphasized that this development is changing all the rules of the game, not just in the economy but in politics as well. Three elements of this transformation are particularly pertinent to the law. First, the WTO demands a level of legal and bureaucratic transparency that is utterly foreign to the traditional Chinese system. Unbridled official discretion and secrecy will have to give way to published rules and procedures. International monitors will carefully scrutinize government actions. Regulations bearing on foreign companies will have to be more fairly administered. Second, the Chinese government and private firms cannot meet the WTO's demanding fair trade requirements unless they become much more efficient. As China seeks to transform its protected economy into an intensely competitive one, it must find ways to lower the transaction costs of doing business there. This means overhauling its systems of banking, licensing, intellectual property, bankruptcy, and virtually every other area of private law. Finally, China will have to establish a public law that assigns significant roles to independent judicial review in general and administrative law in particular.

These new demands on Chinese law explain why Chinese experts invited us to advise them on administrative law reform, and why American experts are advising the Chinese in other legal areas as well. In addition to areas such as bankruptcy, commercial law, securities regulation, and financial institutions, some projects are more surprising. For example, Shanghai is seeking help in establishing systems of professional licensure and other forms of consumer protection. It is also trying to develop professional and trade associations, in order to improve communications between the government and the business communities that are the source of China's economic dynamism.

American experts are providing advice on how to revamp the country's antiquated court systems, which are simply overwhelmed by the burgeoning caseloads and legal complexities produced by the new economic order. In fact, the spanking-new intermediate appellate court in Shanghai is a model for what judicial administration reform can accomplish; the court now boasts up-to-date computer technology and efficient caseload tracking systems. But this success is a conspicuous exception to the deep morass into which the Chinese courts have sunk.

China is not a complete novice when it comes to the demands of transparency, efficiency, and administrative regularity. For many years, the government has had the good sense to allow certain enterprise zones in a few regions, a policy that North Korea may be copying. These zones are in effect laboratories for a post-WTO economy. They are relatively free of the heavy-handed command-and-control techniques traditionally used by the party apparatchiks who try to manage the economy. Not surprisingly, these enterprise zones are flourishing. The two most important ones are Guangdong Province in the southeast, and the great port city of Shanghai.

Any visitor to Shanghai—even a native New Yorker—is astonished at the entrepreneurial dynamism driving that city's growth. This energy is evident wherever one turns—the crowded shops lining every street; the choking auto traffic; the sea of well-dressed and well-fed workers; the wharves crowded with shipping; the feverish construction of office buildings and infrastructure in Pudong, a previously desolate district of Shanghai across the Huangpu River; and the rapid population growth, despite China's one-child population policy.

China's hunger for law, however, remains highly selective. While the government knows that the rule of law will be essential in a post-WTO economy built largely on foreign investment, this conviction does not extend much beyond the civilian economy. The immense military establishment is largely exempt, still operating on the traditional command-and-control model and running according to its own rules. The most glaring challenge to the rule of law, of course, is the political system, which still dances to the tune of the Communist Party. The party has permitted elections for some local posts, but that is the extent of its experiment with democracy. Everyone recognizes Mao's revolutionary ideology of heroic self-sacrifice, popular idealism, mass support, and socialist legality as utterly hollow and fraudulent. One of our translators, a talented graduate of a top American law school and a corporate lawyer in Beijing, insisted that he did not know a single individual in China—urban or rural, rich or poor, educated or not—who believed that this ideology is anything more than a mask for official cynicism and exploitation.

Deng's genius as a dictator in the 1980s was to begin to relax controls on the economy while maintaining an iron grip on the polity. This impressive feat is very hard to sustain, as the habits of freedom, once entrenched in one sphere, tend to expand into others. In fact, embryonic ideas about transparency, efficiency, regularity, and even rights have percolated into the criminal justice and civil administrative systems—though implementing these ideas is another matter entirely. Deng's epigone, Jiang Zemin, continued with this high-wire act, though Jiang has little of Deng's personal stature or panache.

Indications that Jiang and his ruling clique have begun to lose their balance are growing. One sign is the rising chorus of complaints about official corruption, an ancient Chinese tradition whose costs have become unsustainable. Corruption's pervasiveness demoralizes and infuriates ordinary citizens and imposes a heavy tax on business. A second sign is the government's hysterical crackdown on the Falun Gong, Christians, Buddhists, and other potentially independent power centers. This overreaction reveals the regime's illegitimacy for all to see. A third sign is the abject poverty in rural China, another ancient pattern but one that has become intolerable to those who see daily TV images of the luxuries and freedoms enjoyed by their fellow citizens in the large cities.

Hu Jintao, Jiang Zemin's successor, has given few clear signs of which changes his accession will bring to China's legal and political cultures, although optimists reading the tea leaves divine that he harbors reformist leanings. More than a personnel shift at the top of the party bureaucracy will be needed to establish the rule of law in China, yet institutionalization of these legal values is precisely what will be required in order to transform China from a dangerous, unpredictable, tyrannical giant into a nation with which the United States and the rest of the world can safely do political, diplomatic, and economic business.

∽ **33** ∽

India: What the Raj Wrought

In recent years, China has been the leading new market for legal services in a rapidly globalizing world. Soon, however, that distinction may go to India. It is already the world's largest democracy and, with a population of 1.1 billion, projected eventually to be the world's largest country. China enjoyed a big head start; foreign direct investment there dwarfs that in India, and China conducts more trade with us. But this could quickly change as Indian entrepreneurship, already greater than that in China, starts attracting more foreign capital, and as India's advantages, including English and the rule of law, loom larger.

India now bars foreign lawyers from opening offices there, but the gates may open as the World Trade Organization and other nations pressure India to relax its trade barriers for professional services. Once the gold rush to India starts, American firms planning offices there will need to know something about the exotic society—and the advanced, if imperfect, legal system—that awaits them.

Actually, many societies await them there. India is a nation of contrasts and incongruities. The flat desert vastness of Rajasthan and the soaring cathedral-like spires of the snow-capped Himalayas. The arid plains of the Deccan and the Iowalike fertility of the Punjab. The axle-to-axle, cacophonous, frenetic congestion of Old Delhi's lanes and the verdant serenity of New Delhi's embassy row. The Stone Age workshops in Calcutta's slums and the high-tech campuses of Bangalore. The tropical, spacious backwaters of Kerala in the south and the grim, teeming urban jungles of Uttar Pradesh and Bihar in the north. The intense spirituality of pilgrim destinations like Dharamsala, Rishikesh, and Varanasi, and the equally fervent materialism of Mumbai business and Bollywood. Indeed, many streets look like a history of urban transport compressed into a single bursting diorama: Human-drawn sledges, ox-drawn carts, rickshaws powered by human legs or small engines, buses, trucks, and cars, and of course the endless parade of animals—cows, pigs, goats, dogs, and sometimes monkeys, camels, and elephants—all move at their own pace through the wholly unregulated traffic. Only inches away (there are few sidewalks), countless people are sleeping, eating, conversing, doing business, and performing ablutions. The words bedlam and chaos do not quite capture the sheer energy, vitality, and congestion of this ubiquitous scene. Yet somehow the traffic actually moves. While there are frequent accidents and near misses, road rage seems far less common than on the comparatively empty and well-regulated American roads.

India is probably the most culturally diverse country on earth. India's constitution now lists twenty-two official languages, and hundreds of local and regional tongues are spoken daily. English, the language of government and higher education, is taught at Indian schools, but many students do not stay there long enough to master it. Even fluent English speakers are often unintelligible to the American ear, as frustrated callers to Bangalore-based help lines know. George Bernard Shaw's quip about America and England—"two countries separated by the same language"—applies even more to India.

Linguistic diversity intersects with—and reinforces—diversities of religion, region, and caste to create a bewilderingly complex, fragmented political system driven by scores of disciplined parties. (It is illegal for Indian legislators to defect from their party leaders.) India has the world's largest Hindu, Sikh, and Jain populations, and the second-largest Muslim population, after Indonesia. It also has large Buddhist, Parsi, and Christian communities. Even the 85 percent Hindu majority is divided by deity-of-choice (Shiva and Vishnu predominate) and by other fissures. Profound regional divisions exist. In the north, Aryan culture and languages, centuries-long domination by Muslim invaders, and caste-based parties and ideologies have bred massive poverty and corruption. The south speaks Dravidian languages, receives large foreign remittances and cultural ideas from its millions of migrants working abroad, boasts high-tech areas, inhabits a tropical, seacoast environment, and in some areas has matrilineal family and property arrangements. And although the law long ago abolished the despised status of untouchability, caste remains highly salient. Indians can identify thousands of subcastes through surname, occupation, and reputation. This is particularly true in the rural areas, where 70 percent of Indians live. Caste-based parties demand higher constitutionally required quotas in legislatures, colleges, and the civil service and would extend these quotas to private firms with at least ten employees.

India's Moghul and British conquerors, while often tolerating these diversities, also cynically exploited them for imperial ends. Their well-honed divide-and-rule tactics culminated in the 1947 partition that carved Pakistan out of the British Raj and unleashed intercommunal violence—savage even by Rwandan and Balkan standards—that still haunts India today. This bitter diversity-driven legacy presents an extraordinary challenge to India's cohesion. Its survival, not to mention its robust democracy and recent economic growth, is a political achievement that evokes wonder and respect.

India's hard-won national unity remains fragile, still threatened by strong centrifugal forces and endemic corruption. Its twenty-eight states implement a single body of national law, but within and among states parochial ethnopolitical identities, historical passions, and separatist pressures continually swirl. To relieve these pressures, the national government has had to carve three new states out of old ones. It also allows Muslim, Christian, Hindu, and Parsi communities to apply their own domestic relations, religious, and personal laws. This privilege, granted by the secular Congress party that created modern India, is under challenge by the BJP, a Hindu nationalist party with long-standing extremist elements. Until the May 2004 elections reversed its steady electoral progress, ending six years of national rule, the BJP pressed for a single, uniform civil code likely based on Hindu practice, and advocated other policies offensive to religious minorities, especially Muslims.

The outcome of these elections, perhaps the biggest political upset in Indian history, is a Congress-led coalition relying on a resurgent Communist party, other leftist groups, and some corrupt state and local machines. Most pundits see this as a victory for secularism, a spasm of deep anti-incumbent sentiment, and a rejection of economic liberalization policies that benefit the educated minority. These policies, critics say, have bypassed the vast drought-ridden agricultural sector where most Indians still live in utter destitution—a huge population that the BJP's much-derided "India Shining" campaign theme seemed to ignore.

THE COST OF CORRUPTION

Most analysts believe that corruption is even more corrosive, perhaps, than minority disaffection and separatism. There is no reason to think the situation has improved since the 1980s, when Rajiv Gandhi estimated that almost 85 percent of money spent on public antipoverty programs was lost to corruption. Young lawyers and students are especially demoralized; they bemoan the absence of any role models in politics. This sentiment was reinforced by the devastating defeat in the recent elections of Chandrababu Naidu, the top elected official of Andhra Pradesh, whose capital city, Hyderabad, is nicknamed "Cyberabad" because it is a world symbol of technological prowess and progress. Before his defeat, which reflected a variety of factors, Naidu was India's icon of modernization and one of the few internationally recognized politicians in India.

In a parody of scrupulosity, government officials do essentially nothing for the forty days before an election lest they be accused of using their powers to aid the incumbents. Candidates for office routinely violate the unrealistically low limits on campaign receipts and expenditures. They view the mass of poor voters as reliable "vote banks" whose support can be bought with alcohol or small favors in ways reminiscent of the urban political machines of premodern America. This disgusts many well-educated citizens who then decline to vote. Whistle-blowing is uncommon. Until very recently, investigation of officials' wrongdoing required approval by their superiors. Freedom of information is not yet a well-developed right. Many newspapers are highly partisan. Party leaders enforce discipline with the rigor of a maximum-security prison warden. Politicians exert great influence over prosecutors.

The Supreme Court of India is widely admired (perhaps excessively so, as discussed below), but lower-level judges are often reputed to be on the take. Baksheesh, or bribery, is as common a topic of conversation as biryani. Dynastic succession in political office is the rule, not the exception.

PROSPERITY AND POVERTY

Even against this dismal backdrop, India's economic future should be bright. It boasts a large and growing middle class, many highly trained workers (over two million college graduates a year), widespread English language fluency, low labor costs, and generous remittances from prosperous nonresident Indians throughout the world. According to respected journalist Gautam Adhikari, Indians or Indian Americans launched 40 percent of Silicon Valley start-ups, and almost 10 percent of America's millionaires come from this group. Economic growth has been robust since the early 1980s, although still well below that of China and many other developing countries. The poverty rate has declined significantly, but, as discussed below, it remains above 25 percent, by India's very low standards. The much ballyhooed IT industry, centered in the southern cities of Hyderabad and Bangalore, was the subject in 2004 of a series of admiring columns by Thomas Friedman, the influential New York Times columnist. Exports of software and technology services have more than quadrupled since 2000, reaching $15 billion this year. Many U.S. jobs could be susceptible to outsourcing in India, a threat denounced by John Kerry in the presidential campaign but that leading trade economists view as exaggerated.

Beyond the IT industry, however, the economic picture is more sobering. India still bears the scars of the misguided statist and protectionist policies of founding father Jawaharlal Nehru and Indira Gandhi, his daughter. By 1990, India's share of world trade had contracted to 0.4 percent, one-sixth its share at Independence. India's recent growth spurt, then, is very heartening. It is usually traced to liberalization policies adopted by the Narasimha Rao government in 1991 or, alternatively, to new probusiness attitudes in the early 1980s. In any event, bureaucratic controls continue to limit productivity in many areas today, making it hard to get things done efficiently—one reason why corruption thrives. Power failures occur with a disturbing regularity. Air India Limited, the national airline, is a poor, much subsidized imitation of its dynamic private competitors. Market-oriented reforms are much discussed but slow to take root. The state controls seven of India's ten largest companies; state-owned banks control 90 percent of deposits, and the national railroad is the largest commercial employer in the world.

The political drag created by vested interests is of course one reason for this inertia. Another is India's huge, meddlesome civil service. According to a survey, business managers spend 16 percent of their time dealing with government officials. Career bureaucrats staff government agencies to just below the ministerial level, giving the relatively few political appointees less leeway to introduce and implement new liberalization policies. Rather than struggle against these status quo forces, some of India's best physicians, engineers, and entrepreneurs go abroad to find more dynamic and rewarding outlets for their talents.

The results of the recent elections have created enormous market uncertainty driven by concerns that the new center-left government will undo privatization, discourage foreign investment, and take costly populist measures. The Indian stock market rendered its verdict—by plummeting as soon as the results were announced—although it later recovered somewhat with the naming of the new prime minister, an admired economist who designed the earlier liberalization.

Other impediments to more rapid growth exist: the lingering effects of a harsh feudal caste system; gender inequality; primitive transportation, electricity, sanitation, and other infrastructure; a public-sector budget deficit (largely in the states) approaching 10 percent of GDP; a backward agricultural sector that remains dependent on monsoons for irrigation; restrictions on foreign ownership of property; and the failure of many states to invest heavily in primary and secondary education. Such conditions leave 35 percent of adult Indians illiterate and even more at destitution levels that westerners can scarcely imagine. A 2004 survey in *The Economist* finds that an estimated 300 million Indians survive on less than $1 a day, 160 million lack clean water, and a tragically wasteful system for distributing India's ample food stocks leaves almost half of small children underweight. If it is any consolation, they live in family and spiritual communities that seem less demoralizing and isolating than the American underclass experiences with far better material conditions.

India's labor force of four hundred million is tragically underemployed. Knots of able-bodied men stand (or squat) on most urban streets doing either obvious make-work or nothing at all. AIDS contagion, already alarming in some states, could break out to reach South African levels.

On a more hopeful note, a few states like Kerala and Mizoram (a tribal area bordering Burma) have managed to achieve almost universal literacy, low fertility and infant mortality rates, and almost equal female and male births, despite widespread poverty. Even these states, however, do not generate enough jobs to sustain their growing populations, forcing many of their best and brightest to migrate abroad. One stunning measure of the brain drain: The almost two million Indians living in the United States make up this country's wealthiest ethnic minority; nearly 30 percent of these families earn over $100,000 a year.

A BRITISH LEGAL LEGACY

India's proudest inheritance from the British was its legal system and the professional civil and military service that would implement it. Most of the founding generation's political and legal leaders, like Nehru, Mahatma Gandhi, B. R. Ambedkar, and Vallabhbhai Patel, were educated in England, where they creatively combined their anti-imperialist fervor with an Anglophilic respect for British legal culture. Almost sixty years after Independence, even the most nationalistic Indians revere this colonial legacy. Few colonized peoples have done as well as India in gaining the political-ideological maturity to cast off a despised imperial rule while appropriating some of the empire's best traditions.

Indian legal education, as in Britain, has traditionally been a three-year highly specialized course of study at the undergraduate level. Several programs, including elite national law schools that now operate with state and central government funding in Calcutta, Bangalore, Hyderabad, Bhopal, and Jodhpur, have begun to move to five-year programs, which will include some nonlaw courses. Even today, however, the law schools tend to have large lecture classes, sporadic interactions with students, little interdisciplinary analysis, few clinical programs, limited training in legal research and writing, and an emphasis on rote learning. The vast majority of professors lack training in nonlaw fields and conduct little original research.

Most Indian lawyers practice alone with tiny offices on or near the street. At the high end, lawyers spend almost all their time as advocates before the Supreme Court of India in New Delhi, or before the state high courts. As in the United States, the law of India's states must yield to inconsistent national law, and many high court judgments are appealable to the Supreme Court of India. The legal profession generally enjoys less social prestige than engineering, medicine, or high-tech work, and some of India's most talented young people (law graduates included) aspire to highly competitive positions in the relatively well paid and secure Indian Administrative Service, rather than in private-sector jobs. This may change, however, as privatization initiatives take hold.

India's vision of a judicial system carefully meting out justice through judges who are as independent as those in Britain and the United States remains largely unfulfilled. American researchers Marc Galanter and Jay Krishnan find that "Indians avail themselves of the courts at a low rate, and the rate seems to be falling." Even so, the courts stagger under mind-boggling caseloads and delays. Criminal defendants can spend years in jail before reaching trial. The civil court backlog of twenty-four million cases proceeds at the pace of Dickens's *Jarndyce v. Jarndyce*; great heaps of litigation documents spill over from clerks' desks onto floors and into hallways. Relatively few cases settle. A twenty-year-old reform, *lok adalats* ("people's courts"), follows a number of earlier efforts to improve ordinary citizens' access to justice. They are usually modeled on informal, indigenous, village-based courts. But a new study by Galanter and Krishnan concludes that *lok adalats* generally operate in a peremptory, top-down manner that provides little of the speedy, fair, deliberative, grassroots justice that was promised.

Even more demoralizing than its slow pace and inefficiency, the judicial system is also seen as corrupt. Lawyers believe that many lower court judges (and even some on the high courts) take bribes, favor certain litigants, and do not really know or apply the law. The judges' ethical standards are thought to be little better than those of politicians. An outsider, of course, cannot readily assess the accuracy of this view. The Chief Justice of India, after consultation, can rotate high court judges among the various states and require that the chief judges of these courts come from other states—a mandate largely designed to reduce corruption opportunities. In a far-flung country like India where the quality of life can vary enormously from state to state, this power to reward and punish other judges could intimidate without having to be exercised.

Many good-government advocates who are desperate for change and do not know where else to turn have cast their lot with the Supreme Court of India, making it a primary focus of their reformist hopes. It is easy to see why. The twenty-six-member court is perhaps the most prestigious organ of government in India, and is certainly among the most powerful and autonomous. The constitution confers remarkably broad authority on the court, which has energetically extended this authority to (if not beyond) its outer limits. For example, it has even invalidated duly enacted constitutional amendments, ruling that they violate the spirit and intention of the constitution's framers.

Much of the court's constitutional and statutory review occurs in highly controversial disputes. In April, for example, it ordered the retrial of twenty-one Hindus acquitted on charges of burning fourteen Muslims alive in a bakery during religious riots that many believe BJP members instigated. It did so under constitutional powers ensuring judicial fairness. In many cases, the court has mandated specific and complex public policies that politicians and bureaucrats have either rejected or failed to adopt. For example, it has banned older vehicles from the streets of New Delhi, late-evening noise, and polluting industries within miles of the Taj Mahal. It has also ordered the cleansing of the holy Ganges River.

The court has remarkable procedural authority to engage in such policy making through "public interest litigation" under Article 32 of the constitution. The court also creatively interprets regulatory statutes, the constitution's broad "directive principles," and its open-ended substantive provisions. The court has, for example, transmuted the "right to life" into a right (albeit still aspirational) to a dignified and safe life.

Under Article 32, the court has eliminated virtually all standing require-ments, allowing any concerned citizen to apply to it or to a state high court to redress any legal wrong—political, environmental, dignitary, social, or otherwise—suffered by any person or group of people who by reason of poverty, disability, or disadvantage cannot sue on their own behalf. These cases also receive priority on the judicial docket. Not surprisingly, lawyers have filed a very large number of them. Indeed, an angry Supreme Court panel ruled in March that most of these cases have nothing to do with the public interest or purposes of Article 32. This ruling followed an earlier case in which it had felt obliged to issue guidelines designed to prevent frivolous and abusive claims, apparently with little effect.

The Supreme Court's power extends well beyond substantive decisions in particular cases. In a remarkable 1993 decision, it interpreted the consti-tution to empower the chief justice of India and his most senior colleagues to determine, in effect, who is appointed to fill vacancies both on the court itself and on the state high courts. The court does not brook vigorous crit-icism of itself or its rulings. In a 2002 case involving Arundhati Roy, the celebrated Indian writer and social activist, the court held that her sharp attack on one of its environmental decisions scandalized the court, tar-nished its dignity, and thus constituted contempt of court—although the court, citing its own "magnanimity," reduced her sentence to one day in jail. In these and other ways, the justices seem to have succeeded in intim-idating journalists, the bar, and the legal academy from engaging in the kind of feisty assessment of their decisions that in America is routine. The court claims to welcome constructive criticism short of contempt, but the potentially severe penalties for crossing this uncertain line inevitably chill debate over its performance. This in turn could threaten the court's integrity, the quality of its work, and perhaps the rule of law itself.

No one can deny India's extraordinary achievements and future prom-ise. Out of the wreckage of the British Raj and a congeries of ancient cultures and feudal principalities, it built a dynamic nation-state with uncommon respect for and tolerance of the astonishing diversity of its people—and rel-atively little violence, outside of Kashmir. Its economy is finally on the right track, powered by a large, growing middle class, immense internal and regional markets, and first-rate technical training. Its civil society esteems strong families, communal solidarity, higher education, and a generative mix of spirituality and materialism. Its democracy (like most, including ours) is not pretty to watch but remains remarkably robust and secure. Its legal institutions—the courts, bar, legal education, bureaucracy, and consti-tutionalist ethos—are probably stronger and more mature than those in any other developing country. This last is not faint praise; instead, it recognizes what is a kind of historical-cultural miracle. When American lawyers finally arrive in India, they will find much there to dismay them but even more that is promising, intriguing, admirable, and even inspiring.

– PART VII –

THE FUTURE OF LIBERALISM

L iberal values—constitutionalism, the rule of law, limited but democratic government, individual freedom, a flourishing, independent civil society—are America's precious inheritance, a legacy of hard-fought struggles in other nations, especially England. These values, transformed in the unique crucible of our culture and institutions, are also America's great gift to the world.

In these final five essays, I consider various aspects of American liberalism in an effort to assess how it is dealing with and being shaped by new challenges. The essays are in a sense bookends, with the first written in the wake of the 1980 election of Ronald Reagan and the last written after the 2004 reelection of George W. Bush. The first, an op-ed piece for the *New York Times*, explores an intriguing paradox about American liberals: They believe that we should use the state to actively and self-confidently intervene to reform the *social* environment in many ways, while at the same time believing that the *natural* environment is too complex for us to alter intelligently.

The second essay maintains that America's growing cultural diversity confers enormous functional advantages. By facilitating social learning and adaptation, diversity can help us to solve or manage the new problems that the future will inevitably throw up for us. The next essay considers how we can best get along with one another in an increasingly diverse and contentious society in which minority (and sometimes majority) grievances and sensitivities to slights, real and imagined, abound and are in a sense encouraged. I propose two modest but elusive remedies: greater candor and thicker skins. Another essay explores the demand for greater civility in public discourse, which might seem obviously desirable, like motherhood and apple pie. I show, however, that although civility is indeed a virtue in most contexts, we should not allow it to be used, as it sometimes is, to enforce orthodoxy, flatten vigorous expression, or suppress substantive disagreement.

The final essay is a fitting, and I hope provocative, conclusion to the book. Here, I present my analysis of the 2004 elections by distilling what

I take to be the absurdities and hypocrisies of some other postelection commentary, the realities that these pundits ignore, two tragedies that the elections confirmed, and some strategies for the revival of a healthy Democratic party, a revival in which I believe all Americans—and certainly militant moderates—have a strong stake.

～ 34 ～

Rethinking Liberalism: A Paradox Unresolved

For liberals, President Reagan's election is a time for reflection, an unaccustomed respite from the thought-impoverishing responsibilities of power. Although unregenerate defenders of hallowed dogma remain, more thoughtful liberals wish to reassess their alternative to Reaganism. They have repaired to the academy, "think tanks, and the private sector, eager to fashion a creed suitable to today's *zeitgeist.*" Once they roost, what next?

They might well begin by examining some apparently contradictory premises of contemporary liberalism. Just as a house is no sturdier than the structures upon which it rests, a political program reflects the strength or weakness of its underlying assumptions. These foundations, buried long ago under campaign rhetoric, political expediency, and programmatic commitments, must now be exhumed for critical scrutiny. The 1980 debacle has given liberalism an urgent reason—perhaps its last opportunity—to do so.

There are, alas, many apparent inconsistencies from which to choose. One with striking policy implications is the varying attitudes of liberals toward stability and change in different realms of affairs. Consider the liberal Democrat's approaches to changes in the environment, the economy, the society, the polity, and foreign affairs. His environmental strategy is premised upon ecological principles: Nature is wondrously, endlessly complex and diverse; everything in this natural world is systematically linked to everything else; despite awesome scientific advances, these linkages remain obscure; nature's apparent defects often turn out to be functional for the ecosystem as a whole; changes introduced into one part of the system, even for benign purposes, disturb other parts and ramify unpredictable, often undesirable consequences. Liberals wearing environmental hats observe that aerosol sprays seem to contribute to skin cancer, and industrial activity to a possibly devastating greenhouse effect. They conclude that society should create a strong presumption against introducing significant change into the natural order, one that can be overcome only after we perform painstaking impact analyses and adopt safeguards demonstrating that we know what we are doing before we do it. The liberal environmentalist's rhetoric—"go slow," "small is beautiful," "less is more"—reflects this pronounced aversion toward change.

Turning to other domestic policy areas, however, he readily rejects or ignores these hard-won ecological insights. Systemic change is his goal—the more fundamental, the better. The status quo enjoys no presumptive legitimacy; imperfections imply governmentally enforced reform. Wearing his consumerist hat, the liberal exchanges caution for audacity, insisting that government manage energy markets of stupefying intricacy with only the crudest of regulatory tools. As social reformer, he urges the state to regulate promotion practices, parental choices, and other equally delicate transactions without delaying until the social consequences can be predicted. Likewise, ecology is irrelevant to the liberal political reformer. He would never disturb the natural food chain but cannot quite believe that "equalizing" political struggle has weakened parties, strengthened incumbents, and magnified news media influence.

In taking these positions, the liberal affirms his belief in government's ability to improve people's lives, its power to realize moral ends by mobilizing collective will. Yet when confronted with massive injustice, terror, and genocide against vulnerable people elsewhere in the world, he will often swiftly abandon the certitudes of the activist reformer, turning again to the quietism of the ecologist: We know too little to intervene intelligently; we should acquiesce in the natural ebbs and flows of power rather than attempt artificially to modify them; we cannot be the world's policeman. These laissez-faire principles, distilled from our Vietnam experience, distinguish today's liberal most markedly from his pre-1965 counterpart.

I described these diverse attitudes as "apparent" contradictions. It may well be, however, that these assumptions about stability and change in different realms can be harmonized and that the strategies of extreme caution toward changes in nature, boldness regarding domestic reform, and passivity in the face of foreign convulsion can be reconciled on some principled level. Perhaps social reality is more easily comprehended than the natural or international orders. Perhaps those who regulate domestic activity can more readily discern what justice requires than can those who design foreign policy. Perhaps misguided, incompetent interventions in nature are more damaging than those in domestic affairs. Or perhaps (as I believe) liberalism seriously underestimates ecology's relevance to human and institutional behavior. Until these tensions are squarely faced, contemporary liberalism will strike many as an incoherent doctrine for the complex worlds of the future.

∽ **35** ∽

Diversity: Society's Teacher

Diversity can be socially functional. A functionalist theory posits that a society—usually viewed as an organic whole—orients its norms, practices, and institutions toward ensuring its survival and the successful attainment of its goals, whatever they may be. Every society, of course, is at least minimally functional in this sense. As many critics have noted, vulgar functionalism, like vulgar Darwinism, comes perilously close to tautology—and to a status quo tautology at that. Whichever elements of a system exist for a long time are assumed to be functional, else neither they nor the system of which they are a part would have managed to survive. On the other hand, diversity is not *necessarily* functional for a society; much depends on that society's particular values. Certain kinds of diversity can, under some common social and political conditions, threaten the prosperity, harmony, governance, and even the survival of human communities.

More sophisticated functionalists like Robert Merton have shown that all societies have dysfunctional aspects. If we focus on several features that any complex organism must possess in order to prosper, we can rescue a functional view of diversity from a tautological circle that obscures its distinctive social advantages, failures, and risks. Which are those features? The most important, I believe, is a society's capacity to learn and to adapt swiftly and creatively to changing conditions. This learning capacity in turn depends upon the society's ability to generate, aggregate, process, disseminate, deploy, and (as necessary) correct the information it needs in order to discover what its collective purposes are and might be, and then to pursue them effectively.

Social learning of this kind must be a central goal of every group, whether it be liberal, communitarian, or utilitarian. Nevertheless, some groups are far better at it than others. I can best make this point by considering several domains in which diversity can facilitate this social learning process, even though it may at the same time create certain social problems. First, diversity is important, even essential, to the strength and survivability of biological communities. We might usefully understand this as the functional equivalent of social learning in human communities, albeit in a form that processes and exploits new information through biological processes rather than through cognitive ones. Many people value the invigoration of the biota as an ultimate good, as something to be valued for itself. Some may conceive of this as part of a divine plan or manifestation. Others who are theologically agnostic or even atheistic may believe that humans owe a secular, moral duty of environmental stewardship to ourselves or to future generations. Still others may simply be awed by the sublime, ineffable beauty and power of the living world and feel obliged not to mar it.

Diversity-driven strengthening of the biota can also be valued as an instrumental good, one that serves a variety of fundamental human needs: agricultural productivity, public health, medicinal innovation, natural resource management, and others. Until quite recently, for example, the level of biodiversity was widely thought to be relatively unimportant to the functioning of ecosystems. Darwin and other nineteenth-century scientists viewed the process of speciation as functional for subpopulations seeking a biological niche in which they could survive and reproduce in the face of scarce resources and other hostile environmental conditions. Little discussed was the notion that biodiversity not only benefits the species that occupy those niches, rendering the natural world more interesting, exotic, and beautiful for human observers, but also supports and promotes the health of the larger ecosystem.

Accumulating scientific evidence now strongly suggests that biodiversity contributes to the stability of larger ecosystems. In extreme cases, biodiversity may even prevent species extinction or accelerate the recovery from the biological effects of such extinctions. Like climate, soil type, moisture, fire, storm, and other such factors, species diversity seems to help cushion the damaging effects of environmental stresses, preventing the collapse or degradation of species into weakened states that are more vulnerable to temporary ecological disturbances. Recent agricultural experiments, moreover, indicate that crop diversification can vastly increase disease resistance and yields, much more so than standard pesticide applications on monoculture crops.

Diversity facilitates social learning in the economic domain as well as the biological. Corporations have developed a managerial "diversity rhetoric" that affirms the problem-solving propensities of a diverse workforce and its conduciveness to the so-called new economy. But *homo economicus* finds other virtues in diversity. In approaching their decisions to invest, produce, and consume, individuals confront uncertainties that would be extremely costly, if not impossible, for them to resolve on their own. The price system in a competitive market, however, elicits, impounds, sifts, and transmits much of the information that they need in order to make these decisions, and it does so at a very low individual cost. Other things being equal, the more numerous the market's participants and the more diverse their experiences, the better and more valuable this information is likely to be. More participants bring to the market more diverse local knowledge and preferences that bear on economic decisions. The price system can quickly evaluate and aggregate this information, enabling participants to adjust their decisions swiftly. A competitive market also rewards success and punishes failure, as defined by participants; it encourages experimentation, enabling participants to refine their conduct and decisions in order to attract more resources. In contrast, a monolithic or thin market or one that is otherwise not workably competitive tends to weaken and distort these signals, inducing participants to learn the wrong lessons and make the wrong choices.

Religious diversity has also fostered social learning in numerous ways. These include the lessons the Framers took from the long history of religious wars in Europe and intolerance in early America, the role of religions in easing immigrant assimilation, the social reforms for which religious groups campaigned to great effect, and the work of faith-based organizations in providing public goods and social services that in most other advanced democracies are supplied directly or indirectly by governments. Without this extensive and growing network of privately provided public goods, America's tradition of limited government could not have been sustained into the twenty-first century, when the public demands more such goods. Precisely because these religious groups address society's most fundamental needs, deal with its most intimate relationships, and effectuate its most important (largely noncommercial) transactions, they generate information that is of incalculable social value and cannot be obtained in any other way. In addition to their work on specific moral and policy issues, religious groups have often served society as a kind of canary in the mine, signaling hard-to-discern trouble ahead. Robert Fogel puts it this way:

> Evangelical congregations have been very effective instruments for detecting the negative effects of new technologies and changes in economic structure on the lives of their parishioners and for advancing programs of reform. These congregations might be called America's original focus groups. . . . Such interactions also made it possible for leaders to formulate programmatic demands and develop strategies that could mobilize home and far-flung congregations. It was this process of early program formulation and the preexisting network of organizations with passionate members and earnest leaders that made the evangelical churches the leading edge of populist reform movements.

This reformism is by no means limited to evangelical groups; it was true of most Christian and Jewish congregations in nineteenth- and twentieth-century America.

Social learning is also advanced by political diversity. The federal system, for example, both enables and encourages the states and other political subdivisions to experiment with their own programmatic approaches to a wide variety of public issues. Louis Brandeis's view of the states as "little laboratories" of social learning is probably even truer today than it was in his day. During the 1990s, social and political developments enhanced the states' policy autonomy and fiscal resources. At the same time, several new lines of Supreme Court decisions interpreting the Commerce Clause and the Eleventh Amendment to the U.S. Constitution began to constrain federal government authority over the states, an authority that had relentlessly expanded since the 1930s until it had come to seem virtually limitless. Concurrently, many states modernized their governance structures and processes in order to increase their effectiveness in policy initiation and implementation. These efforts have borne much fruit; state-level policy innovations now set the agenda for national debates in a host of policy areas. Some examples are term limits, health care regulation, voter registration rules, antismoking efforts, gun control, the death penalty, working conditions, environmental standards, tax law, consumer protection, campaign finance, special education, energy deregulation, conservation, and educational choice.

A particularly interesting and revealing instance is Congress's overhaul in 1996 of the welfare system. This was a far-reaching reform that followed—substantively as well as chronologically—several years in which different states experimented with different approaches, sometimes under waivers granted by the Clinton administration to relieve those states of federal law requirements that all state programs conform to uniform national standards. In Wisconsin and some other states, these experiments showed promising results in moving welfare recipients into jobs and in reducing their dependency without generating the increased homelessness, child abuse and abandonment, and other indicia of immiseration that most commentators had predicted. Although powerful political pressures would probably have ensured a far-reaching welfare reform in any event, these experiments contributed greatly to the political viability and the specific programmatic content of the 1996 law.

The policy failures of states can be as influential in shaping national policy debates as their successes. During the 2000 election campaign, the Democrats were able to cite the inability of state programs to attract insurers into the market for prescription drug coverage for the elderly as evidence that could be used to discredit Republican proposals to extend that approach to the nation as a whole. In the aftermath of the election itself, the failure of Florida's electoral machinery and the likelihood of similar failures in other states have spawned a political groundswell in support of national legislation to remedy the problem.

For all of diversity's functional virtues in promoting social learning and adaptation, diversity can also be dysfunctional. Sanford Levinson points to many examples in the decision theory and organizational behavior literatures indicating that diversity can adversely affect group performance in a variety of contexts by interfering with the ability of people to communicate, define common goals, and pursue them effectively. Indeed, the chaos of the Tower of Babel in Genesis made this now-obvious point long before social science confirmed it.

Finally, diversity may contribute to another, more ideological kind of chaos, which may be functional or dysfunctional depending on how the society values shocks and disruptions to its normative equilibria. So-called critical theory seeks to create precisely this kind of disruption—one might call it the "shock of nonrecognition"—by insisting that diversity-talk, like other dominant discursive patterns, is a social construct that serves both to advance a particular political agenda or ideology and to disguise it. In the critical view, a discourse does this by normalizing and naturalizing itself, seeming to project a perspective on reality that is value-neutral, common-sensical, and unproblematic. Critical theory seeks to unmask this ruse so as to reveal what is "really" going on beneath the discursive surface. To be sure, the more candid of these theorists readily concede that they are, inescapably, as fully engaged in a power-seeking, ideological competition as those whom they criticize.

To mention critical theory under the rubric of functionalism might seem very odd indeed. After all, opponents of critical theory often attack it for being cynical and nihilistic—a dog that has fun chasing its own tail when it is not busy denying its parents, eating its young, and covering its tracks. Yet a critical perspective on diversity remains functional. It tends to raise important questions about diversity-talk that a smugly integrationist society might otherwise miss. The struggle to answer these questions can help to clarify diversity's various meanings—including some darker ones. One of my colleagues, for example, has characterized diversity rhetoric as a misleading slogan that society's winners use to mollify its losers, tossing them some extra points for being different in some (irrelevant) way. A second critical take on diversity, akin to Robert Cover's warning that law wreaks violence on the distinctive ways of life (*nomei*) it regulates, emphasizes what minorities lose when they assimilate and how and why they often resist doing so. A third exposes the comforting but often unexamined assumptions that make different versions of assimilation and multiculturalism seem more natural, humane, and liberal than they truly are.

⌁ 36 ⌁

Punctilios for a Diverse Society: Candor and Thicker Skins

Much of the work of diversity management must be done not by government but by *us*. Most conflicts that diversity engenders occur when almost three hundred million Americans and more than thirty million aliens interact with one another in countless ways as they proceed with the ordinary business of life. Relatively few of these interactions are problematic for society, and fewer still are suitable for legal intervention. Indeed, projecting more law into these low-level interactions would generally make the challenge of managing diversity even more formidable.

The range of such interactions is much too vast, complex, opaque, unpredictable, and resistant to formal sanctions to be well regulated by legal rules. Even if that were not so, the Constitution and practical politics severely constrain such intrusions into private conduct and relationships.

Inevitably, then, these interactions will largely be governed not by legal rules but by the intricate, often ineffable punctilios of everyday life—what Alan Wolfe calls "morality writ small." If law cannot much affect these punctilios, what can? Novelists, social scientists, humanists, and politicians make their living by seeking answers to this question, of course, yet the reasons why people think, feel, and behave as they do remain notably obscure. If it is rigorous explanation and prediction that we seek, we are likely to be disappointed. But if what we want are normative prescriptions about how people in a diverse America should treat one another, we shall find an overwhelming social consensus on some basic precepts.

These precepts are perfectly serviceable for practical purposes even though—perhaps *because*—they leave some important terms undefined. Here are some of the most important precepts. All people should receive respect, dignity, fair treatment, and the benefit of the doubt unless and until they show by their conduct that they do not deserve these things. Diverse cultural practices and beliefs should be permitted so long as they neither violate the law nor offend moral decency as defined by the larger communities in which they occur. The law and those in authority should not play favorites. People should feel free to identify with racial, religious, ethnic, and other limited groups so long as this is not inconsistent with a common American citizenship. People's private feelings and thoughts are their own business, not the government's, but conduct that adversely affects others is subject to censure or sanction. Religion—almost any religion—is good for society, as are hard work and strong families. People are responsible for their behaviors and destinies—or at least we should treat them as if they were. Government should not interfere with people's freedom without strong public justification. People should not look to the government to do for them what they can do for themselves. People should cultivate an interest in and sympathy for those who are different, trying by an act of moral imagination to put themselves in a stranger's shoes before judging her.

Most of these punctilios should not be controversial, and they are by no means unique to today's diverse America. Indeed, most of them would likely have been endorsed even by a generation of Founders who owned slaves, denied women full citizenship, barred nonwhites from naturalizing, established state churches, viewed Englishmen as a superior breed, and believed that the English language revealed a special genius for liberty and self-government. But if most of these precepts have a long pedigree in America, the same cannot be said of the level of diversity today. Both the fact and the ideal of this diversity are largely post-1965 phenomena.

These recent developments necessitate, in my view, at least two new
punctilios: more candor in debating how to manage diversity, and thicker
skins as we conduct this debate. Both of these changes are essential; indeed,
more candor will surely increase our need for thicker skins.

Candor. Candor is the easiest to justify, as it seems like an unexceptionable virtue. It certainly should be, yet I find that there is remarkably little
of it. In order to manage diversity intelligently, citizens and officials must
identify and confront squarely the inescapable value conflicts, empirical
tradeoffs, and confounding ironies generated by diversity policies. For
example, ethnoracial profiling is morally justified in certain situations, and
our leaders should not pretend otherwise. Laws that respect family and
group diversity by protecting their autonomy also enable private power
holders to behave illiberally toward those subject to their authority. Acute,
endemic, and largely unacknowledged conflicts exist between the values of
diversity and substantive equality. The crucial question of precisely how to
compromise these competing values needs careful normative and empirical exploration, and then frank appraisal. This requires that we tease out
the relevant interests, comprehend the precise nature and extent of the conflict, and consider alternative ways to strike acceptable compromises. This
in turn demands honesty and rigor, not evasion and superficiality.

Thicker skins. The need for thicker skins is more complicated and controversial than the need for more candor, and it is also harder to achieve. As we
interact in an increasingly diverse world, I claim, we should strive to cultivate greater resilience in individuals, not greater delicacy. Unfortunately, as
one commentator puts it, America has become, "a world of endless slights."
Of the myriad examples of this hypersensitivity, I shall mention just a few
that have come to my attention recently even without my searching for
them. A group of Holocaust survivors expresses horror and indignation
about an exhibition of artistic uses of Nazi imagery mounted by the Jewish
Museum in New York City. A Korean American student at Yale takes such
offense at a college dining hall worker's joking proposal to add "dogs and
kimchi" to the menu that he protests to the worker's superior. Although the
worker apologizes as soon as he learns that offense was taken, the student
still files a report that will go on the worker's record. A group, "9/11 People
against Racism," posts a large sign near a New York State thruway exit
ramp proclaiming "This community does not tolerate racism against
Muslims, Arabs and people of color," only to elicit protests by Jews, gays,
and lesbians complaining that they also face discrimination and should not
be left out if others are being named. The *New York Times* reporter who inter-
viewed people in this community found that many residents "read the sign
to mean that it was O.K. to discriminate against everyone else—so long as
they were not Arabs or Muslims or people of color. Others took it as a rep-
rimand and bristled that it was done in such a public way, as if accusing the
[community] of being bigots in need of character education." A Chinese

American complains that the term "Chinese wall," used in its ordinary colloquial sense in a lawyers' magazine, is a "euphemism for exclusion" and is "insensitive, outdated, and outright offensive." An earnest District of Columbia official feels obliged to resign after a barrage of public criticism for having correctly used the word "niggardly." A large school district adopts an "antiharassment" policy barring any verbal or physical conduct that creates an intimidating or hostile environment, including jokes, name-calling, graffiti, and innuendo, as well as making fun of a student's clothing, social skills or surname, with punishments ranging up to suspension, expulsion, or firing. A regular *Yale Daily News* columnist who is a woman of color recounts how she reacted when four white boys in a car turning into a parking lot waited and whistled while a group of white girls on the sidewalk ahead of her walked past the entrance, but said "No, no, no. We go first" when she tried to do so. Saying nothing more about the boys' behavior than this, she describes the deep emotional crisis (weeping, hatred, physical collapse, intense bitterness, and inconsolable sadness) into which this incident propelled her. A law professor taps a female student on the shoulder in class to illustrate the principle that even an innocent touching, if unconsented and unprivileged, constitutes a tort, and she sues him for assault and battery, seeking compensatory and punitive damages because, according to her lawyer, the touching "exacerbate[s] and bring[s] to the surface once again her vulnerability to men with authority and power."

I shall not attempt to persuade the reader that these examples describe egregiously intolerant, uncharitable, self-absorbed, self-indulgent, and irrational (not to say humorless) conduct on the part of the complainants, and unconstitutional overreaching in the case of the school district. Nor shall I try to prove that such examples abound in American life today. The reader who denies these two propositions need not read any farther, for I shall proceed as if they were true. The reactions I describe—and much conduct that is less extreme—are corrosive in a society as diverse, interactive, plain-spoken, casual, and free-wheeling as ours. When used to justify political or legal sanctions against the putative offenders, such behavior is not only perverse but dangerous. It chills personal interactions by denying them the lubricating pleasures of spontaneity and humor. It discourages candid discussion or artistic expression on vital public issues. It enlists formal and informal sanctions in order to reduce what should be robust give-and-take. It invites us to open our wounds, magnify our fears, and parade our sensitivities, to imagine injuries and motivations that do not exist, and to view others, without basis, as enemies. It rewards cant, hyperbole, and reductionist rhetoric while penalizing moderation and reason. It denies others the slack it gives to itself. It encourages us to seek security in groups of people who look, think, or worship like us rather than to venture out into the public square where our common citizenship is forged. It makes a mockery of the law when the law is brandished to stigmatize what often is only just ignorance, boorishness, confusion, ill-considered speech, clumsy provocation, misjudgment, rough or poor humor, and other infelicities.

As individuals in a turbulent, vibrant, feisty, competitive, jostling society of diverse strangers, we do better to respond to such conduct with constructive engagement, forceful rebuke, pointed rebuttal, and internal shrugging of shoulders and biting of tongues. Even when the offender intends to humiliate or dehumanize, the schoolyard adage "sticks and stones can break my bones but names will never hurt me" is a much sounder foundation for coexistence in such a society than the all-too-familiar swift turn to law and other strong reprisals. This means developing thicker skins and deeper tolerance, reserving the law and other heavy artillery for incitements to violence, traditional defamations, and other extreme cases.

It is unfair that the people who need the thickest skins and the most self-restraint are often those who already feel under siege. To them, more self-restraint will seem like an added burden and an unjust imposition on their all-too vulnerable status. Why, they may wonder, should they have to practice it rather than those who offend them? Four considerations, however, can help palliate this unfairness, if not assuage the hurt and indignation.

The first concerns the social value of even offensive speech. Those who practice incivility are morally obligated not to offend others without justification, and under certain conditions this may even amount to a legal duty. But the arguments for and against tolerating such incivilities are not equal; they generally favor the speech (if not the speaker). There is a compelling social interest in people feeling free to express themselves without undue external or internal censorship. This interest in spontaneity is compelling not only because of the truth-value the speech may contain (even hurtful speech may contain some), but also for other reasons. The offense may provoke socially useful speech in response. (Self-)censorship risks inhibiting more than what is false or offensive. The social interest in spontaneity is shared ex ante by *all* members of society, including those who ex post will find particular spontaneous utterances offensive. This interest, moreover, extends beyond constitutionally protected speech to include inhibitions of expression caused by informal norms and practices. Sometimes other values such as privacy and modesty must override this interest, but it remains one with which we must always reckon.

A second consideration reducing the unfairness from a punctilio of thicker skin is that incivility today transcends class, status, and ethnoracial grouping. This has always been a feature of American popular culture to some degree. Exalted social status has never protected a group from crude and hurtful forms of public mockery, although high status may make it easier for them to absorb or deflect it. My point is not to compare public criticism of elites with verbal abuses directed at low-income groups and minorities, but to emphasize that such incivilities are in an important sense indiscriminate and that all Americans, rich or poor, must learn to deal with them.

Third, the informal social norms condemning such hurtful conduct are stronger than ever before—in some cases, too strong for our own good. These condemnations are now reinforced by political and market mechanisms, not to mention legal ones. Public and private critics of the Boy Scouts' antigay policy, for example, have moved swiftly against the organization. Business, political, religious, and civic leaders almost reflexively denounce and sanction antiminority slurs by celebrities, employees, and others. Laws against hate speech and hate crimes have proliferated, and political correctness often rushes in where laws fear to tread.

Finally, all of the alternatives to developing thicker skins are unappealing, unconstitutional, or unworkable. Consider some examples. Employment discrimination law punishes speech and conduct by workers that may offend some coworkers' sensibilities but that do not otherwise harm them. This well-intentioned remedy, however, has introduced formality, legalisms, and incentives that stifle enjoyable and productive interactions, making matters worse for all but the most prickly employees. Campus and other institutional speech codes supposedly adopted to respect diversity have regulated thought and conduct in ways inimical to diversity. Political correctnesss—on and off campus, by the left and the right—tends to suppress and flatten the eccentricity, heterodoxy, obliqueness, and complexity so essential to realizing the diversity ideal.

This ideal is still in its infancy, and all of us are responsible for guiding it to maturity and beyond. Like all abstract conceptions, the diversity ideal will be rudely buffeted by the brute experiences of its implementation. Indeed, particular versions of this ideal have generated strong resistance that should chasten anyone who embraces these particular versions and should humble any others who want government to pursue different ones. Yet these failures have not tarnished the luster of the ideal itself; it retains a powerful, compelling allure. Much in American culture demands and nourishes diversity, even as we grope to understand what it means, how much it costs, whether law can effectively manage it, and which other social processes, if any, might do it better. We have only begun to ask these immensely difficult questions. I take some comfort in the fact that no other society on earth is better equipped to answer them than America at the dawn of the twenty-first century.

ᨆ 37 ᨆ

Civility: A Sometime Virtue

Who can be against civility? Polite behavior, after all, lubricates our social relationships. It takes the edge off of our anger and aggressiveness. It shows respect for others. It reminds us that we are part of a community (the Latin root is *civis*, for citizen) with obligations to our fellow members. Good manners, we have been told since childhood, are necessary for getting along with others. All true.

But three recent events—one legal, one political, and one academic—give me pause. They suggest that with civility, there can be too much of a good thing (though recall Mae West's leering avowal that "too much of a good thing is . . . *wonderful*"), but also that sometimes it may actually be a *bad* thing.

Consider first the legal incident. The Supreme Court of South Carolina has just extended—for the second time—its deadline for members of the bar to take a one-hour civility class and promise to behave in and out of the courtroom, taking a pledge of "civility, not only in court, but also in all written and oral communications." To be sure, the Palmetto State may be particularly sensitive to incivility. The *New York Times* reporter reminds us of what every schoolboy used to know—that South Carolina sent a lawyer to Congress who earned the sobriquet "Bully" Brooks by beating his distinguished colleague from Massachusetts unconscious with a cane on the floor of the Senate. (The reporter adds that the father of South Carolina icon Strom Thurmond killed a political enemy who had insulted him in the street).

The court's requirement raises a number of intriguing questions. Can the civility trainer teach the lawyers anything that they do not already know? The ethical rules governing lawyers exhort them to represent their clients "zealously" while also behaving courteously, presumably on the assumption that there is no conflict between these two dictates. But is that assumption always true? Since lawyers engaged in transactional work already have strong incentives not to insult those with whom they hope to conclude deals, civility training seems most relevant to litigation. There, lawyers typically engage with their opponents in zero-sum wrangling: They and their clients win when and to the extent that their opponents lose. Does civility mean that litigators can no longer use cross-examination, oral arguments, and briefs to mock their opponents' arguments (and thus the opponents who have advanced them) as stupid, deceptive, hypocritical, deluded, incompetent, and destructive of the rule of law, if not of the Republic? Needless to say, one can always find easy cases of incivility: A woman complained to the South Carolina Supreme Court that the lawyer who was taking her deposition told her "You are a mean-spirited, vicious witch and I don't like your face and I don't like your voice." But (assuming that the allegation is true) a lawyer so utterly lacking in self-control is as likely to gain it in an hour of civility training as Jack the Ripper would benefit from a day in charm school or Jose Canseco from a lecture against steroids.

The South Carolina example suggests some larger points. First, except in the clearest and least worrisome cases (like this out-of-control lawyer), it is hard to say where civility ends and incivility begins. Context is everything. The same aggressive questioning of a hostile witness in a courtroom would, on the street, at a dinner party, or even in a law school classroom, be considered highly rude, assaultive, or even defamatory. The less an interaction is structured by established rules or norms, the more blurry the line between what is and is not civil. And in a society as diverse and dynamic as ours is, more and more interactions occur in situations lacking such rules or norms. Second, civility is seldom the only virtue in play, at least in the interesting cases. A lawyer, we saw, is obliged to be not just a civil interlocutor but also a zealous advocate. A prison guard's duty is not only to protect his charges but also to impose stern discipline and even violence when appropriate. A citizen convinced that he is being arrested unjustly should assert his rights to the officer respectfully but aggressively even if, as often happens, this only offends and enrages the officer.

Political interactions sometimes remind us of the limits of civility. In March 2005, Senate minority leader Harry Reid was quoted as having publicly called Federal Reserve chairman Alan Greenspan a "political hack" when Greenspan testified in ways that seemed to support some of President Bush's proposals for Social Security reform. Greenspan, of course, is widely venerated for his sagacity and stewardship of monetary and other economic policies over the course of several decades. As a result, he enjoys a de facto immunity from strong public criticism that has no equal in Washington—or perhaps in world affairs. (Even the Pope attracts more harsh criticism than Greenspan.) For one to question not only his economic judgments but his motives and nonpartisanship is to take on the sacred cow essential (many think) to a bull market (pun intended).

Reid's comment was immediately denounced as a gross breach of political civility, and even some members of his own party backed away from this arrant indecency. Yet why should this be so? Greenspan exercises enormous power; he controls Fed decision making, which in turn influences virtually every aspect of the American, and hence the global, economy. Indeed, within his realm he enjoys more power than either the President or Congress because he is subject to few if any of the checks and balances that limit them at every turn. If he errs, we all pay the consequences. Although he does work under a number of informal constraints, they are relatively loose and imposed largely by his own sense of prudence. It is only a slight exaggeration to say that Greenspan, who at his age has no expectation of other office, is accountable to no one but himself.

The institutional independence of the Fed, on the whole, has been a great virtue. In a constitutional structure designed to subject public officials to constant pressure, the United States has been well served by an arrangement that leaves the Fed relatively free to regulate the economy with a view toward long-term goals and stability and with little regard to the short-term interests of politicians seeking an electoral advantage. But this same independence poses a serious problem in a democracy because if the Fed chooses to abuse its power, no obvious legal or political remedy is readily at hand. Were Greenspan to exercise his immense discretion in order to support one or another party or for some other improper reason, the peril to the institution, and indeed to the nation, could be incalculable.

My point is that if Senator Reid genuinely believes that Greenspan is in fact abusing his precious public trust, it is not uncivil for Reid to say so—as clearly and effectively as he can. If upon careful reflection he concludes that Greenspan habitually behaves in this fashion, then "political hack" is not too strong an appellation. He may be right or wrong in his judgment—I think that he is wrong—but his public responsibility as a leader of a great party and as a senator is to reach that judgment conscientiously and then express it without mincing words. Whether he can achieve that goal by using a more restrained, less inflammatory term is indeed an important question he should (and presumably did) ask himself. But if he cannot and if he is convinced that he is right, then in my view civility must bow to effectiveness.

My third case is the public agony of Larry Summers, the controversial president of Harvard. In January, as everyone but Rip Van Winkle must know by now, Summers offered some closed-door, off-the-record luncheon remarks to a conference of professors to discuss diversifying the science and engineering workforce. Focusing on the underrepresentation of women in tenured professorships in those fields at first-tier research institutions, he indicated that he meant to be provocative and then listed four hypotheses that might cause the underrepresentation. First, women might be less willing to spend the eighty-hour weeks in the laboratory required to attain those rarefied positions, given the competing demands of parenting and family responsibilities. Second, the aptitudes of men and women, and the variability of aptitude within each group, might differ, and that even slight differences in aptitude and variability could account for the different proportions at the very top of those professions. The third and fourth hypotheses were different socialization of men and women, and discrimination. All four probably played some role, Summers said, but the first and second—willingness to spend eighty-hour weeks in the lab, and aptitude—probably explained "a fair amount of this problem." He emphasized that this was conjecture, his "best guess after a fair amount of reading the literature and a lot of talking to people," and cited supporting reasons and studies. Urging that more studies be done, he suggested possible lines of research and noted that he "would like nothing better than to be proved wrong." All in all, these might seem like provocative (as promised), thoughtful, and constructive remarks aimed at an important problem about which he and his audience were both deeply concerned and more needs to be learned. One might even say that Summers' talk exemplified what the leader of the world's most prominent university should be about, not just fund-raising and managing his immense enterprise.

The reaction, chronicled the next day on the front page of the *New York Times* and most other media outlets, was swift and harsh. An MIT professor told the *Times* that Summers's words made her feel so ill that she had to leave the room; some others walked out in protest. Still others denounced Summers as unfit to lead a great university, demanding his resignation. In the weeks that followed, he consulted widely with his critics and apologized for his remarks. Even so, the Harvard faculty subsequently voted a lack of confidence in his leadership and the calls for his resignation continue.

Rather than refute his hypotheses on the merits, his assailants accused him of sexism and worse. Days later, one of his tartest critics, *Times* columnist Maureen Dowd, cited a new study published in *Nature* showing that the second X chromosome in women makes them, in Dowd's words, "more different from each other than we knew—creatures of 'infinite variety,' as Shakespeare wrote . . . So is Lawrence Summers right after all?" But having finally raised the $64,000 question—in fact, Summers's suggestion about differences in scientific aptitude at the high end was explicitly about intragroup variability—Dowd did not pursue it; instead she went on to joke about many *other* differences between the sexes.

A recurring charge against Summers was incivility, sometimes termed "arrogance." But although Summers can indeed be arrogant, the transcript of his talk reveals neither discourtesy nor high-handedness—merely an offer of provocative hypotheses, a call for more research, and some sensible suggestions about how it might be pursued. Like the attack on Senator Reid, the demand for civility and apology seems designed to silence and humiliate him, settle other scores, and change the subject from his substantive speculations to his style and motive. The hidden agenda is to discourage influential people from asking forbidden questions about sensitive issues like gender difference. Other critics think it "irresponsible" for the president of Harvard to raise such questions unless he has an iron-clad study and an army of footnotes to support him. But the most important questions are not so clear-cut, so this is really a prescription for bland blather and reassuring pieties, not vigorous intellectual inquiry leading to often discomfiting truths. Coming from our top scientists, this augurs ill for their vocation—and for the rest of us who rely on them to help us with our truth-seeking.

Civility, then, turns out to be a complicated thing and only a sometime virtue. Highly desirable in its proper sphere, it can be a social vice elsewhere. A robust democracy must learn to tell the difference.

∿ 38 ∿

The 2004 Elections: A Militant Moderate's Interpretation

As George W. Bush prepares for his second term, the chattering class (of which I am a tenured member) is still debating and digesting the larger meanings of the 2004 elections. Much of this conversation is ill-informed, tendentious, and nakedly partisan. As a political independent and militant moderate, I like to think that I have no ax to grind other than a passionate love for my country. Skeptical of all simplifying ideologies, I hold that most things are more complicated than they seem, especially in politics. Here, then, are some brief observations about the kind of polity that America is—and what we might become.

ABSURDITIES

Some explanations of recent events are just silly. One example is the claim that Bush's reelection marks a triumph of the kind of fundamentalist religious culture that H. L. Mencken mocked in the 1920s—then, with good reason. Writer Christopher Hitchens exaggerates only slightly when he says that many who today scorn the religiously zealous imagine "a God-bothering, pulpit-pounding Armageddon-artist, enslaved by ancient texts and prophecies and committed to theocratic rule." Even the brilliant Garry Wills, who should know better, contends that religious conservatives have declared war on the Enlightenment, science, and democracy.

In fact, American society has liberalized even the most fundamentalist religions over time. Uncompromising traditionalists are vastly outnumbered by adherents who have managed to make their peace with the modern world. Christian groups are no different. According to Andrew Kohut and associates, "one-third of committed evangelicals and 41 percent of committed Catholics believe that legal abortions should be available to women in at least some circumstances other than rape, incest, or to save the life of the mother, and well over half of the members of these two groups support the distribution of birth control information in public schools. Thirty-three percent of committed evangelicals, and nearly as high a percentage of Mormons, believe that government regulation is necessary for the public good; 28 percent of both groups think that the federal government does a better job than it is often given credit for." Citing a new Pew Foundation survey of American religions, *The Economist* reports that substantial majorities in all religious groups agree that the disadvantaged need government help "to obtain their rightful place in America" even if it means higher taxes, and also support stricter environmental rules and a high priority to fighting HIV/AIDS abroad. Liberal secularists should not mimic Falwell-like bigots by ignoring the diversity among and within religious groups lumped together as the "religious right," and by promoting religious stereotypes that would rightly offend them if applied to racial or gender groups.

HYPOCRISIES

The postelection analyses reveal (surprise!) that hypocrisy is nonpartisan. Many liberals who boast their broad tolerance and generosity of spirit, it turns out, are neither tolerant nor generous in characterizing their opponents' views on guns, partial-birth abortion, Iraq, the international criminal court, the Kyoto treaty, the military, school vouchers, and a host of other issues. Not taking these views seriously makes it easy for liberals to dismiss them as stupid, bigoted, unsophisticated, xenophobic, and selfish. They act as if genuine debate on the merits would only serve to dignify the political equivalent of flat-Earthism.

Conservatives, for their part, often abandon principles for tactical reasons. Staunch states-rights advocates support federal tort reform legislation. So-called strict constructionists lionize U.S. Supreme Court justices who propagate a radical jurisprudence that has overturned numerous federal statutes based on strained and novel readings of the Constitution. Fiscal conservatives lobby for massive special interest subsidies and tax cuts that produce record deficits. Proponents of limited government often favor further state intrusion into our private lives and civil liberties. Worshipers of our sacred Constitution propose to amend it at the drop of a hat to advance some crusade-of-the-moment.

REALITIES

An interesting feature of postelection analysis is what it does not discuss. Many pundits have glossed over some of the most politically salient facts of American life. This ostrich-like evasion, of course, is not confined to one party, position, time, or place. Still, Democrats' recent losses suggest that they are particularly prone to it.

The most notorious "newly discovered" fact is Americans' religiosity, a faith in faith unique among postindustrial democracies. Some 85 percent of Americans believe in heaven, 65 percent in the devil, and 75 percent in angels that affect human affairs. (Scoffing cosmopolitans should acknowledge that some of their own pet pieties are also unempirical, and that unprovable religious convictions may still be socially vital.) A Pew Foundation survey in 2001 found 25 percent of adult Internet users had gone online to find religious and spiritual material—more than the number who had visited gambling sites, participated in online auctions, or traded stocks online, and a sharp increase from only a year earlier. An abiding mystery, then, is how Democratic politicians who should be in the business of knowing their market could have failed to exploit this unmistakable religiosity. Their inattention is especially stunning because Bill Clinton, their only two-term president since FDR, was (in Professor Marci Hamilton's words) "the most religiously activist president in history."

The hype about a "transformative" election has also obscured the remarkable continuity of public opinion over time. In *The Rational Public,* political scientists Ben Page and Robert Shapiro show that opinion has changed little in the last fifty years on a broad range of controversial policy issues. Many pundits seized on the 22 percent of exiting voters who cited "moral values" as their top concern, yet this response to a very ambiguous question was similar to those in earlier elections—including those Clinton won. Another sign of continuity: Only three states changed colors in 2004, with the split of the U.S. House of Representatives, state legislatures, and governorships hardly shifting. The election was a tremor, not an earthquake.

Some political facts do change. Majority views of racial, religious, and ethnic minorities, for example, have grown far more positive, and attitudes toward gays and lesbians have gone from widespread hostility to broad support for equal treatment with remarkable speed. Indeed, civil unions and same-sex marriage became mainstream political issues only five years ago, yet 62 percent of voters now support one of these reforms (at least where courts do not force it on them). These shifts reveal another reality: Political centrism dominates public attitudes. Although the GOP has steadily gained on Democrats in registration for several decades (this election merely continued the trend), exit polls found 29 percent self-identifying as moderates. For all the talk about the campaign's divisiveness and the mapping of blue states massed on the coasts with red states occupying the vast in-between, voters' moderation persists. Political scientist Morris Fiorina's new book, *Culture War?,* contrasts their centrism with the polarization among political and media elites.

Another reality: The vast majority of Americans are now middle-class; an even larger share (some 90 percent) *think* that they are. Most live outside cities, invest in the stock market, own their homes, drive two cars, go to restaurants, have little use for labor unions, and seldom interact with the poor. Although economic vulnerability still shadows the middle class, they do not respond well to crude appeals for soak-the-rich tax proposals, Naderite populism, or other class-based animosities. Few are rich— but most still hope to be.

TRAGEDIES

The election highlighted two facts that imperil our political health. First, blacks remain isolated on the Democratic party's left wing. While Bush gained more support among Latinos, Jews, other minority groups, and even blacks (by 2 percent), blacks remain the most reliably loyal Democrat group; the party takes that bloc for granted with largely symbolic gestures such as affirmative action and showcasing black celebrities. (Some, like Al Sharpton, hurt their cause.) Yet the party opposes important reforms like school choice that most blacks think would truly help them. They would increase their political influence by forcing politicians to court them as swing voters who demand a high price for their support. Barack Obama's landslide victory for the U.S. Senate seat from Illinois shows that exceptionally attractive black candidates can escape this isolation, winning independent and Republican voters. Alas, Obama is just that: exceptional.

A second perilous isolation is that of opinion leaders in the media and the academy. More than 80 percent of national journalists are far more liberal than the electorate, while Fox, Drudge, and conservative talk radio are militantly conservative. Their bellicose crossfire tends to drown out quieter centrist voices. The liberal-conservative ratio on faculties, especially in law, humanities, and social sciences, is now at least 7:1 and likely to keep rising, according to a recent study. Leading foundations also tend to be quite liberal. This overwhelming orthodoxy among opinion leaders who preach incessantly about the virtues of diversity is of course hypocritical. More important, it betrays the public that relies on them for the balanced, rigorous information and analysis that shape civic discourse.

STRATEGIES

All Americans—both empowered conservatives and disempowered liberals—have a vital stake in the revival of a Democratic party that can seriously contest, and often win, national elections. As journalist Jonathan Rauch recently argued, our national well-being requires a government in which each party holds enough power to keep its opponents honest. Historically, as political scientist David Mayhew shows, divided government has been good government.

As the defeated Democrats go back to the drawing boards and the Republicans savor their victory, what kinds of changes can an independent moderate suggest to nourish the competitive national politics we so desperately need? Here are a few modest proposals.

1. *Reduce unwarranted incumbent advantages.* Long cycles of one-party rule are bad for the polity. Triumphalist Republicans forget at their peril that the shoe was recently on the other foot. In 1994, the Democrats had controlled Congress for almost all of the preceding forty years, during which Republicans seemed (and felt) irrelevant except when they could win the White House.

An important reason for these overlong cycles is that state legislatures control the decennial redistricting of House seats and use their power largely to protect incumbents. They do their job effectively; in this year's election, only seven incumbents were denied reelection, and in only thirty-seven of the 435 contests were the losers even arguably close. Again, this gerrymandering is a game that both parties play when they can. No panacea exists, but we could make redistricting less partisan, as Iowa has. We also need to analyze how well the new campaign finance law worked. Many observers (including me) predicted that it would restrict challengers' access to funds, limit parties' political advertising, and otherwise weaken them. The early evidence suggests that in fact the parties became stronger, raising a great deal of money, much of it in small donations. Still, the law's longer-term effects on competition and free speech remain to be studied.

2. *Reform election law.* Given the recent experiences with voting equipment failures, disputed voting rules, legal challenges, and near-deadlock in the electoral college, Congress should revisit the election law it enacted after the 2000 debacle, legislate more interstate uniformity in federal elections, and provide more funds for implementation. These elections are too important to be left to the largely unreviewable discretion of local boards staffed by patronage appointees who are ill-equipped to do the nation's vital work. Even without constitutional amendment, we can also reform some of the electoral college's worst features—for example, ensuring that third-party candidates with little support cannot throw the election into the House, and that faithless electors cannot flout the people's choice.

3. *Advance more attractive candidates and policies.* The Democrats were terminally foolish to run a Massachusetts liberal (arguably the most liberal in the Senate) for president for no better reason than that he boasted a gallant war record. John Kerry has demonstrated few coalition-building skills in his long Senate career, and gave independent voters few reasons to support him. He did as well as he did because even a weak Democratic candidate can win 48 percent of the vote when his opponent runs on an unpopular war and an uncertain economy.

Moderate candidates are hobbled by the parties' nominating processes, which empower party activists: teachers, unionists, and racial minorities for Democrats; progun groups, small-business owners, and religious conservatives for the GOP. These people do not truly represent the parties' actual and potential voters in the general election. The militantly antiwar, Michael Moore–populist supporters of Howard Dean and Ralph Nader pulled Kerry so far left during the primaries that his centrist moves as nominee opened him to "flip-flop" ridicule. Both parties, but especially the Democrats, need to make their selection processes more centrist-friendly.

Democrats can also win votes by attacking unfair, growth-stifling policies. The regressive payroll tax is ripe for reform, and income tax simplification could appeal to the middle class. Social Security can be fixed with moderate changes such as raising both the retirement age and the taxable income ceiling. Health insurance changes linking consumer choice, cost-sharing, and coverage for catastrophic expenses can gain support from the middle class and employers whose competitiveness is threatened by the current system.

4. *It's national security, stupid!* Democrats will never regain power until voters again believe that the party will energetically use American power—multilaterally if possible, unilaterally if necessary—to protect vital national interests and complete difficult, unpopular missions once under-taken. Rightly or wrongly, a majority of voters trusted Bush to do this while doubting Kerry's conviction and tenacity. And 89 percent of the half who thought (rightly or wrongly) that the Iraq war has increased our security voted for Bush, as did most of those who saw terrorism as a top issue. People vote as they do for many reasons, of course, but terrorism and Iraq were more decisive than the same-sex marriage ban (approved in solidly blue Oregon and Michigan), evangelical voters (whose share rose only slightly), or most other "moral" or wedge issues that many Democrats want to believe defeated Kerry.

Wishful thinking is no strategy for winning the next election.

CREDITS

Essay 1 (Affirmative Action I) was originally published as "Affirmative Action" in *Brookings Review* (Winter 2002): 24–27.

Essay 2 (Affirmative Action II) was originally published September 9, 2003, on *The Jurist* website (http://jurist.law.pitt.edu/forum/symposium-aa/index.php).

Essay 3 (Affirmative Action III) was originally published in *The American Lawyer* (June 2003): 67–69. © 2005 ALM Properties, Inc. All Rights Reserved. Further duplication without permission prohibited.

Essay 4 (Groups and Equal Protection) was originally published as "Groups in a Diverse, Dynamic, Competitive, and Liberal Society: Comments on Owen Fiss's 'Groups and the Equal Protection Clause'" in *Issues in Legal Scholarship*, The Origins and Fate of Antisubordination Theory (2003): Article 15. http://www.bepress.com/ils/iss2/art15.

Essay 5 (Race Matters) originally appeared in *Reconstruction* 2 (1994): 84–89.

Essay 6 (Slavery Reparations) was originally published December 9, 2002, on *The Jurist* website http://jurist.law.pitt.edu/forum/forumnew78.php).

Essay 7 (Housing Integration) was originally published in the *New York Times*, August 8, 2002, A25.

Essay 8 (The Pledge of Allegiance) was originally published in *The American Lawyer* (September 2002): 65–69. © 2005 ALM Properties, Inc. All Rights Reserved. Further duplication without permission prohibited.

Essay 9 (School Vouchers) was originally published in *The American Lawyer* (February 2001): 63–64. © 2005 ALM Properties, Inc. All Rights Reserved. Further duplication without permission prohibited.

Essay 10 (Military Recruitment) was originally published in *The American Lawyer* (January 2004): 57–59. © 2005 ALM Properties, Inc. All Rights Reserved. Further duplication without permission prohibited.

Essay 11 (Expressive Groups) was originally published in *The American Lawyer* (September 2000): pp. 67–69. © 2005 ALM Properties, Inc. All Rights Reserved. Further duplication without permission prohibited.

Essay 12 (Professors and Profession) was originally published in *The American Lawyer* (July/August 1998): 85–86. © 2005 ALM Properties, Inc. All Rights Reserved. Further duplication without permission prohibited.

Essay 31 (Immigrant Voting) was originally published in the *Los Angeles Times*, August 1, 2004, Part M, p. 5.

Essay 32 (China) was originally published in *The American Lawyer* (November 2002): 73–75. © 2005 ALM Properties, Inc. All Rights Reserved. Further duplication without permission prohibited.

Essay 33 (India) was originally published in *The American Lawyer* (November 2004): 100–105. © 2005 ALM Properties, Inc. All Rights Reserved. Further duplication without permission prohibited.

Essay 34 (Rethinking Liberalism) was originally published in the *New York Times*, May 31, 1981.

Essay 35 (Diversity) is reprinted by permission of the publishers from *Diversity in America: Keeping Government at a Safe Distance* by Peter H. Schuck (Cambridge, MA: Harvard University Press), copyright © 2003 by the President and Fellows of Harvard College.

Essay 36 (Punctilios for a Diverse Society) is reprinted by permission of the publishers from *Diversity in America: Keeping Government at a Safe Distance* by Peter H. Schuck (Cambridge, MA: Harvard University Press), copyright © 2003 by the President and Fellows of Harvard College.

Essay 37 (Civility) was originally published in *The American Lawyer* (June 2005). © 2005: 81–84. ALM Properties, Inc. All Rights Reserved. Further duplication without permission prohibited.

Essay 38 (The 2004 Elections) was originally published in *The American Lawyer* (January 2005): 61–65. © 2005 ALM Properties, Inc. All Rights Reserved. Further duplication without permission prohibited.

INDEX

ABOUT THE AUTHOR

Peter Schuck has taught at Yale Law School since 1979, where he holds the Simeon E. Baldwin professorship. The author of many books and articles on a wide variety of subjects, he is often called upon for public commentary and expert testimony. His most recent books are *Diversity in America: Keeping Government at a Safe Distance* (2003), *The Limits of Law: Essays on Democratic Governance* (2000), and *Immigration Stories* (coeditor, 2005). Before joining the Yale faculty, he was a federal official, a "public interest" lawyer, and a lawyer in private practice. A recipient of Guggenheim, Fulbright, and other fellowships for his scholarly work, he lives in New York City where he is also affiliated with NYU Law School. He and his wife of almost forty years have two grown children.